Schools and Students At Risk

*Context and Framework
for Positive Change*

Schools and Students At Risk

Context and Framework for Positive Change

Edited by Robert J. Rossi
American Institutes for Research

Teachers College, Columbia University
New York and London

Published by Teachers College Press, 1234 Amsterdam Avenue
New York, New York

This work was supported under contract RR 91–172011 awarded to the American
Institutes for Research by the Office of Educational Research and Improvement,
U.S. Department of Education. Any opinions, findings, and conclusions expressed
in this book are those of the authors and do not necessarily reflect the views of the
supporting agency.

Library of Congress Cataloging-in-Publication Data

Schools and students at risk : context and framework for positive
  change / edited by Robert J. Rossi.
     p.   cm.
  Includes bibliographical references.
  ISBN 0-8077-3326-1. — ISBN 0-8077-3325-3 (pbk.)
   1. Socially handicapped children — Education — United States.
  2. Minority children — Education — United States.   3. School
management and organization — United States.   4. Educational change-
-United States.
  LC4091.S34   1994
  371.96'7'0973 — dc20   93-44316

ISBN 0-8077-3326-1
ISBN 0-8077-3325-3 (pbk.)

Printed on acid-free paper

Manufactured in the United States of America

99 98 97 96 95 94   8 7 6 5 4 3 2 1

For Andrew and Rachel, Who are Soon to be Students

Contents

Foreword

As an advisor to the important evaluation of educational reforms for students at risk, conducted by the American Institutes for Research and directed by Bob Rossi, I am honored to write the foreword for this book because it is one of the major outcomes of the project, and more important, it is a comprehensive exploration of the conditions that impact students who are at risk of failing in school. I attended the conference in San Francisco where many of the papers that subsequently became chapters in this book were presented. What was striking to those in attendance at that conference was the diversity of approaches to the topic of educational reforms for students at risk. This was not surprising because these students are themselves diverse and so are the circumstances that cause them to be at risk. This book emphasizes that there are solutions to the problems that these students are experiencing and that many of the solutions rest with the adults who are responsible for setting policies and managing the complicated social systems that provide varying levels of support.

School dropout statistics collected from schools that serve mainly poor and minority students across the nation indicate that a large portion of these students are being underserved. We really do not know the number of school dropouts and their problems because states and school districts use different definitions to determine who is a dropout, and different formulas to calculate the dropout rate. However, even with these differences, there remain wide disparities in the dropout rates within school districts between schools with large concentrations of poor and minority students and schools with few of these students.

This book reemphasizes that students who are at risk, due to the negative effects of their educational, social, cultural, and psychological situations, are more likely to drop out of school. The consequences for dropping out of school have changed dramatically. In earlier times, there was limited social stigma to dropping out. It mainly meant going to work at an earlier age. Now, in a world that is increasingly technological, there is little or no work for school dropouts, and there is a social stigma of being underemployed or unemployed.

School systems have tried to address the needs of students who are at risk by offering school reforms that included stronger doses of the same program offerings or multiple components of school dropout prevention programs. In many instances, the planning has been based on the belief that dropping out of school is voluntary and internally motivated. However, as a director of research and evaluation in a large urban school district, I learned after being responsible for the evaluations of several dropout programs that dropping out of school, many times, was an involuntary and externally motivated action. Because of the "hostile and non-supportive" educational and social environments of some schools, students felt that they were pushed out of school. Some school environments, reflecting district policies, school staff attitudes and beliefs, and limited support systems, did not provide the cohesiveness to hold students in school and to assist them to complete their goal of earning a high school diploma. We know that many high school dropouts later earn a GED or an adult school diploma, but in-between there are the lost years of underemployment and unemployment. We also know that many dropouts never return to school and are thus relegated to the lowest socioeconomic tier of poverty.

In the school district where I was an evaluator for many years, there was a program, although it was not called a dropout prevention program, that offered many of the common dropout prevention elements — a continuous psychological support system and scaffolding for individual students, a respect for cultural diversity, an alternative offering of quality education, and an alternative means to earn graduation credits. The School-Age Mothers Program began in spite of a prevailing attitude that to help pregnant students would encourage others to follow in their "faulty" footsteps and become pregnant also. Yet in the positive environment of the program, the female students were encouraged to continue with their education and not lose school time or credits to earn their high school diplomas. Through the years, as the program successfully graduated potential school dropouts, the School-Age Mothers gained credibility as a successful dropout prevention program and eventually became institutionalized as an alternative educational program in the school district.

This program and thousands of programs across the nation demonstrate that educational reforms for students at risk require extras — extra help and understanding of students' circumstances, extra efforts to develop nonpunitive policies and policies that eliminate obstacles for attending school, and extra focus on changing attitudes and beliefs that negatively impact on those students who are potential dropouts or are returning to school after dropping out.

The chapters in this book bring differing perspectives to the task of ameliorating the conditions that increase the number of students who are at risk and generate school dropouts. Better insights about the contents of necessary reforms are gained from reading the chapters. This is a valuable document for persons in schools with the responsibility for setting reform policies and for planning new programs in response to policy initiatives.

Floraline I. Stevens
National Science Foundation

Preface

In September 1992, the American Institutes for Research (AIR) and the Johns Hopkins Center for Research on Effective Schooling for Disadvantaged Students began a joint effort to study educational reforms for students at risk. Funded by the Office of Educational Research and Improvement within the U.S. Department of Education, the scope of work was rather singular in that it provided for the collection of papers on relevant topics by foremost scholars and practitioners of these reforms. In addition, it encouraged the gathering together of researchers and practitioners to hear and to discuss the papers with their authors in large and smaller discussion groups. Our meetings were held in April 1992 and were well-attended; they provided the authors and project staff with a sense of the interests of the field, as well as food for thought in bringing these papers to final form. This collection represents the products of all our work.

Before turning to the general description of the contents and organizing rationale for the volume, one subtle but important development in perspective relating to the general topic-area is worth noting. When we began, we were reasonably comfortable using the adjective *at-risk* to refer to children and youth who were experiencing difficulties in school. However, we now find this term troubling because it has become almost standard practice in the field to refer to entire groups of children (e.g., black or Hispanic children) as "at-risk" populations, implying that somehow these children are inherently "at risk." No child is inherently at risk; rather, children are put at risk by external disadvantages. For this reason, we use the phrase "children (or youth) at risk" to refer to individuals who are subject to one or more risk-producing conditions or circumstances. If these conditions were to be eliminated or their effects were to be significantly reduced, the children in question would no longer properly be termed "at risk."

The chapters included in the four main parts of this volume make clear why any attribution of "at-riskness" to individuals should be a concern. In Part I we are introduced to the nexus of factors that *put* children and youth at risk of failure and to the approaches that have been taken by educators and other concerned professionals to ameliorate their conditions. Part II describes the dangers, for children, of systems that fail to recognize and to appreciate their distinctive abilities to learn. In Part III, the chapters relate what is now being learned about how far and how fast schools, districts, and city- and statewide programs must go to stop the failures that have been permitted for too long. Finally, Part IV provides a stock-taking and a look ahead. The authors challenge us with unifying and new perspectives on how we must think of schools and schooling if students who are at risk of failure are to be well-served.

I am grateful to the U.S. Department of Education for their support and to Harold Himmelfarb of OERI, who helped shape our plans. The insights of James McPartland of Johns Hopkins University regarding potential topics were instrumental in developing a balanced perspective, and the willingness of his colleague Samuel Stringfield to assist in the review of selected chapters was a great help. The critical reviews of selected chapters by G. Alfred Hess, Aaron Pallas, Charlene Rivera, and Floraline Stevens also helped to improve the final products. Certainly my most grateful thanks go to the authors who invested their time and energy in addressing these most difficult subjects.

To the many researchers and practitioners who were involved in the review and discussion of the themes presented by our authors, I can only acknowledge that I could never thank them enough. Special thanks are due to George Bohrnstedt of AIR, who provided both encouragement and support for the work and who was an active participant in discussions related to specific chapters, and to Katie Goya of AIR, who oversaw assembly and production of the manuscript in its final stages and worked energetically to ensure that all production deadlines were met. My sincerest gratitude is reserved for Susan Liddicoat of Teachers College Press and Phyllis DuBois of AIR. Susan's in-depth and perceptive critique of every chapter spurred us to do our best, and Phyllis's capable and sensitive skills in working over the text and with the authors in making final refinements helped to ensure that our best efforts were reflected on every page.

Schools and Students At Risk

*Context and Framework
for Positive Change*

Part I

CONTEXT AND HISTORY OF REFORM EFFORTS

The chapters in this part set the stage for understanding current efforts at school and system reform. In Chapter 1, Alesia Montgomery and Robert Rossi describe the range of conditions and circumstances that may put children at risk of educational failure. Following a brief review of extant theories that have been used to describe the relationships between educational performance and individual development, these authors provide an alternative conceptual schema that interrelates student resources and behaviors and school resources and opportunities within the larger societal context. This model clarifies the sources of "at-riskness" and suggests what the roles and constraints are for schools in the learning process.

Nettie Legters and Edward McDill, in Chapter 2, provide a wide-ranging description of the school-based efforts that have been made to assist students who suffer the effects of many risk factors. Their summary of initiatives and longer-term commitments to helping students who are failing in school captures the good intentions and considerable investments that have been made from the 1960s to today. As they address emerging issues for policy, they challenge educators to refine evaluation systems, develop and disseminate more accurate projections of resource requirements associated with specific interventions, and plan for the coherent allocation of resources across the grade levels.

CHAPTER 1

Becoming At Risk of Failure in America's Schools

ALESIA F. MONTGOMERY AND ROBERT J. ROSSI

It is popular to reminisce about "the good ol' days" when the quality of public education for all students was presumably high and the challenges posed by student diversity were supposedly minimal. However, in early twentieth-century America, the overwhelming majority of young people lacked high school diplomas (Hodgkinson, 1985). The quality of education that poor children, children of color, and immigrant children received was vastly inferior to that provided for children of higher socioeconomic status. Policy makers did not view developing poor children's "critical thinking skills" as a priority. Destined for low-wage labor, poor children were required to learn basic skills and the disciplined work habits suitable for factory positions (Tyack, 1974). And children of color often received instruction that devalued their cultural backgrounds and discouraged them from aspiring to the "white man's condition" (Odum, 1968).

If we are now a "nation at risk," it is not due simply to recent educational, demographic, or social trends, but rather it is — to a large extent — the culmination of disastrous, persistent, and in many cases intentional disparities in our schools and society. Many young people today are becoming at risk of failure in America's schools for the same reason that their parents and grandparents became at risk: limited educational opportunities and incentives. And some young people are also becoming at risk due to age-old problems beyond school walls: poor nutrition, inadequate health care, dangerous neighborhoods, abuse, and neglect.

Media reports, however, often suggest that new "societal plagues" such as "broken homes" and "crack-addicted mothers" are the primary causes of academic failure. News stories that emphasize family dysfunction fail to explain the underlying conditions that historically have made life in impoverished areas difficult for families and children. And they overlook the significant influence of school climate and resources on student performance.

Subsequent chapters describe emerging strategies to create a challenging learning environment that meets diverse student needs. In this chapter, our purpose is to develop a conceptual framework for understanding the societal, student, and school processes that influence student performance — processes that may begin as soon as a child enters school.

STUDENT BACKGROUND

In almost every school, regardless of students' race and class, teachers can identify children who underachieve because of problems beyond school walls. Some children may do poorly at school because they feel that nobody at home cares about them. Other children may underachieve because their basic needs for food, shelter, health care, and safety are unmet. And some children with low social status may see little reason to exert effort in the classroom because they do not believe their efforts will increase their chances for upward mobility.

Family Life

Of all the conditions outside school thought to place children at risk, single-parent homes are perhaps the most frequently cited. However, research findings on the relation between family structure and student performance are mixed. For example, analyzing data from *High School and Beyond*, Ekstrom, Goertz, Pollack, and Rock (1987) find a correlation between single-parent homes and dropout for whites and Hispanics (but not for blacks). In contrast, a more recent analysis of *High School and Beyond* data indicates that the effect of father absence on dropout is nil for all gender/ethnic groups except for non-Hispanic white females, who are significantly *more* likely to drop out if a father is present in the home (Fernandez, Paulsen, & Hirano-Nakanishi, 1989). Family atmosphere rather than family composition is probably most predictive of dropout (Stroup & Robins, 1972). Anecdotal comparisons of children from "intact" and "broken" homes may be biased (Guttman, Geva, & Gefen, 1988). Studies of the effects of family structure on children may often fail to control adequately for parents' age, education, socioeconomic status, and support systems. Thus, although it makes intuitive sense that two-parent homes might tend to offer more resources than single-parent homes, we must be cautious about making broad generalizations concerning the negative effects of single-parent homes on children.

Severe neglect or abuse has a less ambiguous effect on children: Babies whose parents fail to show affection and provide educational stimulation (e.g., teaching the child new words) are at risk of developing learning and emotional problems (Werner & Smith, 1982). And children who suffer physical or sexual abuse are much more likely to exhibit psychological problems (Green, 1978). Although many severely abused children become remarkably well-adjusted adults, battering places children at increased risk of lifelong emotional/behavioral problems, impaired intellectual functioning, and permanent physical or neurological damage (Perry, Doran, & Wells, 1983).

Reported rates of child abuse are higher among lower-income groups than among higher-income groups. However, it is difficult to determine the accuracy of child abuse estimates. Parents and children may be reluctant to describe instances of abuse, and hospitals may be reluctant to report abusive parents with high socioeconomic status (Hampton & Newberger, 1985). Many child abuse studies have had disproportionate percentages of poor families in their samples; thus, it is often difficult to untangle parental abuse/neglect effects from poverty effects. Some of the developmental problems attributed to parental misconduct may be caused by poverty (e.g., poor nutrition, high mobility, unsafe surroundings).

Child abuse and welfare services are often overwhelmed with the number of children that need assistance, and thus many cases of severe abuse/neglect may be inadequately investigated and addressed (Dugger, 1992). Due to limited resources for monitoring and follow-up, interventions such as foster care placements may, in some cases, actually increase the danger of bodily or emotional harm.

Health and Nutrition

Poor health and untreated physical conditions may slow a child's academic progress. Recurrent illness may interfere with attentiveness and attendance, and vision or hearing problems may make class participation difficult. Rural children, low-income children, and nonwhite children are at higher risk for health-related problems than their urban, high-income, white counterparts, but have less access to health care (Aday & Andersen, 1984). Homeless children in particular are at high risk for a variety of health problems, including elevated lead levels (Alperstein, Rappaport, & Flanigan, 1988) and tuberculosis (Centers for Disease Control, 1985).

A small but significant percentage of children are born with conditions that place them at risk of health and developmental problems. For example, Hack and co-authors (1991) find that very low birth weight children with subnormal head size at 8 months are at increased risk of poor cognitive function, lower academic achievement, and abnormal behavior at 8 years of age.

In some cases these problems might be prevented by adequate prenatal care or changes in mothers' lifestyle (e.g., drug use) during pregnancy. The problems of cocaine-exposed children have been documented by researchers (e.g., Chasnoff, Burns, Schnoll, & Burns, 1985) and sensationalized in the media as the crisis of "crack babies." While it is true that some cocaine-exposed children have severe mental and physical disabilities, new findings suggest that cocaine exposure does not always lead to developmental problems — most children exposed to cocaine test within the normal developmental range without the help of treatment (Viadero, 1992). Even cocaine-exposed children who show signs of poor health and developmental delay may improve with the help of early intervention programs. However, treatment can be expensive (Chasnoff, 1991).

The media focus on the crisis of "crack babies" obscures the endemic problem of prenatal exposure to legal and illicit drugs, including alcohol and cigarettes (Kline, Stein, & Hutzler, 1987). Media reports often fail to recognize that maternal drug use cuts across socioeconomic groups: The prevalence of drug use among pregnant whites, for example, may be significantly underreported (Chasnoff, Landress, & Barrett, 1990).

Poor children, however, may be especially vulnerable to maternal drug abuse because of other environmental risks (Viadero, 1992). Earlier studies that found severe "crack" effects may not have adequately controlled for complicating factors associated with poverty (e.g., poor maternal nutrition) that pose a threat to many impoverished children and may contribute to the health problems of infants exposed to cocaine.

Regardless of maternal drug use, poverty poses significant risks to infants. In a longitudinal study of newborns in an eight-county area of California, Braveman, Oliva, Miller, Reiter, & Egerter (1989) find that lack of insurance is associated with higher rates of adverse neonatal outcomes (including low birth weight) in uninsured black, Latino, and Asian infants relative to insured white newborns. The greater the poverty, the greater the risk — homeless women are less likely than other low-income women to receive adequate prenatal care and are more likely to deliver a baby of low birth weight (Chavkin, Kristal, Seabron, & Guigli, 1987).

Community Conditions

Poor communities, especially those in the inner cities, are often stereotyped as uniformly blighted and dangerous. However, in spite of the poverty of these communities, many residents attempt to provide safe, attractive environments for children. In even the poorest inner cities, there are often pleasant streets with well-maintained buildings and concerned neighbors.

However, it is true that many sections of inner cities are unsafe for children. As Halpern (1991) notes, "[Children] in some neighborhoods face the possibility of walking into danger on every trip to and from school, and on every trip up and down the stairs of their apartment building" (p. 7). Many inner-city children reside in neighborhoods so crime-ridden it is dangerous to play outside (Kotlowitz, 1991). Young people in these communities have fewer programs and a narrower range of activities to participate in than do young people in affluent suburbs (Littel & Wynn, 1989). Adult leadership in these communities may be ineffective and disorganized, and in the absence of parental authority young people may seek protection, camaraderie, and "career opportunities" in gangs and the drug trade. The murder rate for young black men in these communities is so high that Gibbs (1988) refers to them as an "endangered species."

Although poor rural areas usually lack the level of violence characteristic of some inner cities, they also may be discouraging, hostile environments for children (Auletta, 1982). The declining economies of many rural areas intensify these problems (Green & Schneider, 1990). Recreational and educational opportunities for rural youths and adults are often limited.

Youth programs and informal social networks (e.g., concerned, mutually supportive neighbors) sometimes serve as "mediating structures" that protect young people from the risks of living in poor communities (Woodson, 1981). However, involvement in inner-city youth programs may sometimes stigmatize participants. In middle-class areas, youth programs are often viewed as opportunities to encourage and develop children's talents. In poor areas, youth programs are frequently thought of as interventions to discourage involvement with drugs or crime—although many participants may never have considered becoming involved in illegal activities (Littel & Wynn, 1989). Children may receive a hidden message from these programs that, because of the color of their skin or where they live, little is expected of them. Success may be negatively defined or attributed to the intervention or both—if the participants don't grow up to become thugs, the program is a success.

Social Status

Ogbu (1978) argues that "caste" or involuntary minorities—ethnic or racial groups drawn into the social order against their will and traditionally discriminated against—develop patterns of low academic achievement because of biases in the social structure and in employment opportunities. Even when the educational attainments of involuntary minorities are the same as those of whites, they often do not achieve the same degree of success in college and the job market (Braddock & McPartland, 1987; Steele, 1992). In addition to perceiving limited job opportunities, some young people of color may underachieve because, tiring of the pressure to refute racist devaluations, they "disidentify" with academic achievement (Steele, 1992).

Children of color whose parents are recent immigrants to America may not experience the same biases as other young people of color, but they may also feel alienated (Huang, 1990; Olsen, 1988). Southeast Asian immigrant children, for example, tend not to be stereotyped in the same ways as other young people of color and usually adjust well to U.S. society. However, in ways that are similar to native-born children of color, some Asian immigrant youths experience alienation and harassment that may lead to academic or behavioral problems.

In recent years, researchers have drawn parallels between the tendency for some young people of color to become academically disengaged and the school experiences of female students, young people with disabilities, and gay students. The parallels are interesting because they suggest that low social status may negatively impact student performance regardless of economic status.

Some researchers, for example, argue that because female students are discouraged from pursuing male-dominated professions, many young women see no reason to excel in subjects (e.g., math and science) preparatory for these professions (Chester, 1983; Earle, Roach, & Fraser, 1987). Similarly, young people with disabilities may suffer from the low expectations of others (Biklen, 1988). Citing research that indicates gay students are more likely than other youths to attempt suicide, to abuse drugs or alcohol, and to experience academic problems as a result of harassment and low social status, some researchers argue that these young people should also be identified as "at risk" and provided with supportive services (Uribe & Harbeck, 1992).

SCHOOL CLIMATE AND RESOURCES

Many students who exhibit at-risk behaviors (e.g., poor attendance) may not have any background risk factors—they may be placed at risk by the quality of their school environment. And many students who do have background risk factors may be placed at increased risk by a poor school climate or inadequate resources. We discuss the effect of school environment below.

School Climate

School climate is often as palpable as the weather. Some schools have a warm, friendly ambience, while others have a cold, foreboding environment that permeates classrooms and offices. It seems probable that school climate would influence student performance, and the research to date supports this conclusion (Comer, 1988; Firestone & Rosenblum, 1988; Fraser & Fisher, 1982). Subsequent chapters provide a comprehensive analysis of policies and programs to improve school climate.

School administration and support services must be especially sensitive to the needs of students with responsibilities or problems outside school (e.g., working students, teen mothers). Unfortunately, school climates are often inhospitable to these students. Teen mothers, for example, may be refused excused absences for prenatal/postnatal care, tracked into specific courses, and discouraged from full participation in extracurricular activities (Snider, 1989). Students with emotional problems may never have their difficulties treated because many schools have inadequate psychological services (Tuma, 1989). Even when counseling services are available, children of color may not have access to counselors who are sensitive to multicultural concerns (Gibbs & Huang, 1990). Guidance counseling also may be inadequate. For example, Suarez-Orozco (1989) reports that many Central American refugee children may be inappropriately tracked into vocational classes because counselors assume they are not "college material."

Highly mobile students may particularly suffer from inadequate administrative and support practices. Migrant children, for example, may lose academic credits or experience delays in enrollment due to lack of communication and coordination between schools (Morse, 1988; Phillips, 1985). And schools are often unprepared to address the myriad problems that homeless children must face (Molnar, Rath, & Klein, 1990; Nichols-Pierce, 1992).

School Resources

Over the past 30 years, various studies have documented huge expenditure disparities among districts and schools (Barton, Coley, & Goertz, 1991; Kozol, 1991; Sexton, 1961; Taylor & Piche, 1990). The tax bases in poor areas are limited, and community members are often less able to donate time and resources to schools than are community members in wealthier areas.

Do school resources make a difference for student performance? Some researchers argue that, controlling for student background, school expenditures are not related to student performance. The findings of the well-known Coleman report (N = 569,000 students nationwide) suggest that family and peer influences, not school resources, are the important determinants of student performance (Coleman et al., 1966). Analyzing over 20 years of research on expenditure differences since the Coleman report, Hanushek (1989) concludes that the accumulated evidence confirms there is no systematic relation between school resources and educational outcomes.

Disputing these findings, other researchers point to new studies that indicate school resources do influence student performance. Describing a study conducted for the state of Texas involving more than 2.4 million students in 900 districts, Ferguson (1991) reports that school inputs predict students' scores on standardized reading and math tests. Better teacher literacy skills, smaller class sizes, and more years of teacher experience are correlated with better student test performance, controlling for family and community background factors (i.e., single-parent households, poverty, parental education, English as a second language, race, and other demographic variables).

Do school resources influence student outcomes? Comparisons of aggregated expenditure data do not provide evidence of a strong correlation between expenditures and outcomes; however, certain school resources, such as high quality staff, that obviously require funds, seem linked to student achievement. Disengaged students are not the only students at risk—many, if not most, students at risk persist to graduation in impoverished schools that find it difficult to provide challenging educational opportunities.

INTERACTIVE RISKS AND RESOURCES

It is misleading to assess the risks posed by home or school characteristics in isolation from one another. As students progress through school, the cumulative effects of various risks and the interaction of risks and resources over time may lead to achievement disparities.

Parent and teacher expectations that pose no risk to children in and of themselves may cause problems if they are in conflict, producing cultural dissonance. A growing number of researchers argue that merely providing multicultural materials will not bridge the gap between diverse student and teacher backgrounds — learning context must also allow for differences in the values, skills, and learning styles children bring to the classroom (see the chapters of Part II, this volume). Cultural dissonance does not inevitably lead to problems in the classroom, but research suggests that bridging the gap between home and school may facilitate learning for all students, including those at high risk.

Furthermore, there are cumulative, interactive effects between risk factors and resources. Differences in early childhood resources may lead to a widening achievement gap over time between children. Walberg and Tsai (1983) argue that early investments in child care have a "Matthew effect" — initial advantages in educative and personal resources increase the likelihood that children will have the motivation and skills to invest in and profit from schooling, resulting in cumulative advantages over time. Various studies support this argument (e.g., Berrueta-Clement, Schweinhart, Barnett, Epstein, & Weikart, 1984), providing evidence for the importance of early intervention to aid troubled students and schools. However, a "fade-out" effect may occur if successive grades fail to build upon preschool influences and address age-specific needs (see Chapters 2 and 12, this volume).

ANALYZING EDUCATIONAL PERFORMANCE

How well do past and present theories of academic failure "fit" recent research? We analyze some of these theories below, and then we incorporate previous research into a somewhat more inclusive model that illustrates how risk factors, resources, and their interactions may lead to differing degrees of school success.

"Cultural Deprivation" Versus "Socioeconomic Disadvantages"

During the 1960s, many researchers argued that *culturally disadvantaged* black and low-income youth were disabled by a home environment that failed to stimulate intellectual development, reward student achievement, and support school completion (Deutsch et al., 1967). The "cultural disadvantage" perspective has two main flaws: (1) It suggests the average low-income family is dysfunctional, and (2) it views cultural difference as cultural deficit. Although the reported incidence of family risk factors (e.g., neglect/abuse) is higher for low-income families, there is no evidence that the average low-income home fails to foster healthy child development. And although recent research *does* suggest that cultural dissonance may lead to problems in the classroom, that should not imply the home culture is inferior or inconducive to learning. Rather, it suggests that teachers, parents, and students must adapt (not necessarily assimilate) to each other.

Other researchers have asserted that *socioeconomic disadvantages* constrain educational opportunities for poor children and children of color (e.g., Bowles & Gintis, 1976). Research does suggest that structural problems in schools and society may explain much of the variance in student performance. However, while sociological factors may explain broad disparities in student outcomes, they do not explain the performance variances between individuals with similar socioeconomic backgrounds or among schools that serve similar demographic groups.

Student Engagement

Researchers increasingly conceptualize poor educational performance as the outcome of a process of *disengagement* that may begin as early as a child's entry into school (Finn, 1989; Kelly, 1989; Natriello, 1984). According to this model, students who do not identify with, participate in, and succeed in school activities become increasingly at risk of academic failure and dropout. To improve student achievement and persistence, the school climate must foster "investment" behavior — schools must encourage student involvement in academic and extracurricular activities by stimulating students' interest, increasing their personal resources (e.g., remediating skill deficiencies), and rewarding their efforts.

Models of engagement offer powerful explanations for academic progress and student persistence to graduation. No matter the quality of educational opportunities, if students are not engaged with schoolwork, the likelihood of academic success is low. However, to determine the *value* of student persistence, that is, the degree to which students learn useful skills, we must incorporate assessments of educational quality into measures of engagement. Otherwise, we may design "engaging" reforms that do little more than encourage students to persist in schools and academic tracks that are still separate and unequal, and to succeed in educational programs that may be irrelevant to the intellectual and social demands students must face as adults.

AN ALTERNATIVE MODEL OF STUDENT PERFORMANCE

A student's personal, home, community, and school characteristics should not be studied in isolation — all of these variables contribute to student performance, and they are strongly interactive. Recognizing these interactive dynamics, we integrate various theoretical perspectives to explain the variety of reasons that some students fail and others succeed. In particular, we build upon Rossi and Gilmartin's (1980) conceptual framework for the study of educational performance.

As shown in Figure 1.1, we argue that academic progress is primarily an ongoing function of (1) the quality of student resources (e.g., abilities, family support, educational opportunities) and (2) the incentives and pressures perceived by students to invest these resources in academic achievement. Past "returns" on educational investments have a cumulative impact on a student's ability and desire to achieve academic success and to persist in school.

This model combines elements of various engagement models (e.g., Bean & Metzner, 1985; Tinto, 1975). Two distinctive elements of this model are (1) we note that the perception of the effects of engagement may change over time and influence subsequent engagement, and (2) we distinguish between academic engagement and intellectual development. In order to provide quality education, schools must foster intellectual development as well as encourage student interest and involvement in the classroom. Ideally, intellectual development enhances understanding of the self and the environment *and* adds to a young person's academic proficiencies.

In this conceptualization, "risk factors" are variables that decrease the probability that a student will possess the ability, willingness, or opportunities for academic engagement and intellectual development. Being an African-American child, for example, is not a risk factor, while experiencing adverse treatment in or outside the classroom because of one's race or ethnicity *is* a risk factor.

"Resources" (e.g., good health, high quality instruction) are variables that increase the probability that a student will possess the ability, willingness, or opportunities for engagement and intellectual growth. The absence of basic resources (e.g., adequate nutrition) may place a child at risk, while the presence of special resources (e.g., private tutoring in advanced subjects) may give a child an advantage in relation to his or her peers (Reed, 1975). If an improvement in resources eliminates the risk factors that threaten academic progress, a student should no longer be considered or labeled "at risk."

Student Resources

As Bronfenbrenner (1979) points out, the multiple social systems that young people participate in have an "ecological" relation to each other.

FIGURE 1.1 A model for understanding academic progress

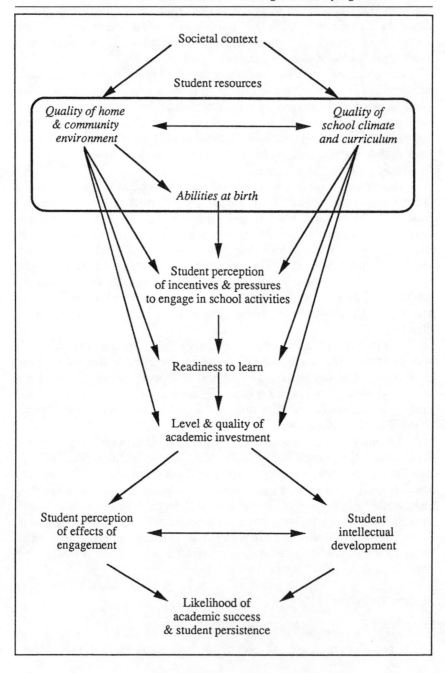

The levels of parental and community resources may influence neonatal health and abilities at birth; developments at home may lead to changes in student behavior, and changes in community demographics and responses may directly or indirectly lead to changes in the school environment. High academic achievement is most likely when schools, homes, and communities contribute to students' ability, willingness, and opportunities to invest in education. Academic failure is most likely when a student has few or no sources of encouragement, practical support, and educational opportunities.

The model presented here, however, does not suggest that schools, homes, and communities must all function optimally in order to prevent educational failure. Resources in one social system may mediate risk factors in another social system. For example, an intellectually stimulating home may compensate for inadequate schooling, and a supportive, orderly school may mitigate the effects of a dangerous, chaotic neighborhood.

Student Perceptions of Incentives and Pressures

Many theories of engagement focus on the incentives for student involvement (Tinto, 1975). The attraction of interesting and relevant assignments, the satisfaction of personal accomplishment, the pleasure of group participation, the desire to acquire skills necessary for a lucrative career, and other rewards may encourage student achievement and persistence. Incentives to do well academically must be greater than incentives to engage in competing activities.

In addition to incentives, research suggests that pressure is also a powerful inducement for student engagement. For example, Clark (1983) notes that students whose parents set firm but not harsh rules and expectations tend to do better than students who lack parental discipline. "Pressure" has negative connotations, so people often talk of "challenging" students rather than pressuring them. However, while "challenge" describes the "pull" of encouragement or stimulating curriculum, it fails to convey the "push" of punishment or loss of rewards. Successful students often have parents, teachers, and peers who "push" them to do their best academically. These students know that if they fail to show effort, they may experience undesirable outcomes such as reproaches from teachers, loss of privileges at home, or criticism from their friends. However, pressure to achieve seemingly unattainable goals may result in disengagement and dropout.

As shown in the diagram, abilities at birth may influence students' perceptions of the incentives and pressures to engage in school activities. If students have strong talents in certain areas, engaging in those activities may be especially appealing and rewarding to them. A student with a high aptitude for mathematics, for example, may find math assignments inherently rewarding, and she may also enjoy the praise she receives from her teachers and parents. Conversely, students born with conditions that make learning or class participation difficult may see little incentive to engage in activities that appear hard and unrewarded.

However, the degree to which students perceive goals as attainable and the extent to which they are aware of academic rewards are not necessarily accurate reflections of reality. As Alva and Padilla (1989) point out, the presence or absence of support from family members, school personnel, and others may shape students' attitudes about their abilities and influence their performance. In addition, differences in personality, culture, or learning styles—and changes in employment opportunities or social status—may lead to differences or changes in the types of learning contexts perceived as "rewarding." It is not enough for schools to provide learning opportunities that are viewed by school staff as excellent: Schools must understand and communicate the relevance of these opportunities to students' lives, and schools must bolster students' confidence in their abilities to take advantage of these opportunities.

Readiness to Learn

As indicated in Figure 1.1, students' readiness to learn is the product of the interaction between the environment, the school, and students' perceptions of the incentives and pressures to engage in school activities. Each of these factors helps to structure a student's readiness to learn. The degree of "fit" between a child's abilities and the demands of school life, the extent to which there is consonance between home and school expectations, and the extent to which school activities appear rewarding all influence a child's readiness to meet school requirements.

Environmental and school factors contribute varying levels of assets that may affect students' readiness to engage in school activities. The most important of these resources are those that meet children's health and developmental needs. Although children's characteristics may differ, they all have the same basic needs for food, clothes, and shelter; safety and stability; adequate health care; guidance and loving support. If these basic needs are unmet, a student is at risk of being inattentive, unresponsive, and uncooperative in school.

Exceptionally skillful parenting, richly supportive communities, and other resources may increase children's ability and willingness to learn, giving them an advantage in school.

Level and Quality of Academic Investment

Student investment is key to academic success and student persistence. If students invest time and effort in school activities, the likelihood that they will achieve academic success increases. Students' readiness to learn is key to academic investment. If students lack the skills or desire to engage in classroom assignments, their investment in these activities is likely to be low.

In addition, as shown in the model, a student's home and school may influence the level and quality of student investment. Given similar levels of student effort, the academic investments of a student with excellent educational opportunities are likely to be more productive than those of a student with poor educational opportunities. Lack of exposure to challenging subject areas or inadequate instruction in these areas may limit skill acquisition. Home exposure to challenging educational opportunities may compensate for or complement school exposure, and vice versa.

Limitations of the Model

It is important to note that this model, like many other models of student engagement, is an attempt to explain and predict academic progress for individual students at risk—it does not deal with all the factors that affect educational equity or social mobility. Although it may be used as a conceptual tool for understanding the performance of students and schools, it does not fully suggest how to change *patterns* of educational inequities and mediocrity.

To fully understand and address the factors that perpetuate social disparities and place students at risk, we need a conceptual framework that, at the very least, compares the quality of educational opportunities across schools and social groups. Educational disparities are not simply the result of risk factors that cause emotional or physical harm, or that alienate students from school—many students at risk of developing low skill levels are emotionally and physically healthy, and they enjoy a relative amount of academic "success" in warm, caring (yet substandard) schools. For many of these students, cumulative disadvantages in educational opportunities may place them in danger of being unable to compete with more advantaged, better educated students in college or the job market. Reforms that raise the educational performance of all socioeconomic groups will not necessarily reduce school inequities—school reforms may cause identical rates of academic progress for all groups, leaving the same degree of educational disparities between groups. And improvements in standardized test scores or attendance should be applauded, but they should not be our sole gauge of progress toward educational excellence and relevance—the range and level of skills acquired may be inadequate for the demands of adult life. Specifying the range and level of skills that diverse students need to acquire—and developing a detailed strategy for providing the school inputs and external resources necessary to cultivate these skills—is beyond the scope of this chapter and is a subject of ongoing debate among those involved in school reform.

Yet there is a growing consensus on effective school practices for all students, including those at high risk—a consensus that hopefully will serve as a foundation for conceptualizing and addressing patterns of inequity across schools. The research on effective school strategies is examined in subsequent chapters.

REFERENCES

Aday, L. A., & Andersen, R. M. (1984). The national profile of access to medical care: Where do we stand? *American Journal of Public Health, 74,* 1331–1339.

Alperstein, G., Rappaport, C., & Flanigan, J. M. (1988). Health problems of homeless children in New York City. *American Journal of Public Health, 78,* 1232–1233.

Alva, S. A., & Padilla, A. M. (1989). *A contextual interaction model of academic invulnerability among Mexican-American students.* Stanford, CA: Center for Educational Research at Stanford.

Auletta, K. (1982). *The underclass.* New York: Vintage Books.

Barton, P. E., Coley, R. J., & Goertz, M. E. (1991). *The state of inequality.* Princeton, NJ: Educational Testing Service.

Bean, J. P., & Metzner, B. S. (1985). A conceptual model of nontraditional undergraduate student attrition. *Review of Educational Research, 55*(4), 485–540.

Berrueta-Clement, J. R., Schweinhart, J. J., Barnett, W. S., Epstein, A. S., & Weikart, D. P. (1984). *Changed lives: The effects of the Perry Preschool Program on youths through age 19.* Ypsilanti, MI: High/Scope Educational Research Foundation (Monograph No. 8).

Biklen, D. (1988). The myth of clinical judgment. *Journal of Social Issues, 44,* 127–140.

Bowles, S. S., & Gintis, H. M. (1976). *Schooling in capitalist America.* New York: Basic Books.

Braddock, J. H., II, & McPartland, J. M. (1987). How minorities continue to be excluded from equal employment opportunities: Research on labor market and institutional barriers. *Journal of Social Issues, 43*(1), 5–39.

Braveman, P., Oliva, G., Miller, M. G., Reiter, R., & Egerter, S. (1989). Adverse outcomes and lack of health insurance among newborns in an eight-county area of California, 1982–1986. *New England Journal of Medicine, 321,* 508–513.

Bronfenbrenner, U. (1979). *The ecology of human development: Experiments by nature and design.* Cambridge, MA: Harvard University Press.

Centers for Disease Control. (1985, July 19). Drug-resistant tuberculosis among the homeless — Boston. *Morbidity and Mortality Weekly Report, 35,* 429–431.

Chasnoff, I. J. (1991). Drugs, alcohol, pregnancy, and the neonate: Pay now or pay later. *The Journal of the American Medical Association, 266,* 1567–1568.

Chasnoff, I. J., Burns, W. J., Schnoll, S. H., & Burns, K. A. (1985). Cocaine use in pregnancy. *New England Journal of Medicine, 313,* 666–669.

Chasnoff, I. J., Landress, H. J., & Barrett, M. E. (1990). The prevalence of illicit-drug or alcohol use during pregnancy and discrepancies in mandatory reporting in Pinellas County, Florida. *New England Journal of Medicine, 322,* 1202–1206.

Chavkin, W., Kristal, A., Seabron, C., & Guigli, P. E. (1987). The reproductive experience of women living in hotels for the homeless in New York City. *New York State Journal of Medicine, 87,* 10–13.

Chester, N. L. (1983). Sex differentiation in two high school environments: Implications for career development among black adolescent females. *Journal of Social Issues, 39*(3), 29–40.

Clark, R. M. (1983). *Family life and school achievement. Why poor black children succeed or fail.* Chicago: University of Chicago Press.

Coleman, J., Campbell, E. Q., Hobson, C. J., McPartland, J., Mood, A. M., Weinfeld, F. D., & York, R. L. (1966). *Equality of educational opportunity.* Washington, DC: U.S. Government Printing Office.

Comer, J. P. (1988). Educating poor minority children. *Scientific American, 259*(5), 42–48.

Deutsch, M., Bloom, R. D., Brown, B. R., Deutsch, C. P., Goldstein, L. S., John, V. P., Katz, P. A., Levinson, A., Peisach, E. C., & Whiteman, M. (1967). *The disadvantaged child.* New York: Basic Books.

Dugger, C. W. (1992, September 8). Troubled children overwhelm care system. *New York Times,* pp. A1, A17.

Earle, J., Roach, V., & Fraser, K. (1987). *Female dropouts: A new perspective.* Alexandria, VA: Youth Services Program, National Association of State Boards of Education.

Ekstrom, R. B., Goertz, M. E., Pollack, J. M., & Rock, D. A. (1987). Who drops out of school and why? Findings from a national study. In G. Natriello (Ed.), *School dropouts: Patterns and policies* (pp. 52–69). New York: Teachers College Press.

Ferguson, R. F. (1991). Competitive salaries, teacher quality, and student performance. *Research Bulletin.* Cambridge, MA: Malcolm Wiener Center for Social Policy.

Fernandez, R. M., Paulsen, R., & Hirano-Nakanishi, M. (1989). Dropping out among Hispanic youth. *Social Science Research, 18,* 21–52.

Finn, J. D. (1989). Withdrawing from school. *Review of Educational Research, 59,* 117–142.

Firestone, W. A., & Rosenblum, S. (1988). Building commitment in urban high schools. *Educational Evaluation and Policy Analysis, 10,* 285–299.

Fraser, B. J., & Fisher, D. L. (1982). Predicting students' outcomes from their perceptions of classroom psychosocial environment. *American Educational Research Journal, 19,* 498–518.

Gibbs, J. T. (1988). Health and mental health of young black males. In J. T.
    Gibbs (Ed.), *Young, black, and male in America: An endangered species*
    (pp. 219–257). Dover, MA: Auburn House.
Gibbs, J. T., & Huang, L. N. (1990). A conceptual framework for assessing and
    treating minority youth. In J. T. Gibbs, L. N. Huang, & Associates (Eds.),
    Children of color: Psychological interventions with minority youth (pp. 1–
    29). San Francisco: Jossey-Bass.
Green, A. H. (1978). Self-destructive behavior in battered children. *American
    Journal of Psychiatry, 135*, 579–582.
Green, B. L., & Schneider, M. J. (1990). Threats to funding for rural schools.
    Journal of Education Finance, 15, 302–318.
Guttman, J., Geva, N., & Gefen, S. (1988). Teachers' and school children's stereo-
    typic perception of "the child of divorce." *American Educational Research
    Journal, 25*, 555–571.
Hack, M., Breslau, N., Weissman, B., Aram, D., Klein, N., & Borawski, E.
    (1991). Effect of very low birth weight and subnormal head size on cognitive
    abilities at school age. *New England Journal of Medicine, 325*, 231–237.
Halpern, R. (1991). *The role of after-school programs in the lives of inner-city
    children: A study of the Urban Youth Network after-school programs.* Chi-
    cago: University of Chicago, Chapin Hall Center for Children.
Hampton, R. L., & Newberger, E. H. (1985). Child abuse incidence and report-
    ing by hospitals: Significance of severity, class, and race. *American Journal
    of Public Health, 75*(1), 56–59.
Hanushek, E. A. (1989, May). The impact of differential expenditures on school
    performance. *Educational Researcher, 18*(4), 45–51, 62.
Hodgkinson, H. (1985). *All one system: Demographics of education – kindergar-
    ten through graduate school.* Washington, DC: Institute for Educational
    Leadership.
Huang, L. N. (1990). Southeast Asian refugee children and adolescents. In J. T.
    Gibbs, L. N. Huang, & Associates (Eds.), *Children of color: Psychological
    interventions with minority youth* (pp. 278–321). San Francisco: Jossey-Bass.
Kelly, D. (1989, March). *Slipping in and out of the system: Continuation high
    schools and the process of disengagement.* Paper presented at the annual
    meeting of the American Educational Research Association, San Francisco.
Kline, J., Stein, Z., & Hutzler, M. (1987). Cigarettes, alcohol and marijuana:
    Varying associations with birthweight. *International Journal of Epidemiol-
    ogy, 16*, 44–51.
Kotlowitz, A. (1991). *There are no children here.* New York: Doubleday.
Kozol, J. (1991). *Savage inequalities.* New York: Crown.
Littel, J., & Wynn, J. (1989). *The availability and use of community resources
    for young adolescents in an inner-city and a suburban community.* Chicago:
    University of Chicago, Chapin Hall Center for Children.
Molnar, J. M., Rath, W. R., & Klein, T. P. (1990). Constantly compromised:
    The impact of homelessness on children. *The Journal of Social Issues, 46*(4),
    109–124.
Morse, S. (1988, October). *Characteristics of migrant secondary students: Out-
    reach meeting report.* (ERIC Document Reproduction Service No. ED 319
    550) Florida State Dept. of Education, Tallahassee, and State University of
    New York, Geneseo College.
Natriello, G. (1984). Problems in the evaluation of students and student disengage-

ment from secondary schools. *Journal of Research and Development in Education, 17,* 14–24.

Nichols-Pierce, M. (1992, April). *Socio-political organizations and diverse populations: Responding to the educational needs of homeless students.* Paper presented at the annual meeting of the American Educational Research Association, San Francisco.

Odum, H. (1968). The education of Negroes. In I. A. Newby (Ed.), *The development of segregationist thought* (pp. 63–69). New York: Columbia University Press.

Ogbu, J. U. (1978). *Minority education and caste: The American system in cross-cultural perspective.* New York: Academic Press.

Olsen, L. (1988). *Crossing the schoolhouse border: Immigrant students and the California public schools.* San Francisco: California Tomorrow.

Perry, M., Doran, L., & Wells, E. (1983). Developmental and behavioral characteristics of the physically abused child. *Journal of Clinical Child Psychology, 12,* 320–324.

Phillips, K. R. (1985). *The educational disadvantages of junior high and high school migrant students in Wisconsin. Part one of a supplementary school program for the children of migratory agricultural workers in Wisconsin.* Paper presented at the State Superintendents' Conference for Supervisors and Directors of Instruction, Madison, WI.

Reed, R. J. (1975). Ethnicity, social class, and out-of-school educational opportunity. *Journal of Negro Education, 44,* 316–334.

Rossi, R. J., & Gilmartin, K. J. (1980). Social indicators of youth development and educational performance: A programmatic statement. *Social Indicators Research, 7,* 157–191.

Sexton, P. C. (1961). *Education and income: Inequalities in our public schools.* New York: Viking Press.

Snider, W. (1989, May 17). Study: Schools violating rights of pregnant girls. *Education Week, 8,* 34.

Steele, C. M. (1992, April). Race and the schooling of black Americans. *Atlantic Monthly,* pp. 68–78.

Stroup, A. L., & Robins, L. N. (1972). Elementary school predictors of high school dropout among black males. *Sociology of Education, 45,* 212–222.

Suarez-Orozco, M. M. (1989). *Central American refugees and U.S. high schools: A psychosocial study of motivation and achievement.* Stanford, CA: Stanford University Press.

Taylor, W. L., & Piche, D. M. (1990, December). *A report on shortchanging children: The impact of fiscal inequity on the education of students at risk.* U.S. House of Representatives, Committee on Education and Labor, 101st Congress, 2nd Session, Washington, DC: Government Printing Office.

Tinto, V. (1975). Dropout from higher education: A theoretical synthesis of recent research. *Review of Educational Research, 45,* 89–125.

Tuma, J. M. (1989). Mental health services for children: The state of the art. *American Psychologist, 44*(2), 188–199.

Tyack, D. B. (1974). *The one best system: A history of American urban education.* Cambridge, MA: Harvard University Press.

Uribe, V., & Harbeck, K. M. (1992). Addressing the needs of lesbian, gay, and bisexual youth: The origins of Project 10 and school-based intervention. In K. M. Harbeck (Ed.), *Coming out of the classroom closet: Gay and lesbian students, teachers, and curricula* (pp. 9–28). New York: Harrington Park Press.

Viadero, D. (1992). New research finds little lasting harm for "crack" children. *Education Week, 11*(19).

Walberg, H. J., & Tsai, S. (1983). Matthew effects in the classroom. *American Educational Research Journal, 20*, 359–373.

Werner, E. E., & Smith, R. S. (1982). *Vulnerable but invincible: A longitudinal study of resilient children and youth.* New York: McGraw-Hill.

Woodson, R. L. (1981). *A summons to life: Mediating structures and the prevention of youth crime.* Washington, DC: American Enterprise Institute.

CHAPTER 2

Rising to the Challenge

Emerging Strategies for Educating Youth At Risk

NETTIE LEGTERS AND EDWARD L. MCDILL

What can be done to effectively engage and educate students who are at risk of low achievement, failure, and eventually dropping out of school? What can be done for students who perform reasonably well but whose educational programs provide them with substandard or limited educational opportunities and experiences, leaving them at a disadvantage as they move on to college or work? These questions have been a central concern of many educators over the past 3 decades and have given rise to a vast number of compensatory programs designed to provide extra help to chronic underachievers and equalize distribution of educational resources and opportunities.

In this chapter, we examine a sample of strategies and programs that outline the terrain of both traditional and emerging resources to the challenge of educating at-risk students (see also Natriello, McDill, & Pallas, 1990; Slavin, Karweit, & Madden, 1989). We begin with a brief look at the ways schools traditionally have addressed academic and socioeconomic student diversity. We then turn to an overview of current and emerging strategies and programs that appear to hold particular promise for educating youths who are at risk. Finally, we raise some issues central to the success of any serious reform strategy.

TRADITIONAL RESPONSES: SORTING AND SELECTING

One of the most enduring characteristics of public education in the United States is the socioeconomic and ethnic heterogeneity of its student body. In general, schools have responded to student diversity with various systems of sorting and selecting students into more homogeneous learning groups.

Grouping/Tracking

One of the most pervasive and controversial forms of instructional grouping is the placement of students in homogeneous learning groups within a grade, or even within a classroom, according to evaluations of their academic performance. This long-standing and widespread practice is often called "ability grouping" at the elementary level and "tracking" at the high school level, where students can be separated into distinct academic, general, and vocational streams — a structure that can have consequences not only in terms of the quality of education they receive but for peer group formation, likelihood of graduation, and future educational and employment opportunities.

There is a growing body of both qualitative and quantitative evidence, however, that suggests ability grouping and tracking, as currently practiced, are poor methods for dealing fairly and effectively with student diversity. Students from low-income and minority backgrounds are disproportionately represented in lower groups or tracks. Moreover, the less selective programs and lower-level classes are often stigmatized and likely to provide poor climates for learning, with lower expectations for student achievement (see, for example, Braddock, 1990; Oakes, 1992).

Retention

Like tracking, the practice of holding back students who fail to demonstrate required levels of achievement has also been a typical response to the challenge of educating low-achieving students. However, like tracking, the bulk of the research evidence shows that retention, as it is currently practiced in most schools, has few positive effects on student learning (see Shepard & Smith, 1989, for a collected review).

Special Education

One of the most important trends in recent years has been the substantial increase in the numbers of students with mild academic handicaps who are receiving special education services. Slavin (1989) points out the striking fact that, while the percentages of students categorized as physically disabled and mentally retarded have stayed at about the same levels from 1976 to 1989, the numbers of students categorized as learning disabled have increased by more than 250%. Reporting that almost 90% of this increase represents the entry into the special education system of low achievers who would not have been served in special education in the 1970s, he concludes that "special education has assumed a substantial burden in trying to meet the needs of students at risk of school failure," even though "research comparing students with mild academic handicaps in special education to similar students left in regular classrooms finds few benefits for this very expensive service" (pp. 15–16).

Chapter 1 Pull-Out Programs

The largest federal education program that provides extra help to students at risk of failure is the national Chapter 1 program. Chapter 1 began in 1965 as Title I of the Elementary and Secondary Education Act of 1965 (Public Law 89–10) and continues today as the primary source of funding for a wide range of academic and social programs serving over 5 million at-risk students nationwide. The most widespread delivery strategy of Chapter 1 services is the "pull-out" model, in which students who are having difficulty in a particular subject typically are removed from their regular classrooms for 20 to 40 minutes a day to participate in subject-specific, small group remedial instruction (Slavin, 1989). However, Stein, Leinhardt, and Bickel (1989) cite several disadvantages to the pull-out approach, and several evaluations of the program in the mid-1980s concluded that Chapter 1 programs displayed only modest positive effects on reading and math skills. In addition, these gains did little to close the gap between low-achieving students and their more advantaged peers, and students' progress was rarely sustained beyond 2 years after participation in the program (studies summarized in Natriello and co-authors, 1990, pp. 72–78).

Tracking, retention, special education, and Chapter 1 pull-out programs are primary ways in which schools have attempted over the years to respond to diversity and the needs of underachieving students. In practice, however, the research evidence available suggests that these strategies add few extra benefits and often may do more to limit than to increase learning opportunities.

CURRENT AND EMERGING STRATEGIES

Changes in Chapter 1

The size and scope of Chapter 1 make the program an important bellwether for change in educational programs for youth at risk. One of the potentially most significant changes brought about by the 1988 Hawkins-Stafford amendments (Public Law 100–297) was the provision for greater flexibility in the coordination of program resources with the regular school program, by enabling schools with 75% or more students eligible for free lunch to use Chapter 1 funds for school-wide programs (LeTendre, 1991). There is both potential and challenge inherent in the school-wide project (SWP) approach, however. For example, teachers and principals report that the flexibility of the SWP enables them to create more effective learning environments for all students. At the same time, Winfield (1991) cautions that the success of the SWP option depends on adequate support for change at the central office or district level and on the availability of adequate resources for on-site assistance.

Few argue with the intent of the Hawkins-Stafford reauthorization to provide for greater flexibility in the use of Chapter 1 funds and encourage a focus on student outcomes. Few also would take issue with the way in which many schools are taking advantage of this flexibility. The program improvement mandates accompanying the bill, however, have been the subject of some criticism. Under the new program improvement requirements, schools that are not making sufficient progress toward bringing students up to grade-level performance must recast their programs so that they will produce measurable gains in student progress. On the face of it, this is a reasonable, even laudable goal. However, several researchers argue that the requirements may have a variety of negative effects, including potential for error in identifying schools "needing improvement," a feeling of being stigmatized among staff of those programs so identified, an evaluation model that encourages the use of standardized tests and gains measured in Normal Curve Equivalents (NCEs), possible greater incidence of retention in order to boost test scores, and an increased tendency by schools to focus on narrow instructional objectives that are easily measured (see, for example, Clayton, 1991). At the time of this writing, Chapter 1 will be up for reauthorization again shortly, and several federal evaluations are being counted on to assess the quality and delivery of services and to identify exemplary programs and practices.

EARLY INTERVENTION

Early intervention programs, targeting very young children, are often regarded as the most cost-effective education interventions. These programs are designed to ensure that students enter and progress through school "ready to learn." Although the advantages of early intervention without follow-up programs in later grades may be overemphasized, early childhood programs can help provide a firmer foundation for later school success (Slavin, Karweit, & Wasik, 1992).

Preschool

Preschool and kindergarten environments that are developmentally appropriate and provide learning experiences that develop the child's language and symbolic competencies, can help all children enter school at higher levels of readiness. Head Start, created in 1965, was the first national program for preschoolers and remains one of the most well-known and popular federal initiatives. Since 1965, Head Start has served a total of 12.5 million children; in 1991 it received nearly $2 billion to operate approximately 1,350 projects serving over half a million children nationwide (U.S. Department of Health and Human Services, 1992).

The scientific basis of Head Start's effectiveness is somewhat arguable, however. In 1985, CSR, Inc. conducted a review/meta-analysis that synthesized results from more than 200 separate evaluations conducted over a 20-year period. They concluded that Head Start does show some statistically significant effects on students' cognitive and socioemotional development. However, the study reported a frequent "fade-out" effect whereby students' cognitive and affective gains disappeared by the end of the first year of regular school (McKey et al., 1985). At the time of this writing, the national Head Start office reports that another comprehensive evaluation of the Head Start program will be conducted in the near future.

Kindergarten

Nearly all children (98%) attend kindergarten. Researchers have studied both the organizational and curricular features of kindergarten programs to determine their effects on cognitive and affective outcomes in young children. Karweit's syntheses of the research literature in this area show modest evidence that full-day programs are more effective than half-day programs for students at risk, but show little evidence that extra-year kindergarten programs provide extra benefits to children, at risk or otherwise (e.g., Karweit, 1992). She argues that more lasting effects on children do not come from adding time to the child's kindergarten experience, but rather are brought about by participation in learning environments that are both individually and developmentally appropriate and that develop the child's language competencies and understanding of the functions of written and print materials.

Karweit (1989) examined 21 validated kindergarten programs, seven of which are still active (KITE, TALK, CLIMB, STAMM, Early Prevention of

School Failure, KINDERMATH, and the Kenosha Model). Karweit (1992) further describes five programs—KITE, Early Prevention of School Failure, Books and Beyond, Writing to Read, and STaR. Of these, KITE (Kindergarten Integrated Thematic Experiences) is shown to produce the largest effects on students' reading and math. The program incorporates two well-evaluated programs, Astra's Magic Math and Alphaphonics, to provide students with a kindergarten day integrated around a theme that emphasizes language and cognitive, physical, and socioemotional development.

Success for All

Approaches in the elementary grades that deliver extra, intensive academic help to students when they most need it have been found to have substantial positive effects on students' mastery of reading skills and comprehension abilities (e.g., Madden, Slavin, Karweit, Dolan, & Wasik, 1991). Success for All, for example, is an elementary school restructuring program that takes advantage of the new option to use Chapter 1 funds for school-wide projects. The goal of the project is to do everything necessary to ensure that all students will perform at grade level in reading, writing, and mathematics by the end of third grade. Strategies used in the program include one-on-one tutoring, regrouping for reading, a family-support team, frequent assessments of learning with immediate help on problems, and individual academic plans for each student. At the time of this writing, the program has been implemented in 36 urban elementary schools that have high minority and low-income student populations. In a first-year evaluation of Success for All, participating children outscored a matched control group on multiple measures of reading readiness and reading comprehension tests (Slavin et al., 1989). As is the case with all early childhood programs, however, follow-up studies that show how participating children fare in later school experiences are needed to determine whether such programs provide the "booster" shot needed to protect students against future school failure.

MULTICULTURAL EDUCATION

Multiculturalism has been the subject of enormous debate in recent years, with the idea of "multicultural education" most often associated with specific changes in curriculum. Proponents decry the Anglo-centric bias of traditional learning materials and argue for the integration of more diverse, positive images, historical role models, and, in general, a more balanced view of history that represents the experiences and perspectives of marginalized groups. Critics of multiculturalism view the kind of curricula being proposed as potentially divisive and even "anti-American" because they encourage students to seek their primary identity in a particular ethnic group rather than in a united American culture (e.g., Schlesinger, 1991). A slightly different version of such criticism is found in Ravitch (1991–92), who distinguishes between "pluralistic" and "particularistic" multiculturalism and argues for the former, which should result in a curriculum that reflects both multiculturalism and the common culture — "the pluribus and the unum" (p. 11).

While the public attention to multiculturalism has focused on balancing curriculum content, Gottfredson, Nettles, and McHugh (1992), in their first report of their evaluation of Pittsburgh's Prospect Middle School's Multicultural Education Center, outline four additional elements of multicultural education: (1) personal development and interpersonal relations of students; (2) fair and effective approaches to individual differences in learning styles that are believed to be linked to cultural influences; (3) multicultural representation in the entire school environment, including staffing, and (4) equal opportunity to learn for all groups. Prospect has adopted a multicultural approach to restructuring that incorporates not only a multicultural curriculum, but cooperative learning and conflict resolution techniques, staff development, parent and community involvement, and, notably, the elimination of tracking. Although a full program evaluation is not yet available, Prospect shows promise in meeting the substantial challenges facing its multicultural restructuring effort.

Another aspect of multicultural education is the issue of bilingual education, which also has been embroiled in controversy and debate since the passage of the federal Bilingual Education Act in 1968 (Public Law 90–247). The conflict can be seen in the general debate over whether bilingual education should be offered in schools as a tool to help minority students assimilate into the American mainstream or as a second-language acquisition that adds to the linguistic resources an individual already possesses (Hakuta & Pease-Alvarez, 1992). Specific examples of this conflict are found in the English-only movement versus the English-Plus coalition, and proposals for a bilingual immersion program in which "both language-majority and language-minority students learn each others' language while continuing to develop their own" (e.g., Cziko, 1992, p. 10).

CHANGES IN CURRICULUM

The content, purpose, and organization of courses and activities shape every student's school experience. In addition to multicultural education efforts, other initiatives reject the special education model of offering more of the same content at a perhaps slower pace, by developing and offering a core curriculum that is high level, more engaging, and relevant. These efforts generally focus on developing content that relates to the student's current interests and life experiences or by combining vocational with academic tasks.

Real-World Learning

A number of curriculum projects that focus on real-world experiences for the learning content have been developed to engage students actively in the learning process. Examples range from the microsociety school (Richmond, 1989) to experiential learning projects (e.g., Blumenfeld et al., 1991), from the Foxfire student publishing experience (Wigginton, 1989) to various community service programs (e.g., Nettles, 1991). At the same time, comprehensive plans are being pursued by major national groups to completely restructure the curriculum for active student learning of higher-order competencies through real-world applications in each major subject across the grades (Jackson, 1992). If all students are to benefit from these developments, resources must be available to implement ambitious curriculum changes in all schools, including those attended by poor and minority students and presently not adequately funded for instruction in the traditional curriculum.

Integration of Academic and Vocational Skills

Many middle and high school students are more motivated to work hard if they view classroom learning tasks as useful in the adult world of work. However, traditional vocational education has frequently been criticized as lacking sufficient academic content and failing to prepare students with well-defined marketable skills — problems that have a particularly strong impact on minority and lower-income students because they are disproportionately represented in vocational programs (Braddock, 1990).

Proposals for upgrading the quality of vocational education typically involve some variation of the thesis that programs must provide students with a combination of essential academic skills, rigorous vocational training, and on-the-job experience. Asserting that "learning to know and learning to do are linked," Bottoms and Presson (1989), for example, observe that "allowing students to use academic materials to perform 'real life' tasks or address 'real life' problems is appealing as a method for increasing students' motivation to learn higher level academic concepts in high school" (pp. 2–3). Considerable impetus for the integration of vocational and academic education has come from the reauthorization by Congress in 1990 of the Carl D. Perkins Vocational and Applied Technology Act (Public Law 101–476), which pressed states and local school districts to achieve such a merger. In an empirical survey, Grubb, Davis, and Lum (1991) studied more than 70 secondary schools around the United States and identified several different models for achieving this sort of integration. These models include merging of faculties and course content and creating academies or major programs within a school that focus on a general cluster of careers. Unfortunately, evaluation evidence of these programs is not generally available.

CHANGES IN INSTRUCTION

Accompanying changes in curriculum, changes have occurred in the more traditional forms of instruction—that is, away from the passive teacher-lecture/student-listen mode of instruction to a more active arrangement of learning activities. Recent approaches suggest that effective "instruction" can take place within and outside of the classroom, and that a personal connection with a "teacher" can make a difference in whether a student succeeds or fails. Specific strategies include involving nontraditional teachers such as mentors and race/sex role models, adult and cross-grade peer tutoring, and integrating technology as a tool for instruction.

Adults as Mentors or Advocates

A widely publicized approach to provide students with the support of a caring adult during the middle and high school grades is to use volunteers from the community as mentors or advocates. Although terminology differs in various programs, mentoring is commonly defined as a one-to-one relationship between an adult volunteer and a student who needs support for achieving academic or personal goals. Advocacy, on the other hand, is usually defined as a continuing set of relationships between an adult (volunteer or paid) and members of a group of students, in which the adult provides support and services by intervening on the students' behalf, monitoring participation in programs, or brokering additional services.

Research indicates that using outside adults as mentors or advocates can have modest positive effects on a limited range of student outcomes and that a well-designed program may help some students develop more positive attitudes toward school. The successful monitoring/advocacy relationship does require, however, continuing contacts (such as weekly face-to-face sessions), and these programs often have difficulty locating large enough numbers of adult volunteers who have the time and commitments to sustain relationships with students (McPartland & Nettles, 1991). Having school staff serve in mentor or advisor roles for middle and high school students overcomes the need to depend on outside volunteers and can increase the value of in-school relationships, but resource and scheduling issues are not always easily resolved. A frequent approach is to establish a homeroom-advisory period that meets several times each week to discuss a variety of school, character, and career topics in a group setting. However, recent analyses of data from a national survey of middle schools found no clear evidence of positive effects on students' perceptions of teacher–student relations, suggesting that the typical homeroom-advisory period today may be similar to the traditional superficial homeroom period, which provided few new opportunities for contacts between individual students and a caring adult at the school (McPartland, 1992).

Race/Sex Role Models

The multiple and often serious challenges faced by young African-American males, for example, in American society have prompted the development of various approaches to provide more positive role models for school-aged black male students (Ascher, 1991). These include African-American male classroom teachers for elementary grade classrooms, mentoring programs using black male adults from the community, and peer-tutoring approaches using older students to help young students of the same race and sex. These approaches have focused on various sex and ethnic groups and have been widely reported in the mass media (e.g., Butler, 1987; Hakuta & Pease-Alvarez, 1992; Tifft, 1990), but no careful research has assessed their impact on students.

In spite of the lack of evaluation, there is reason to believe that adding positive race/sex role models may be important particularly to school-aged African-American males (Fordham & Ogbu, 1986). Such programs have become the subject of controversy, however, because they often purposely segregate students by race and/or sex. Further, these programs are in some instances opposed by veteran civil rights organizations because they are believed to lead to tensions between black males and females and might provide support in the larger society for white supremacy advocates (e.g., NAACP Legal Defense and Education Fund, 1991).

Peer Support

A student's peer group will almost certainly be a powerful influence on attitudes and behaviors in school, since status and acceptance from others in the same age group become very important from early adolescence through young adulthood. But the peer influence can be either positive or negative with regard to the school's goals of hard work on classroom learning tasks, depending on the norms that develop within the various friendship groups to which a student may be attached. Several approaches have been encouraged to define positive roles in schools that most students will accept, and to structure classroom tasks and rewards that encourage peer support for academic efforts.

One strategy to assist students during the transition between elementary and middle school or between middle and high school is to pair each entering student with an older one at the school in a peer–mentor relationship that begins the first day of school for the newcomer and lasts throughout the year. In a recent experiment in a racially mixed Baltimore middle school, the older-student mentors were trained for their mentor responsibilities — with communication skills, conflict resolution, and community service concepts — and then were carefully matched with incoming students and scheduled to participate in weekly activities with their mentees, including checks on tardiness and absence patterns, tutoring, and community service projects. Many other examples are available, but without evaluation data the impact of these approaches is unknown.

Cooperative learning is another strategy that utilizes the peer group to attain academic and prosocial goals. Cooperative learning usually involves students working in small teams to accomplish a group goal, such as earning points on classroom tests that count in a classroom competition with other teams. Classroom competition is structured between teams so that each student's individual efforts contribute to a shared group goal, rather than raising the stakes for good grades under the usual classroom competition among individual students. As a result, peer norms are shifted to encourage classroom efforts of individual students rather than discouraging them. An extensive set of careful evaluation experiments confirms the positive effects of these forms of group effort on individual student achievement and peer group acceptance of team members (Slavin, 1990).

Tutoring

One-on-one tutoring is a powerful strategy for providing extra help to youth at all levels. With the recruitment of adult volunteers and various peer-tutoring strategies, school systems are able to provide many underachieving students with the type of one-on-one instruction formerly available only to more privileged segments of society (Cohen, Kulik, & Kulik, 1982).

Reviews of peer-tutoring studies that examine same-age and cross-age strategies show that peer tutoring contributes to the achievement of both tutors and tutees. Cohen and co-authors (1982), for example, conducted a meta-analysis of 65 studies and concluded that peer tutoring has modest positive effects on both tutor and tutee attitudes toward the subjects being taught and their performance in those subject areas, especially when the programs are highly structured. The advantage of highly structured programs in which student-tutors are given explicit instructions is also documented by Slavin (1986).

There has been some controversy over the relative effectiveness of tutoring compared with other types of interventions — reduced class size, computer-assisted instruction (CAI), and the extended school day. Levin, Glass, and Meister (1984, 1986) find that peer tutoring is the most cost-effective strategy for reading and math achievement, while Niemiec, Blackwell, and Walberg (1986) argue that CAI is the most cost-effective. Wasik and Slavin (1990) conducted a "Best Evidence Synthesis" of five programs using adult tutors to prevent reading failure in the early grades: Reading Recovery, Success for All, Prevention of Learning Disabilities, the Wallach Tutorial Program, and Programmed Tutorial Reading. These programs were shown to have more positive effects on student achievement than reduction of class size and student/adult ratio.

Technology

The potential of technology to transform, even revolutionize education has been a source of speculation since the advent of computers in the 1960s. Thirty years later, although many observe that the promise of technology has yet to be fulfilled, it continues to be viewed as a catalyst for change in schools (Bell & Elmquist, 1992). Numerous studies and reports examining how technology is being integrated into classrooms and schools, its impact on student learning, and its importance for educational restructuring identify technology as a key component of the nation's education reform agenda (see, for example, Sheingold & Tucker, 1990).

Many practitioners also assert that information-age technology holds particular promise for educating students at risk, yet few studies examine its actual effects on learning outcomes for students. For example, data from a national survey indicate that the most frequently reported effects of computer use on lower-achieving students are in behavioral and attitudinal areas such as motivation, self-confidence, and self-discipline (Becker, 1986). An analysis of these same data also shows that lower-achieving students are more likely to use computers for developing basic skills in math, reading, and language as opposed to higher-order skills or comprehension and problem solving. In addition, students in low-SES schools and rural schools are more likely to spend computer time on drill and tutorial programs than are students in high-SES metropolitan schools, where computers are used more frequently for more creative applications.

In an effort to move away from simple drill and practice programs for underachievers, the Vanderbilt Learning Technology Center and its Cognition and Technology Group have investigated the potential of interactive videodisk technology to improve learning for children at risk. This ongoing research is grounded in the knowledge base of cognition and child development and identifies active engagement and the need for a learning context accessible to the child as essential to successful learning (e.g., Johnson, 1992). Empirical findings of this research show improved comprehension and ability to make inferences when information is presented to the students through videodisk rather than traditional oral format. Similarly, the Higher Order Thinking Skills program (HOTS) also eschews drill and practice in favor of developing problem-solving and conceptual skills. HOTS combines software with special curriculum and instructional strategies to create a stimulating learning environment for students. For 35 minutes each day, students are challenged by trained teachers to think in more sophisticated ways and to develop hypotheses and strategies for solving problems (Pogrow, 1990). However, HOTS has not yet been evaluated experimentally.

One important barrier to the effective use of technology for students at risk is that students' exposure to technology-rich learning environments may be cut short when they advance or transfer to schools where technology is not effectively deployed. This problem was identified by researchers evaluating the lasting effects of the Apple Classrooms of Tomorrow (ACOT) program in Memphis, who found that once the ACOT students left the technology-rich, student-centered environment for a school where computer availability was limited, they were unable to transfer the skills they had learned (Ross, Smith, & Morrison, 1991).

In sum, there is evidence that technology can be used effectively to improve academic achievement for all students. However, it is clear that technology costs, and that schools with few resources will have difficulty providing their students with equal access to technology-rich learning environments. Moreover, effects will remain limited so long as programs are implemented only in a few classrooms at a school site and are not part of a larger school- or district-wide change effort (e.g., David, 1990). Maintaining access to technology throughout the student's school career, integrating technology so that it is available for all kinds of learning, and deploying uses of technology that move away from traditional teaching and learning methods, are necessary components of a successful technology strategy for educating students at risk.

CHANGES IN ASSESSMENT

Critics of conventional testing and assessment methods argue that such methods do more harm than good by narrowing the scope of instructional efforts. For this reason, alternative forms of assessment aim (1) to have students demonstrate all that they have learned and (2) to motivate rather than discourage students who start out well below average.

Alternative forms of assessment include oral interviews, science experiments, portfolios of students' work over extended periods, public exhibitions where students answer questions on their senior project, and performances of skills in simulated situations (see, for example, Perrone, 1991; Wolf, Bixby, Glenn, & Gardner, 1991). Although interest is now very strong in federal and state agencies to extend these new assessment methods to most if not all schools (and several well-financed development projects are underway), it is still unclear how the interests of low-SES and minority students will fare in this area. While prospects of new uniform high achievement standards and sensitive performance-based assessment methods are to be welcomed as long as *all* students are provided opportunities to demonstrate skills in these ways, the question remains whether the resources will be provided to all schools (including seriously underfunded schools) to put alternative assessment programs into place.

In addition to restricting the ways in which students demonstrate what they have learned, traditional assessment methods can be insensitive to the actual achievement or progress of individual students. As Mac Iver (1991) asserts, "traditional evaluation systems often do not adequately recognize the progress that educationally disadvantaged students make because even dramatic progress may still leave them near the bottom of the class in comparative terms or far from the 'percent correct' standard needed for a good grade" (p. 4). Individualized incentive and reward structures that value students' incremental improvements can motivate students to try harder, foster an intrinsic interest in the subject matter, and improve performance.

The Incentives for Improvement program is implementing such an evaluation and incentive system in four Baltimore public schools. Through the program, teachers help students develop "specific, individualized, short-range goals that are challenging but doable" based on the students' past performance (Mac Iver, 1991, p. 5). Students receive certificates and other awards for improvement as well as for high levels of achievement. In studies using a nonrandomized, matched control group, with a pretest/posttest design to evaluate the program's effectiveness on student performance and on students' motivation to learn, students participating in the program on average received higher grades and had a 10% higher probability of passing than did control students. A modest positive impact on students' perceptions of the intrinsic value of the subject matter as well as on overall student efforts also was found, although no effect on students' self-concept was shown as a result of the program.

ORGANIZATIONAL STRATEGIES

The way in which schools and classrooms are organized has an immediate impact on students' educational experiences. One of the most obvious aspects of school organization, ability grouping or tracking, was discussed earlier in this review. Other aspects such as school size, departmentalization, and organized connections to the world beyond school are also important to consider. Below we examine alternatives to aspects of school organization that have been found to have a negative impact on the learning of students.

Alternatives to Large Schools

Extensive research evidence indicates that a supportive climate for learning can be severely damaged by the very large secondary schools that are typical of the major urban and suburban districts where many minority and low-SES students are enrolled. Although there is no evidence that new smaller schools are now being constructed for the middle and high school grades, many smaller units *are* being created within large schools. Some community school districts in New York City, for example, have developed "schools-within-schools" in which a single building may contain up to five smaller separate schools — including elementary, junior high, special education, and special programs for troubled youth. The separate schools share the building's gym, labs, and studios, and older students from a unit may tutor younger students from another unit. Other examples include the "house" system in Columbus, Ohio, in which groups of 250 high school students remain together in largely autonomous units for their high school careers, and self-contained "academic units" within Philadelphia high schools that have a special vocational-academic focus (Toch, 1991). The "charter" system being developed in urban comprehensive high schools (see Chapter 8, this volume) is another example of this strategy. While these programs are promising, Maeroff (1992), for one, notes that opportunities for sustained, close, positive contacts between students and teachers will only be achieved if schools-within-schools are more than administrative units and provide adult guidance and support for each individual student.

Alternatives to Departmentalization

Most American middle and high schools, and many elementary schools as well, are departmentalized; that is, students receive daily instruction from several different teachers, each specializing in a single subject. The rationale for this approach is that the instructional content of each academic subject requires teachers who are experts in the area, and that instruction will be of higher quality when teachers can take special pride in their subject-matter discipline and can concentrate on preparing a limited number of outstanding lessons each day that are offered to multiple classrooms. Although research supports some of the instructional benefits of departmentalized staffing, the risks that many students will not encounter a climate of caring and support have been more strongly documented (e.g., Bryk, Lee, & Smith, 1990; McPartland, 1990).

Recent research indicates two approaches may help to offset the negative effects of departmentalized staffing. The first is a form of "semi-departmentalization," in which the number of different, specialized teachers assigned to each student is limited. A second way to offset the negative effects of departmentalized staffing is to implement interdisciplinary teacher teams that have specific team responsibilities for the success of each student. During regularly scheduled team planning periods, teachers identify students who need special attention and follow through by providing extra academic help and coordinating problem-solving approaches with students' families. Teams may be especially effective when combined with a teacher-advisory function in which each student has one specific adult in the school who serves as the main point of contact for advice and individual support. Evidence from national data on middle schools, as well as qualitative data, show that both semi-departmentalization and interdisciplinary teacher teams contribute to more positive school climates (Connors, 1992; McPartland, 1990).

Alternatives to Tracking

As pointed out earlier, another pervasive structural feature of American middle and secondary schools that often constitutes a major barrier to positive school climates for students is "tracking." Alternatives to tracking include various approaches to limit the use of separate classes for instruction, and various methods to make the heterogeneously mixed class work well when tracking is eliminated. The adverse effects of tracking can be limited in several ways, including the following: regrouping in only one or two courses (such as math and reading) while keeping all others randomly mixed; assigning students to track levels on the basis of course-specific data (so that a high-track assignment in one subject and a low-track assignment in another subject can occur for the same student); restricting the number of different track levels in the same course (such as a gifted section and a broad general section); and assigning extra resources and the most talented teachers to the classes with the most needy students (Braddock & McPartland, 1990).

Simply eliminating tracking to equalize educational opportunities will produce classes of students with a wide range of backgrounds and achievements in which special problems of student motivation, teacher effectiveness, and classroom climate must be addressed. Student motivation can suffer when earning high grades is too easy for those at the top of the academic distribution and too hard for those at the bottom. Teacher effectiveness can decline when classroom materials for a whole group lesson are poorly matched to the prior preparation of various students, such as reading matter that is geared to a single grade level when student reading skills range over several grade levels. The classroom climate can also be weakened in a heterogeneous class when discipline problems arise with students who cannot earn status through academic accomplishment.

Experiments to modify the structure of classroom competition indicate new directions for giving all students in heterogeneously grouped classes an opportunity to earn recognition and rewards for academic accomplishments. The basic idea is to establish individual benchmarks from which to calculate student improvement for the purpose of rewarding individual efforts at schoolwork. Several studies in the late 1970s (e.g., Beady & Slavin, 1980; Slavin, 1980) developed practical methods for calculating individual improvement points from regular teacher-constructed achievement tests in English and mathematics and demonstrated the motivational potential of frequent rewards to middle grade students on this basis.

Modifications of classroom curriculum materials and learning activities may also help teachers deal successfully with heterogeneous classrooms. The Civic Achievement Award Program (1989), for example, for middle grade social studies is a curriculum for U.S. history, geography, economics, and civics that contains lessons and classroom activities written at two reading levels (5/6 and 7/8). Individual students in a heterogeneous class using this program can work on the same lessons but at whichever reading level is more appropriate. The Literature Project: Reading for Real, for middle grade reading and literature, contains carefully selected literature of high interest for early adolescents from different racial-ethnic and gender groups in specified reading-level categories from grades 4–9. Similarly, new directions in mathematics instruction — away from the scope-and-sequence approach requiring prerequisite knowledge and toward a concept-based curriculum framework—may permit more effective learning activities in heterogeneously grouped classes.

The most commonly used structure to deal with the diversity of students in heterogeneous classrooms—and even to turn that diversity into an advantage—is cooperative learning (described earlier). Cooperative learning methods include a number of approaches for heterogeneously grouped classrooms that create roles of high status and responsibility for each student in the class and establish a positive peer climate for learning. Numerous empirical evaluations have shown positive effects for both below- and above-average students on academic achievement and on student acceptance and respect across race, sex, and social-class boundaries (e.g., Slavin, 1983). Other versions of cooperative learning assign roles to students that emphasize their special strengths, so as to build status in the group and commitment to group learning goals (see Cohen, 1986).

Closer Connections with Work or College

Schools can institutionalize direct connections between success in school and the student's future educational and employment opportunities. In this vein, schools can (1) provide better *information* about student behaviors in school to employment agents and college admissions officers; (2) offer specific employment *opportunities* or college financial aid to students who meet particular school performance standards; and (3) include actual college and work *experiences* as part of middle and high school learning activities.

Employers who hire recent high school graduates typically have little information from schools on which to base their decisions, even though many aspects of school behavior are useful indicators that a job candidate is dependable, can work well as a team leader or member, or has other special job-related talents. Most students know that their high school record of attendance, grades, test scores, and extracurricular activities has little meaning in the employment process, so there is little incentive from the labor market to do well on these criteria. New ways have been proposed for assembling records of academic and nonacademic accomplishments and for providing the information in a timely and convenient form in the job recruitment and selection process. Career Passport and Worklink are two examples of such initiatives (see Charner, 1988; Carlson, 1990).

Many middle and high school students also see little connection between their school behavior and later opportunities for college. In this case the problem is more likely to be an absence of knowledge by students of college admissions processes than a need for better information by colleges about their student applicants. A review of the evaluations of the Upward Bound program in Natriello and co-authors (1990), including the multiphase longitudinal study conducted by the Research Triangle Institute (Burkheimer, Riccobono, & Wisenbaker, 1979), concludes that Upward Bound is successful in getting students to graduate from high school and enter college.

Other strategies and programs also create links between school and employment and college aid. Agreements between local businesses and school systems, for example, can guarantee students job interviews, actual employment, or direct assistance in applying and paying for college, in return for maintaining good high school attendance rates and grade point averages. Similarly, learning activities in the middle and high school grades can be directly connected to the worlds of college or work through school-to-work apprenticeship programs, community college co-op programs, and high school programs to integrate academic and vocational offerings with experiential learning activities. In this way, the transition between different domains becomes a *gradual* experience, rather than school being merely a preparation for the college and career events that *follow* high school graduation.

Parent, Community, and School Partnerships

A final way in which schools can be better organized to serve the needs of young people is by strengthening school–family–community ties. In the past 2 decades, educational practitioners and researchers have begun to realize that schools need help to improve appreciably the academic performance and social behavior of the most disadvantaged segment of the at-risk school population. These are the students who manifest a variety of personal and family problems that persist over time from early in their school careers to well into adulthood and serve as impediments to adequate school performance and prosocial behavior.

To address the versatility and perseverance of these student problems and behaviors, school systems are attempting to implement multifaceted and coordinated approaches in collaboration with public and private community agencies and parents. Long-standing mandates for parental and community involvement exist in the most prominent federal compensatory education programs, but "the shared responsibilities of families, schools, and communities are not well understood nor well-developed in family practice, school practice, or community practice" (Center on Families, Schools, Communities, and Children's Learning, 1990, p. 1).

One way in which schools are addressing the personal problems that impede students' learning is by integrating and coordinating the social services many disadvantaged students need. "Joining Forces" (Levy, 1989) is one *national* effort to help education and human services professionals at both the state and local levels collaborate in aiding children and families at risk. A more recent national programmatic effort is the National Center for Service Integration, established in 1991 with support from the U.S. Department of Health and Human Services. The most ambitious integrated services program at the *state* level is the School Based Youth Services Program (SBYSP), funded at $6 million annually and launched in 1988 by the New Jersey Department of Human Services in collaboration with the departments of labor, education, and health (New Jersey Department of Human Resources, 1988). This New Jersey model has since been adapted by Kentucky as part of its Kentucky Integrated Delivery System (KIDS) program, a collaborative effort between the State Department of Education and the Cabinet for Human Resources to meet the personal, social, and educational needs of students. At the *local* level, San Diego's "New Beginnings" represents a prototypical effort to design and implement an interagency collaboration to improve the lives of disadvantaged families and their children through creation of a new system concentrating on integrated services and prevention efforts.

The integrated services model clearly is an advance over earlier compensatory education models that often ignored the complex of demographic, economic, and social changes that interfered with schools' ability to educate students. The success of this newer approach most likely depends on the ability and willingness of school and human services agencies to develop and implement comprehensive plans to link the school restructuring movement with health and social services programmatic initiatives (Dryfoos, 1991).

EMERGING ISSUES

The discussion in the previous section provides a sample of the many and varied strategies and programs aimed at better educating youth in our schools. It is possible for schools and school systems to be more effective by adopting one or more of these programs and adapting them to meet the needs of their students. However, in our examination of strategies and programs we have consistently observed three troubling phenomena.

First, with few exceptions, there is an absence of well-designed evaluation evidence indicating whether a particular program has actual effects on important student outcomes, such as achievement scores, attendance and promotion rates, or reduction in dropout rates. No concerted effort of funding, support, and coordination is yet to be found that stimulates careful, well-designed evaluations to accompany the large number of interventions continually being developed and implemented by individual districts and schools throughout the nation. Until the scientific basis of educational interventions for youth at risk improves and becomes cumulative, service approaches will remain largely the product of creative and well-intentioned guesswork.

Second, we almost never find realistic cost information for special programs accompanying the program descriptions. Without this information, educators in other locations are unable to estimate the resources needed to implement a particular approach in their schools. Accurate cost information should include not only the direct costs of supplies, equipment, and added staff, but the necessary startup costs of local design and the continuing essential costs of staff development, monitoring, and support for the teachers who will be carrying out the program. It has often been stated that many educational innovations fail not because the ideas were weak, but because poor involvement, support, and supervision of the local staff precluded successful implementation.

Third, no well-grounded strategy has been developed for allocating special resources at different grade levels to help students have successful school careers. If anything, there is a tendency to concentrate extra resources in the early years, with the belief that building a firm foundation of initial skills will be enough.

While it is essential to provide a strong foundation in the early grades, continuing extra resources will often be necessary to sustain the gains made by early interventions. Indeed, a recurrent finding of the existing high quality evaluation research is the "fade-out" effect, where evidence of initial positive impact declines over time and disappears entirely a few years after an intervention early in the schooling process. Poor readers and other problem learners can and should be helped throughout the grades, and we must realize that interventions will be needed to match the developmental and emotional requirements of students of different ages.

REFERENCES

Ascher, C. (1991). *School programs for African American students.* New York: ERIC Clearinghouse on Education, Columbia University, Teachers College.

Beady, C., & Slavin, R. E. (1980). Making success available to all students in desegregated schools. *Integrated Education, 18*(5, 6), 28–31.

Becker, H. J. (1986, August). *Instructional uses of school computers: Reports from the 1985 national survey.* Johns Hopkins University, Center for the Social Organization of Schools, No. 2.

Bell, T. H., & Elmquist, D. L. (1992, February). Technology: A catalyst for restructuring schools. *Electronic Learning, 11*(5), 10–11.

Blumenfeld, P. C., Soloway, R. W., Krajcik, J. S., Guzdial, M., & Palincsar, A. (1991). Motivating project-based learning: Sustaining the doing, supporting the learning. *Educational Psychologist, 26*(3,4), 369–398.

Bottoms, G., & Presson, A. (1989). *Improving general and vocational education in the high schools.* Atlanta, GA: Southern Regional Education Board.

Braddock, J. H., II. (1990). *Tracking: Implications for student race-ethnic subgroups.* Baltimore, MD: Johns Hopkins University, Center for Research on the Effective Schooling of Disadvantaged Students.

Braddock, J. H., II, & McPartland, J. M. (1990). *Alternatives to tracking.* Baltimore, MD: Johns Hopkins University, Center for Research on the Effective Schooling of Disadvantaged Students.

Brown, P. E. (1990). *From school to work.* Princeton, NJ: Educational Testing Service, Policy Information Center.

Bryk, A. S., Lee, V. E., & Smith, J. B. (1990). High school organization and its effects on teachers and students: An interpretive summary of the research. In W. H. Clune & J. F. Witte (Eds.), *Choice and control in American education* (Vol. 1; pp. 135–226). New York: Falmer Press.

Burkheimer, G. J., Riccobono, J. A., & Wisenbaker, J. M. (1979). *Evaluation study of the Upward Bound Program: A second follow-up* (Final Report on Contract No. HEW–300–78–0037 to the U.S. Office of Education). Research Triangle Park, NC: Research Triangle Institute.

Butler, A. S. (Ed.). (1987). *Black girls and schooling: A directory of strategies and programs for furthering the academic performance and persistence rates of black females K–12.* Manhattan: Kansas State University.

Carlson, C. G. (1990). Beyond high school: The transition to work. Princeton, NJ: Educational Testing Service.

Center on Families, Schools, Communities, and Children's Learning (1990). *Proposal to the Office of Educational Research and Improvement.* A consortium of Boston University Institute for Responsive Education, Johns Hopkins University, University of Illinois, Wheelock College, and Yale University. Baltimore, MD: Author.

Charner, I. (1988). Employability credentials: A key to successful youth transition to work. *Journal of Career Development, 15,* 30–40.

Civic Achievement Award Program. (1989). *A civic knowledge and skills development program.* Arlington, VA: Author.

Clayton, C. (1991, Winter). Chapter 1 evaluation: Progress, problems, and possibilities. *Evaluation and Policy Analysis, 13*(4), 345–352.

Cohen, E. G. (1986). *Designing groupwork: Strategies for the heterogeneous classroom.* New York: Teachers College Press.

Cohen, P. A., Kulik, J. A., & Kulik, C. (1982). Educational outcomes of tutoring: A meta-analysis of findings. *American Educational Research Journal, 19,* 237–248.

Connors, N. A. (1992). Teacher advisory: The fourth R. In J. L. Irvin (Ed.), *Transforming middle level education* (pp. 162–178). Boston: Allyn & Bacon.

Cziko, G. A. (1992). The evaluation of bilingual education. *Educational Researcher, 21*(2), 10–15.

David, J. L. (1990). Restructuring and technology: Partners in change. In K. Sheingold & M. S. Tucker (Eds.), *Restructuring for learning with technol-*

ogy (pp. 75–89). New York: Center for Technology in Education, Bank Street College of Education, and National Center on Education and the Economy.

Dryfoos, J. G. (1991). School-based social and health services for at-risk students. *Urban Education, 26,* 118–137.

Fordham, S., & Ogbu, J. (1986). Black students' social success: Coping with the "burden of acting white." *Urban Review, 18,* 176–206.

Gottfredson, G. D., Nettles, S. M., & McHugh, B. (1992). *Meeting the challenges of multicultural education: A report from the evaluation of Pittsburgh's Prospect Multicultural Education Center* (Report No. 27). Baltimore, MD: Johns Hopkins University, Center for Research on Effective Schooling for Disadvantaged Students.

Grubb, W. N., Davis, G., & Lum, J. (1991). *The cunning hand, the cultural mind.* Berkeley, CA: National Center for Research in Vocational Education.

Hakuta, K., & Pease-Alvarez, L. (Eds.). (1992, March). Enriching our views of bilingualism and bilingual education. [Special issue.] *Educational Researcher, 21*(2).

Jackson, P. W. (Ed.). (1992). *Handbook of research on curriculum.* New York: Macmillan.

Johnson, R. T. (1992). Learning technology contexts for at-risk children. In H. C. Waxman, J. W. de Felix, J. E. Anderson, & H. P. Baptiste Jr. (Eds.), *Students at risk in at-risk schools: Improving environments for learning* (pp. 87–104). Newbury Park, CA: Corwin Press.

Karweit, N. L. (1989). Effective kindergarten programs and practices for students at risk of academic failure. In R. E. Slavin, N. L. Karweit, & N. A. Madden (Eds.), *Effective programs for students at risk.* Needham Heights, MA: Allyn & Bacon.

Karweit, N. L. (1992). The kindergarten experience. *Educational Leadership, 49,* 82–86.

LeTendre, M. J. (1991). Improving Chapter 1 programs: We can do better. *Phi Delta Kappan, 72*(8), 576–580.

Levin, H., Glass, G. V., & Meister, G. R. (1984). *A cost-effectiveness analysis of four educational interventions* (Project Report No. 84–A11). Stanford, CA: Stanford University, Institute for Research on Educational Finance and Governance.

Levin, H., Glass, G. V., & Meister, G. R. (1986). The political arithmetic of cost-effectiveness analysis. *Phi Delta Kappan, 68*(1), 69–72.

Levy, J. E. (1989). *Joining forces: A report from the first year.* Alexandria, VA: National Association of State Boards of Education.

Mac Iver, D. (1991, April). *Enhancing students' motivation to learn by altering assessment, reward, and recognition structures: Year 1 of the Incentives for Improvement Program.* Baltimore, MD: Johns Hopkins University, Center for Research on Effective Schooling for Disadvantaged Students.

Madden, N., Slavin, R., Karweit, N., Dolan, L., & Wasik, B. (1991). *Success for all: Multi-year effects of a schoolwide elementary restructuring program* (Report No. 18). Baltimore, MD: Johns Hopkins University, Center for Research on Effective Schooling for Disadvantaged Students.

Maeroff, G. I. (1992). To improve schools, reduce their size. *The College Board News, 20*(3), 3.

McKey, R. H., Condelli, L., Ganson, H., Barrett, B. J., McConkey, C., & Plantz,

M. C. (1985). *The impact of Head Start on children, families and communities.* Washington, DC: CSR, Inc.

McPartland, J. M. (1990). Staffing decisions in the middle grades: Balancing quality instruction and teacher/student relations. *Phi Delta Kappan, 71*(6), 465–469.

McPartland, J. M. (1992, March). *Staffing patterns and the social organization of schools.* Paper presented at the annual meeting of the Society of Research for Adolescents, Washington, DC.

McPartland, J. M., & Nettles, S. M. (1991). Using community adults as advocates or mentors for at-risk middle school students: A two-year evaluation of Project RAISE. *American Journal of Education, 99,* 568–586.

NAACP Legal Defense and Education Fund, Inc. (1991). *Reflections on proposals for separate schools for African male pupils.* Unpublished manuscript.

Natriello, G., McDill, E. L., & Pallas, A. M. (1990). *Schooling disadvantaged children: Racing against catastrophe.* New York: Teachers College Press.

Nettles, S. M. (1991). Community contributions to school outcomes of African-American students. *Education and Urban Society, 24,* 132–147.

New Jersey Department of Human Resources. (1988). *Coming of age in New Jersey: Today's adolescents face new and complex problems.* Trenton, NJ: Author.

Niemiec, R. P., Blackwell, M. C., & Walberg, H. J. (1986). CAI can be doubly effective. *Phi Delta Kappan, 67*(10), 750–751.

Oakes, J. (1992). Grouping students for instruction. In M. C. Alkin (Ed.), *Encyclopedia of educational research* (6th ed.; pp. 562–568). New York: Macmillan.

Perrone, V. (Ed.). (1991). *Expanding student assessment.* Alexandria, VA: Association for Supervision and Curriculum Development.

Pogrow, S. A. (1990). Challenging at-risk students: Findings from the HOTS program. *Phi Delta Kappan, 71*(5), 389–397.

Ravitch, D. (1991–92). A culture in common. *Educational Leadership, 49*(4), 8–11.

Richmond, G. (1989). The future school: Is Lowell pointing us toward a revolution in education? *Phi Delta Kappan, 71*(3), 232–236.

Ross, S. M., Smith, L. S., & Morrison, G. R. (1991). The longitudinal influences of computer-intensive learning experiences on at-risk elementary students. *Educational Technology Research and Development, 39*(4), 33–46.

Schlesinger, A. M., Jr. (1991, Winter). The disuniting of America. *American Educator, 14,* 21–33.

Sheingold, K., & Tucker, M. (1990). *Restructuring for learning with technology.* New York: Center for Technology in Education, Bank Street College of Education, and National Center on Education and the Economy.

Shepard, L. A., & Smith, M. L. (1989). *Flunking grades: Research and policies on retention.* Philadelphia, PA: Falmer Press.

Slavin, R. E. (1980). Effects of individual learning expectations on student achievement. *Journal of Educational Psychology, 72,* 520–524.

Slavin, R. E. (1983). *Cooperative learning.* New York: Longman.

Slavin, R. E. (1986). *Educational psychology: Theory into practice.* Englewood Cliffs, NJ: Prentice-Hall.

Slavin, R. E. (1989). Students at risk of school failure: The problem and its dimensions. In R. E. Slavin, N. L. Karweit, & N. A. Madden (Eds.), *Effective programs for students at risk* (pp. 3–17). Needham Heights, MA: Allyn & Bacon.

Slavin, R. E. (1990). *Cooperative learning: Theory, research and practice.* Englewood Cliffs, NJ: Prentice-Hall.

Slavin, R. E., Karweit, N. L., & Madden, N. A. (Eds.). (1989). *Effective programs for students at risk.* Needham Heights, MA: Allyn & Bacon.

Slavin, R. E., Karweit, N. L., & Wasik, B. (1992). *Preventing early school failure: What works?* Baltimore, MD: Johns Hopkins University, Center for Research on Effective Schooling for Disadvantaged Students.

Stein, M. K., Leinhardt, G., & Bickel, W. (1989). Instructional issues for teaching students at risk. In R. E. Slavin, N. L. Karweit, & N. A. Madden (Eds.), *Effective programs for students at risk.* Needham Heights, MA: Allyn & Bacon.

Tifft, S. (1990, May 21). Fighting the failure syndrome — a radical proposal for black boys-separate classes. *Time.*

Toch, T. (1991). *In the name of excellence.* New York: Oxford University Press.

U.S. Department of Health and Human Services. (1992, January). *Project Head Start statistical fact sheet.* Washington, DC: Author.

Wasik, B., & Slavin, R. E. (1990). *Preventing early reading failure with one-to-one tutoring: A best evidence synthesis* (Report No. 6). Baltimore, MD: Johns Hopkins University, Center for Research on Effective Schooling for Disadvantaged Students.

Wigginton, E. (1989). Foxfire grows up. *Harvard Educational Review, 59,* 24–29.

Winfield, L. (Ed.). (1991). Resilience, schooling, and development in African-American youth [Special issue]. *Education and Urban Society, 24*(1).

Wolf, D., Bixby, J., Glenn, J., III, & Gardner, H. (1991). To use their minds well: Investigating new forms of student assessment. In G. Grant (Ed.), *Review of research in education* (Vol. 17; pp. 31–74). Washington, DC: American Educational Research Association.

Part II

CULTURE AND CULTURAL CONFLICT IN SCHOOLS

In Chapter 3 Edmund Gordon and Constance Yowell provide much of the theoretical basis for this part, in their characterization of the individual–school relationship as one that may be filtered through cultural understandings and misunderstandings. In particular, they argue that dissonance between student and school cultures, when it occurs, negatively affects the levels of individual achievement and general development that are attained. Following up on this theme, Grayson Noley, Rafael Valdivieso and Siobhan Nicolau, and Wade Boykin focus specifically on the cultural conflicts that occur daily in school settings for American Indian, Hispanic, and African-American children and youth, respectively.

Chapter 4 traces the history of schooling in America for its native students, telling a sorry story of neglect and overeager attempts at assimilation. However, Noley describes certain initiatives and current programs that are rooted in the Indian tradition and history of education, and, if continued and nurtured, may finally address the learning needs of American Indians. In a similar way, Valdivieso and Nicolau begin Chapter 5 by reviewing the histories of the various Hispanic groups in the United States and conclude by presenting a list of elements that must be addressed in any educational reform program for the members of these groups. Foremost among their recommendations is the sense that schools must genuinely "reach out" to students and to their families if they are to succeed in promoting learning. Finally, in Chapter 6 Boykin urges that schools adopt a "talent development" approach, based on a deep-structure perspective of cultural diversity. Relating results from an extensive series of studies aimed at distinguishing the salience of Afro-cultural ethos for school-based learning, he suggests that African-American children may be shortchanged in classrooms that fail to seek ways of relating curriculum and teaching methods to underlying, culturally influenced learning styles.

CHAPTER 3

Cultural Dissonance as a Risk Factor in the Development of Students

EDMUND W. GORDON AND CONSTANCE YOWELL

In human social organization, when one's characteristics are at variance in significant ways from the modal characteristics of the social group that has achieved hegemony, one is likely to find little correspondence between the developmental supports provided by the dominant group and the developmental needs of the persons whose characteristics are different. This is a function of the operation of a principle of social economy whereby social orders design and allocate resources in accordance with the modal or otherwise valued characteristics of the social order. Thus we have schools, public facilities, media, and so on that are designed and allocated to fit the needs of persons whose vision and hearing are intact rather than to serve the needs of persons with sensory impairments. Consequently, persons with impairments in these sensory modalities are at risk of developmental and educational failure, not necessarily as a function of the impairments, but because the society is not organized to adequately support the developmental needs of persons whose characteristics are at variance with those that are modal.

Following this line of reasoning, the identification of a population as being at risk of failure is always situational and relative. In its early usage, "at-risk" status was used to refer to persons with identifiable sensory, physical, or intellectual disabilities that were likely to result in their failure to benefit from the normal range of developmental resources generally available. Their risk of failure was related to the goals or objectives the society expected most children to achieve even in the absence of specialized resources, and to the implicit recognition that without such resources expected achievement was unlikely. It was in the latter half of the current century that we began to think of persons as being "at risk" of failure to achieve an adequate education because of their social circumstances. Thus we see in the chapters in this book that little attention is called to persons with physical or sensory disabilities, and major attention is directed at persons whose "at-risk" status is based on their ethnicity, culture, language, or economic status.

This shift in emphasis from one class of indicators to another may be a reflection of a decline in the relative number of persons with mental, physical, and sensory disabilities, the society's enhanced capacity to address the problems of these groups, an increase in the numbers of persons whose social status places them at a disadvantage in the society, and the increasing recognition of the society's lack of success in meeting the developmental needs of this newly recognized group.

In the identification of populations of children at risk of failure to adequately develop or be educated, it is important that both the old and the new categories of persons be included. It is also important, as suggested in Chapter 1 by Montgomery and Rossi, that we recognize the special at-risk status of persons who are doubly or triply at risk; that is, those who fall into two or three of the at-risk categories. An example of such a person is a language minority group member who is female, hard of hearing, and black. For the purposes of our discussions, however, these will be treated as extreme cases, and the more common patterns of at-risk status will be our focus.

Traditionally, at-risk status has referenced the characteristics of the persons so designated. Typical of this approach is Rosehan's (1967) list of attributes of "at-risk" students.

1. They commonly come from broken homes.
2. They are nonverbal and concrete-minded.
3. They are physically less healthy than their middle-class peers.
4. They lack stable identification figures or role models.
5. They lack stable community ties because of their constant migration.
6. They are often handicapped by their color, which provides them with a negative self-image.
7. They are handicapped in the expression and comprehension of language.
8. They tend to be extroverted rather than introverted.

However, it may be useful to utilize a more dynamic conception of the construct. We hold that at-risk status refers not simply to the characteristics of persons, but to an interaction between the traits of such persons and the context in which they live their lives. Being at risk of failure may be an iatrogenic condition; that is, it may be more appropriately conceptualized as a condition or circumstance brought on by the failure or incapacity of the developmental environment to support the needs of the developing person. Consider the fact that all persons who show some of the above characteristics identified with being at risk do not appear at risk in their interactions in many contexts. All persons for whom English is a second language or who claim African-American identity or who have a physical disability do not flounder. In fact, some such persons have relatively uneventful courses of development and achieve quite adequately. In our work (e.g., Gordon & Song, 1992), we have found that many such persons develop in environments that have been specially structured to ensure that appropriate supports are available and that incapacitating barriers are eliminated or circumvented. We conclude that at-risk status is a function of the inappropriateness of developmental environments to the needs of the person and that a focus on these deficient environments may be more productive than a focus on the characteristics of the persons. We can, then, define *at risk* as referring to a category of persons whose personal characteristics, conditions of life, and situational circumstances, in interactions with each other, make it likely that their development and/ or education will be less than optimal.

To better understand the interactions between these characteristics and life situations, it is important to make still another distinction. Gordon (1989) distinguishes between the status and functional characteristics of persons. Status characteristics like ethnicity, gender, class, and language generally define one's status in the social order. Status is likely to influence one's access to resources, the nature of one's opportunities and rewards, what is expected, as well as the character and quality of society's investment in one's development. Functional characteristics refer to the "hows" of behavior and generally to the ways in which persons function. Functional characteristics, often culturally determined, include belief systems, cognitive style, dispositions, language systems, mores, skills, and technologies (ways of doing things). Obviously there are interactions and overlap between status and functional characteristics, but either set of traits can facilitate or frustrate development and education by virtue of its primary characteristics. However, there are secondary characteristics that adhere to each category that may be of greater consequence for development than is the influence of status on the distribution of resources or the influence of function on the organization of behavior. We refer to the personal identification and attribution processes that derive from one's status as well as from one's way of functioning. Both help to define one's concept of self and the manner in which one identifies oneself. Ultimately, even though status and functional characteristics may be the developmental antecedents of identity, it may be identity that provides the energy behind behavioral adaptation. How then do human characteristics in interaction with social circumstances influence the development of identity, and what is the relationship between sources of one's identity and one's being at risk of developmental and educational failure to thrive? We submit that culture is the context and the ubiquitous vehicle.

CULTURE AND HUMAN DEVELOPMENT

Psychologists and anthropologists such as Cole, Gay, Glick, and Sharp (1971) have concluded that regardless of cultural, ethnic, gender, or class differences among human groups, there are no corresponding differences in cognitive and affective processes. Rather, it is held that the basic processes of mentation in the human species — for example, association, recall, perception, inference, discrimination, and so forth — are common and it is prior experiences, situations, and meanings that form the context for the development and expression of these processes. Because experiences, situations, and meanings are culturally determined, the quality of the development of a process, the conditions under which it is expressed, and even our ability to recognize its manifestations are dependent on cultural phenomena that are often mediated through ethnic, gender, or class identity.

Our conception of risk factors offers an example of the importance of discussing the culturally embedded nature of human experience and meaning. In the past, we have framed our conception of at-risk status or vulnerability in terms of risk factors, such as gender, demographic status, social and intellectual resources, genetic history, mobility patterns, and negative or traumatic life events. What we have not accounted for in this conception of at-risk status is the fact that over half of the individuals who may experience the most severe stressors do not report psychological or social dysfunction (Waxman, de Felix, Anderson, & Baptiste, 1992). Gordon, Rollock, and Miller (1990) have suggested that threats to the integrity of behavioral development and adaptation may exist along a continuum, with the degree of threat better defined by existential meaning than by "reality" factors; the individual's reaction to the threat may depend on the actual perception or the connotation that is permitted by the context in which the phenomenon is experienced.

Culture Defined

It is becoming clear, then, that culture is a construct with a wide variety of definitions and conceptions. Authors have often sought to distinguish between material and nonmaterial aspects of culture. Belief systems, attitudes, and attributions are examples of nonmaterial culture, while tools, skills, and artifacts serve as examples of material culture. We hold, however, that at its core culture is responsible for all human behavior. That is, when we speak of culture, we are speaking of both the cause and the product of human affect and cognition.

Both Geertz and Tylor have provided us with widely accepted indices and definitions for culture. In his perception of culture, Tylor (1958) included "knowledge, beliefs, art, morals, law, custom, and any other capabilities and habits acquired by man as a member of society" (p. 1), while Geertz (1973) viewed culture as a "historically transmitted pattern of meanings embodied in symbolic form by means of which men communicate, perpetuate, and develop their knowledge about and attitudes toward life" (p. 89). We see, then, an effort to discuss culture in terms of objects or tools as well as language and shared conceptual schemata. In joining these perceptions of culture, we can derive five fundamental dimensions of the construct.

1. The judgmental or normative is a reflection of society's standards and values, which often provide the constraints within which thought is facilitated.
2. The cognitive dimension consists of categories of mentation (such as social perceptions, conceptions, attribution, and connotations) that are often expressed through language.
3. The affective dimension refers to the emotional structure of a social unit and its common feelings, sources of motivation, and so on.
4. The skill dimension relates to those special capabilities the members of a culture develop in order to meet the demands of their social and techno-economic environment (Ogbu, 1978).
5. The technological dimension refers not only to different or more highly developed technological practices, but more important to the impact of the different information inherent in these practices on cognitive and affective behaviors.

These dimensions serve to emphasize those characteristics by which a culture may be identified or by which the culture of a group may be characterized. It is in this descriptive definition of culture that we begin to see the reference points for one's social or group identity, as well as the experiences that provide a context for one's conception of his or her own (as well as others') patterns of behavior.

Function of Culture

The function of culture in human activity, however, does not end with its role as a descriptive concept. In addition to providing the referents for group identity, culture also provides the stimuli and the consequences of human behavioral patterns. Thus, culture also serves as an explanatory construct. As mentioned earlier, when we discuss cultural information in terms of description, we are articulating the status phenomenon of culture, and in general are both referring to the social identity of individuals (Goffman, 1963) — the group to which I belong — as well as describing the effect of this identity on an individual's access to resources. When we seek to explain behavior, however, and discuss the influence of one's personal identity — the group to which I feel that I belong — we begin to wonder how particular language and belief systems, specific objects and tools, not to mention technological advances, influence or enable the behavior of individuals. When we examine ways of thinking — such as linear and sequential thought, tendency to generate abstractions, field dependence and independence, connotations and taxonomies as well as allowable metaphors — we are becoming aware of culture as a vehicle for cognition. Ultimately, culture provides the constraints within which mentation and affect are enabled.

Furthermore, culture serves as a mediator for learning in two fundamental respects. According to Vygotsky's notions of cognitive development, learning occurs within social interaction; that is, in contrast to the Piagetian conception of self-constructed knowledge. Vygotsky (1978) argued that the development of higher psychological functions is rooted in children's primary social interactions. Learning, based on the cultural-historical theory, consists of three fundamental activities: transmission of knowledge and cognitive skills, cultivation of cognitive abilities, and the encouragement of these cognitive abilities. According to this conception, knowledge in one's culture is socially transmitted by adults and capable peers to children. The adult or capable peer, in joint activity, serves as a role model or expert tutor on a task that allows for cognitive processes to be demonstrated and then practiced and learned. New cognitive abilities emerge as the adult works with the child on tasks that may have originally been too demanding for the child. As the pair work in collaboration, with the adult providing encouragement as well as appropriate feedback, the child gradually begins to take on the responsibility of the task. While initiating the activity within the child's "zone of proximal development," with time the adult begins to remove support as the child becomes more competent at the task. It is in this form of social scaffolding that we see the mechanism for growth and development in cognitive functioning.

We cannot overstate the importance of an individual's group and personal identity in the social interaction that constitutes the learning process. A secondary human characteristic to status and functional characteristics, one's sense of self — mediated by culture — provides the fuel for the social interaction inherent in learning behavior. Not only does human cognition develop through cultural encounters, but it is also through these same social interactions that we begin to recognize and identify our identity. Culture provides the reference points that allow me not only to recognize myself in terms of my gender, class, and ethnicity, but also to acknowledge that I am separate from others. It is this complex sense of self that I bring to the classroom, that must in turn be met and integrated into the dynamic culture of the learning environment in order for optimal development to occur. This interaction between self and the learning environment is dialectical in nature: Not only will the learning process enable me to grow and change in fundamental ways, but my development will clearly have an impact on the culture of the learning environment.

Mechanism for Culture

We have discussed in detail the impact of culture on what one does and how one does it. Similarly, we have also addressed the manner in which culture frames as well as enables one's feelings and thoughts concerning what one does. The question arises, however, by what mechanism does culture serve as the vehicle and context for human activity? This question can be answered across several levels of understanding — biological, psychological, and social. We will begin at the cellular level and work our way up to the arena of social institutions.

Work in the field of cell assemblies and synaptogenesis provides new perspectives on the interrelationships between neural activity, experience, and behavior. Specifically, Hebb (1949) discussed a model for understanding the relationship between brain function and experience. Neural cells differentiate and, based on experience, associate with each other in a manner that forms "cell assemblies." While a single cell may associate with several assemblies, under appropriate stimulation specific assemblies are activated. It is possible to argue, then, that it is culture that provides the stimuli and the context through which experience actively shapes the organization of brain cells. Further, with respect to reinforcement, it is certainly culture that serves to give meaning to the overt expressions of behavioral products of these cell assemblies — meanings and reinforcements, which in turn allow the behavioral products to become established patterns of behavior activity.

In addition to the association or differentiation patterns of cells, the density of synaptic connections is also fundamentally determined by experiences during the late prenatal and early postnatal periods of development. During the process of synaptogenesis, synaptic connections are first overproduced, followed by a later period of selective degeneration. Greenough, Black, and Wallace (1987) have theorized that experience, in its role as activator of neural activity, is responsible both for the organization of synapses as well as for the selection of which of these synapses will degenerate.

Greenough and co-authors (1987) further advanced a theory of experience-expectant and experience-dependent processes to account for the relationship between synaptic connections and experience. Briefly, the experience-expectant theory hypothesizes that relevant or normal experience results in normal neural activity that in turn maintains typical synaptic connections. Conversely, an absence of experience or atypical experience may lead to irregular synaptic connections. In Greenough's second theory, the experience-dependent hypothesis states that specific neural activity, which results in the formation of synapses, is caused by new information processing on the part of the organism.

It is clear, then, that on the biological level we see a dynamic interaction between the environment and human development. This is also true for the interaction between social institutions and human behavioral patterns. Sociocultural context is mediated through institutional structures as well as personal interaction. This sociocultural context, in the form of family, religious institutions, schools, and the like, provides the stimuli (values, norms, skills, and technological devices) that serve to organize cognitive and affective behavior in much the same way that experience shapes synaptic connections. It should be understood, however, that the relationship between culture and social institutions is a reciprocal one. The relations between education and culture serve to exemplify the dialectical nature of change. Our educational system exists as a subset of our broader social context. Over the course of time, our society has moved to embrace the concept of education for all citizens. In turn, however, this educated citizenry is now capable of creating tremendous change within our culture.

On the micro level, the sociocultural context is mediated through personal social interactions. It is here, in teaching interactions that take the form of social scaffolding, that learners develop a system of knowledge structures and affective cognitive skills that are congruent with the values, beliefs, and conventions of their sociocultural group. The interaction between learner and significant other is premised on reciprocity. While it provides the learner with the opportunity to develop personal attributions, dispositions, and motivations to behave in essentially appropriate ways, the growth of the learner creates new demands for the tutor.

Ultimately, it is the social institution that may come to replace or function in parallel with the significant other, as both a source of reinforcement and a vehicle for the normative dimension of culture. It is through the processes of assimilation, accommodation, and adaptation of schemata, that cultural transmission occurs. Schematization represents the mechanism by which conceptual structures come to represent cognitive, conative, and affective components of phenomena experienced. In accommodation, then, the acquisition and replication of stimulus/response/situation triads is related to existing schemata, while in adaptation the existing schemata or emerging conceptual frames are adapted to the demands of currently perceived or changing conditions.

Cultural Conflict

It is in the relationship between social institutions and the learner that high degrees of dissonance can result in failure to learn or a distortion of the learning process. In a society with tremendous cultural diversity and a culturally hegemonic educational system, dissonance between what is learned in personal interaction with the significant other often may come into conflict with demands and expectations of the social institution. Precision of language offers an example of such dissonance. It is not uncommon in some cultures for individuals to use signal words to represent deeper meanings rather than the elaborated language we have come to associate with the academy. In some groups, numbers and time are evoked in the form of estimation rather than the precise calculations and specific references used in high-technology-dominated cultures. In an educational system that allows only for the precision of exact calculation — that is, a system that does not appreciate the potential for cultural differences in the ways that people use numbers — this demand for exactness may place a child at risk of failure to thrive in the school setting.

It should be understood that while some cultures may place a greater emphasis on technological development than other cultures, the notion of a "culturally deprived" people is a misnomer. The challenge for education thus becomes the enabling of bridging between cultures and of the learning of multiple cultures, and the appreciation of multiple ways of viewing things in all students.

It is the failure or inability of the school to bridge between conflicting cultures that renders schooling a risk-inducing phenomenon for many students. Since learning is such a personal achievement, it is critically dependent on the learner's engagement in the process. When the learning process comes to be associated with that which is "not me," that which is alien to me, learning task engagement is interfered with. E. T. Gordon (1992) has described what he calls "resistant culture" to refer to the sometimes elaborate systems of belief and behavior adopted by African-American males to insulate themselves from the demands of acculturation and socialization experiences that they consider alien or hostile to their interests. Some of these adaptations serve prosocial ends. Others are clearly antisocial. In both instances, however, they represent defense mechanisms for the youth and barriers to intervention. Given the ineptness of much that we do for these youth and the actual destructiveness of some of our actions, these adaptations cannot be rejected. Rather they must be understood and taken into account as intervention plans are developed. In the absence of such respect, alienation and resistance in the face of cultural conflict must be expected.

It is these instances of cultural conflict that are so challenging and frustrating in the design of educational services for children who are at risk. Educators who are sensitive to the diversity of at-risk children should be respectful of their indigenous orientations and values, but these are sometimes at odds with the goals toward which education is directed. If it were simply a matter of cultural taste, the choices would be simpler, even if the implementation might not be. However, in some circumstances, what we are dealing with are resistant cultural values that are politically functional but developmentally dysfunctional. Decisions concerning the quality of educational pursuits and the choice of more challenging courses are examples. For some time now we have taken the position that the educator has a professional responsibility to make these hard choices for the student, when the student's risk status renders him or her incapable of making an informed decision. In such cases, the final criterion must be the increasing of options for the student. If the professionally made choice reduces future alternatives for the student, we feel that it is probably not in his or her best interest. If it increases alternatives for choice, we feel that the professional has the responsibility to act.

IMPLICATIONS FOR EDUCATIONAL REFORM

Several implications for educational reform flow from this way of thinking about at-risk status. Among these are

1. The limitations of reform in school governance alone
2. The limitations of the manipulation of standards and accountability based on educational achievement test data
3. The applicability of principles of social justice
4. The pedagogical principles of adaptability and complementarity
5. Concern for diversity, pluralism, context, and perspective

Each of these implications will be discussed in the following sections.

Limitations of Reform of School Governance

Most of the action on the school reform front has been directed at changes in the organizational structure and governance of schools. In a number of school systems across the nation, efforts are underway to increase teacher participation in decisions concerning what happens in schools. This notion rests on the logical conclusion that people are likely to work more effectively when they are pursuing goals and actions of their own choosing—when they feel some sense of ownership of the programs and projects in which they are engaged. The basic idea is consistent with related developments in the industrial sector and is thought to partially explain the reported differences between the productivity of Japanese and U.S. workers.

In what is perhaps the largest current effort to apply this concept, the public school system of Chicago has directed most of its reform efforts at the decentralization of governance and site-based management (see Chapter 10, this volume). The funds from a court decree have been used in large measure (1) to provide staff development in decision making and management in schools implementing site-based management, and (2) to provide modest support for curriculum enrichment. However, available achievement data do not yet suggest that the goal required by the decree, a 50% reduction in academic underachievement, will be reached (Gordon, 1991).

Site-based management seems to have become the current panacea for much that is considered wrong with schooling, despite the finding that such efforts to date have done more for teacher morale than for student achievement (Collins & Hanson, 1991). Most advocates for this approach to school reform argue that real change cannot occur without support from staff, and site-based management is the supposed route to such involvement and support. But active participation in the decision making and management of schools requires more than authorization to participate. It requires know-how, resources, and societal commitment—none of which is in adequate supply. With respect to know-how, until we strengthen the pedagogical and substantive competence of our teaching force, their involvement in decision making and school improvement is likely to be of limited effect. In addition, if the primary goal of many of our efforts at school reform is to reduce the incidence of school failure among those students who present very diverse characteristics to the school and who are currently served poorly by our schools, the current reforms in school governance hardly seen to be the treatment of choice.

Limitations of Efforts at Accountability and Standards

Many of the states and certainly the federal government have staked their hopes for school reform and the improvement of education for children at risk of failure on the imposition of higher standards of academic achievement and some attempts at establishing systems by which schools can be held accountable for their productivity. Now there is no question that the standards by which we judge academic achievement and to which we consistently fail to hold schools accountable are too low. They compare poorly with the standards achieved in other technologically advanced countries. However, it can be argued that our standards and achievement are low not simply because our sights are too low but because our practice of and provision for education are inappropriate to the requirements of educational excellence. Among the most prominent efforts at goal and standard setting are the President's National Goals for Education and the nongovernment New Standards Project. Both have begun by devoting prime attention to the achievement outcomes of schooling. While for some the National Goals would be measured by a new educational achievement test, New Standards proposes a new system of educational assessment. The latter is headed in the right direction with respect to assessment, but both give woefully little attention to the importance of educational inputs.

One cannot argue with the substance of the national education goals, for each iterates a rational expectation of what will be required for meaningful, satisfying, and responsible participation in the social order. The values reflected in such goals send a powerful message to school systems across the country concerning what the nation expects from its schools. However, an extremely negative message is sent by the promulgation of such goals in the absence of the resources, know-how, and national commitment to ensure that schools and students are enabled to meet these goals. Nothing in the national effort speaks to the desperate need for staff development and the improvement of the quality of the labor force in schools. Nowhere in that effort is there attention given to the states' responsibility for ensuring that schools have the capacities to deliver the educational services necessary to the achievement of such goals. Nowhere is there any recognition of the things that must happen outside of schools to enable schools and students to reach these goals. Without attention to these extra-school forces, it is folly to expect that the national effort will address questions of responsibility for ensuring that these enabling conditions will prevail.

In the New York City Chancellor's Commission on Minimum Standards (Gordon, 1986), the case was made for the importance of symmetry in the pursuit of school accountability. After identifying achievement-level targets as standards, the report proposed that standards also be set for professional practice and for institutional capacity. New York City, other school districts, the federal government, and New Standards have yet to seriously engage standards for practice and capacity. Yet if we are to expect that children at risk of failure and other children as well will experience great improvements in their academic performance, it is more likely to come from holding to higher standards those of us who manage their education and guide their learning. Darling-Hammond (1992) has begun the iteration of an approach to such standards of practice and capacity. The problem is that it is relatively easy to arrive at agreement on what students should know and know how to do, while it is very difficult to agree on what the educational inputs should be to achieve these aims without becoming overly prescriptive or what is more problematic politically, without facing questions concerning entitlements and the fixing of responsibility for costs. If the field can ever agree on a set of standards for professional practice and school capability, do we then have a basis for asking the courts to hold schools or states responsible for making them available, especially to children at risk of school failure?

Social Justice and Distributional Equity

As we turn to the actual distribution of educational resources, we encounter different kinds of problems. In their now classic report, Coleman and colleagues (1966) challenged the society to separate school achievement from such social origins as class and race. The nation responded with several efforts directed at the equalization of educational opportunity. Enlightened as these efforts were and despite considerable expenditure of money and effort, educational achievement has continued to adhere to the social divisions by which status in our society is allocated. One of the reasons why this problem may be so recalcitrant is the confusion of distributional equality (ensuring that all have equal access to the educational resources of the society) and distributional equity, which requires that resources be distributed in proportion to need. Persons who need more educational resources cannot be said to have been treated with equity upon receiving an equal share, when what is needed is a share equal to their need. What is required here is a more appropriate conception of justice. Rawls (1971) has advanced a theory of justice that holds acceptable, unequal distribution of resources that favors the weakest members of our society. Our concern for resource distribution sufficient to the needs of persons most at risk of failure is in keeping with Rawls's theory of social justice. Gordon and Shipman (1979) have argued that in the presence of students with widely diverse learning characteristics and conditions of life, standardized educational treatments may be dysfunctional. We may not be meeting the needs of student A when we provide for her the same educational treatment that we provide for student B, just as we do not provide for medical patients with different needs when we dispense the same medical treatments to them. Where there are groups of students known to present themselves at school without the acknowledged prerequisites for optimal learning, social justice requires that they be treated differently in order to serve their needs. We have begun to honor this notion in the court decision in *Lau* v. *Nichols* (414 U.S. 563, 1974), which required that where there are certain concentrations of non-English speaking students, schools must provide some instruction in the students' first language. In such cases, the school's adaptation is to the language characteristics of the students. The courts have not yet extended this concept to include learning styles, cultural referents, temperament, temporal factors, or health/nutritional conditions. Yet if the needs of students who are at risk are to be adequately (and equitably) served, schools must find ways to adapt to the full range of characteristics that place students at risk. Without such adaptation, the values implicit in our conception of social justice and equity are not served.

Adaptability and Complementarity

If we recognize that children come to our schools with varying degrees of readiness for academic learning and differential patterns of support for educational pursuits, it is necessary that schools be adaptable to these different characteristics and circumstances as educators guide students toward the goals of schooling. When we add the fact that students have been differentially acculturated and socialized, giving them quite different cultural schemata, cultural styles, and related attitudes and dispositions, schools have the added task of developing the capacity to complement much of what students bring to school in bridging from where these children are to where they will need to go in the process of gaining a sound, basic education and becoming effective adult members of society. In the service of adaptation, both our students and our schools must give and take as we try to reconcile differences between the worlds of home and school. In the service of complementarity, the focus is on conserving the respective strengths of both students and schools as we construct connections between the two. Complementarity assumes that beneath the surface differences that exist between groups and institutions, the basic human needs and goals are quite similar, and when made explicit, can be brought into facilitating and supportive relationships with one another. For example, the first author and some of his colleagues have been investigating the acquisition of higher-order thinking skills and strategies by inner-city high school students. After considerable effort at teaching such skills, with little success at getting students to transfer what they had learned in the laboratory to regular academic tasks, we discovered that many of these young people already knew and used some of these skills (e.g., "executive strategies") in their daily lives. However, these students were typically unaware of their applicability to academic problems and, consequently, did not use them in school settings. In addition, then, to teaching new skills and strategies, we turned to making the utility and application of such skills explicit. We bridged the two problem-solving situations and made explicit the applicability of these strategies, which they had learned and did apply in the indigenous situation, to the alien situation. Success in using something they already knew from an "old" setting, to solve problems in a new setting, proved to be easier than learning what appeared to be new skills that were to be applied in a new (academic) setting.

Good teachers for years have attempted to adapt learning experiences to the characteristics and circumstances of learners. Bloom's (1976) mastery learning, for example, does not simply require more time on task for those who require it, but introduces variations in methods of presentation to counteract boredom and more fully engage students. Even some of our misguided efforts at ability grouping are based on the idea that different teaching strategies and pace are useful in the teaching of students who differ. Although the aptitude-treatment-interaction paradigm has failed to find support in much of the extant research, even Cronbach and Snow (1977) still find the paradigm appealing. It may well be that Messick (Messick et al., 1976) is correct in suggesting that the problem with the absence of supportive research findings is related to the fact that many of us have been counting the score before we learned to play the game. Cronbach and Snow provide an excellent critique of the technical problems in much of this research. Gordon (1989) has suggested, however, that the prevailing conception of the relationships in the paradigm may be misconceived. He has advanced the notion that it is not the direct interaction between learner characteristics and learning treatments that produces learning outcomes, but that learner characteristics interact with learning treatments to produce learner behaviors (time on task, task engagement, energy deployment, and so on) and that it is these learner behaviors that account for learning outcomes. Without appropriate learner behaviors, achievement is not likely to occur even in the presence of an appropriate match between learner characteristics and learning treatments.

Diversity, Pluralism, Contextualism, and Perspectivism

Concern with the cultural backgrounds out of which learners come forces us to give attention in education to such philosophical constructs as diversity, pluralism, contextualism, and perspectivism. Each of these notions has its conventional meaning, but in education each has special significance. Attention to diversity requires that differences that adhere to individuals and groups be factored into the design and delivery of teaching and learning transactions. We have discussed some of these implications above under adaptability and complementarity. Attention to diversity in schools is often reflected in the individualization or at least the customizing of education relative to individuals' idiosyncratic characteristics.

Pluralism, which is often used as if it were synonymous with diversity, actually refers to the increasing demand that learners develop multiple competencies, some of which will apply generally while others will be more applicable to idiosyncratic settings. All of us find ourselves increasingly in situations where we must meet other than indigenous standards. Thus it is required that we become multilingual, multicultural, multi-skilled, and capable of functioning in multiple environments and settings. So, while education is influenced by and must be responsive to the differences with which learners enter the educational system, the exit characteristics of its students must reflect the pluralistic demands of the society in which they must live.

In a similar manner, education must be sensitive to variations in the contexts from which students come and in which schooling occurs. Here, values and belief systems provide important examples. Engagement in schooling and effectiveness of learning seem to proceed best when there is congruence between the home context and the school context, when the values of the community are not contradicted by the values of the school. Concern for parent involvement in the school is often misplaced on actual presence or participation in school activities. However, we are increasingly persuaded that the critical variable is not participation, but the absence of dissonance between home and school. Where there is support for common values, participation on the part of parents may be a by-product. Nevertheless, while participation is desirable, it is neither necessary nor sufficient, whereas contextual complimentarity, or congruence, is both.

Context refers to environment, surrounds, conditions, situations, and circumstances; context specificity, however, cannot be permitted to preclude the school's attention to perspective. In our concern for perspective we recognize that diverse characteristics and contexts are associated with differences in world views. People who live their lives differently are likely to have different perspectives on things. However, it is dysfunctional for education if students are not able to see the world from the perspectives of persons and peoples who differ from themselves. Cultural variation in populations is associated with people with different characteristics, who come from different contexts, and who may have different perspectives. These differences may place them at risk of school failure if education does not function effectively to build on these differences to enable pluralistic competencies and the capacity for multiperspectivist thought and problem solving. Especially for children who are at risk of failure by virtue of their differences from those children schools find it easy to serve, respectful concern for diversity, pluralism, context, and perspective must be at the heart of educational planning and service.

CONCLUSION

In the current debates around improving education and opportunities for at-risk students, related dimensions of the problem such as multicultural education, educational equity for students who are at risk of failure, and approaches to school reform are most often treated as separate issues. Unless the several components are viewed and treated conjointly, as if they are all parts of a single problem, we continue this separation at the risk of continued educational failure. For those who are other than members of the hegemonic culture—that is, for those whose cultural identity or experience is alien to that of the dominant culture—such identity can be experienced as a risk factor. This recognition of cultural dissonance as a risk factor has implications for what we do in our efforts at the achievement of a higher degree of social justice in and through education.

Sensitivity to the facts of cultural dissonance should reshape the school reform agenda. The focus on change in school governance alone is an insufficient resource and could lead to reforms that are largely irrelevant to the quality of education received by children who are at risk. In addition, the current emphasis on accountability and outcome standards based on educational achievement test data is questionable education policy, especially in the absence of bilateral symmetry in the concern for standards (concern for quality of school and staff inputs that is equal to concern that has been expressed for achievement outcomes) and in the absence of a social contract that guarantees that students are enabled to meet the new standards. Neither the focus on governance alone nor the emphasis on student achievement standards will realize desired outcomes for students who are at risk of failure. Both areas of reform will need to be coupled with a commitment to educational and social justice. With respect to the concern for equity, we argue that social justice requires that educational resources not be equal but be sufficient to the needs that students bring to the schools. This will in some instances require different and unequal resource allocations. In response to the facts of cultural dissonance, that is, cultural diversity under conditions of cultural hegemony, we argue for the creative application of pedagogical principles and practices that reflect and respect adaptability, complementarity, context sensitivity, human diversity, and social pluralism.

Cultural dissonance places students at risk of educational failure. If education is to be made more effective for such students, efforts at the improvement and reform of education must address this risk factor.

REFERENCES

Bloom, B. S. (1976). *Human characteristics and school learning.* New York: McGraw-Hill.

Cole, M., Gay, J., Glick, J., & Sharp, D. W. (1971). *The cultural context of learning and thinking.* New York: Basic Books.

Coleman, J., Campbell, E. Q., Hobson, C. J., McPartland, J., Mood, A. M., Weinfeld, F. D., & York, R. L. (1966). *Equality of educational opportunity.* Washington, DC: U.S. Government Printing Office.

Collins, R. A., & Hanson, M. K. (1991, January). *Summative evaluation report, School-based management/shared decision-making project 1987–88 through 1989–90.* Miami: Dade County Public Schools Office of Educational Accountability.

Cronbach, L. J., & Snow, R. E. (1977). *Aptitudes and instructional methods.* New York: Wiley.

Darling-Hammond, L. (1992). *Standards of practice for learner-centered schools.* Prepared for New York State's Standards for Excellence Project, NCREST at Teacher's College.

Geertz, C. (1973). *Interpretation of cultures.* New York: Basic Books.

Goffman, E. (1963). *Stigma: Notes on the management of spoiled identity.* New York: Simon & Schuster.

Gordon, E. T. (1992, March). *Subaltern culture and assessment.* Unpublished paper presented at the African-American Adolescent Males Seminar, San Diego.

Gordon, E. W. (1986). *Foundations for academic excellence*. Brooklyn, NY: NYC Chancellor's Commission on Minimum Standards, NYC Board of Education.

Gordon, E. W. (1989). *Human diversity and pedagogy*. New Haven, CT: Yale University, Institution for Social and Policy Studies.

Gordon, E. W. (1991, Spring). *Report of consultant panel: Mid-course review of Project Canal, Chicago Public Schools*. Pomona, NY: Gordon and Gordon Associates.

Gordon, E. W., Rollock, D., & Miller, F. (1990). Coping with communicentric bias in knowledge production in the social sciences. *Educational Researcher, 19*, 19.

Gordon, E. W., & Shipman, S. (1979). Human diversity, pedagogy, and educational equity. *American Psychologist, 34*, 10.

Gordon, E. W., & Song, L. D. (1992, January). *Variations in the experience of resilience*. Paper presented at the Conference on Resilience, Temple University Center for Research on Human Development and Education, Philadelphia.

Greenough, W. T., Black, J. E., & Wallace, C. S. (1987). Experience and brain development. *Child Development, 58*, 539–559.

Hebb, D. (1949). *The organization of behavior: A neuropsychological theory*. New York: Wiley.

Messick, S., & Associates. (1976). *Individuality and learning*. San Francisco: Jossey-Bass.

Ogbu, J. U. (1978). *Minority education and caste: The American system in cross-cultural perspective*. New York: Academic Press.

Rawls, J. (1971). *A theory of justice*. Cambridge, MA: The Belknap Press of Harvard University Press.

Rosehan, D. L. (1967). Cultural deprivation and learning: An examination for learning. In H. L. Miller (Ed.), *Education for the disadvantaged* (pp. 38–42). New York: Free Press.

Tylor, E. B. (1958). *The origins of culture*. New York: Harper Torch Books.

Vygotsky, L. S. (1978). *Mind in society*. Cambridge, MA: Harvard University Press.

Waxman, H. C., de Felix, J. W., Anderson, J. E., & Baptiste, H. P., Jr. (Eds.). (1992). *Students at risk in at-risk schools: Improving environments for learning*. Newbury Park, CA: Corwin Press.

CHAPTER 4

The Cultural Context of American Indian Education and Its Relevance to Educational Reform Efforts

GRAYSON NOLEY

In 1540, Tuscalusa,[1] learning of the imminent arrival of the Spaniard Hernando de Soto, sent his son as an emissary to meet and invite this stranger to visit Athahachi, the home of the great Miko. De Soto arrived in Athahachi to a warm welcome, but he immediately made his depredatory purposes known by detaining Tuscalusa as a captive. Tuscalusa, ordered to accompany de Soto to the densely populated and well-fortified town of Mabila, located north of the present city of Mobile, Alabama, did not resist, but he did manage to send a message telling his people to prepare for the possibility of combat with the Spaniards.

De Soto was greeted with the courtesy due a visiting dignitary when he arrived in Mabila and was showered with gifts of obvious value. Once inside the confines of the town, however, Tuscalusa removed himself from de Soto's custody and refused orders to return. Another Miko, who refused to intercede, was slashed by one of de Soto's officers, whereupon the Mabilians forced the Spaniards out of the fortification, severely wounding de Soto himself. When the balance of his army arrived, de Soto ordered an assault that resulted in severe casualties among the Mabilians, many of whom died in fires (Bourne, 1922).

A hundred years later in 1637, the Pequot Indians in southern New England were nearly annihilated, only about 5 years following their first contact with Europeans. They were attacked by English soldiers and their American Indian allies at a time when most of their defenders were absent. Many of those absent were later hunted down, captured, and sold into slavery or killed. Hauptman and Wherry (1990) suggest that the slaughter of the Pequots "clearly fits the most widely accepted definition of genocide" (pp. 76–77), referring to the 1948 United Nations Convention on Genocide.

These two examples of first contacts with Europeans illustrate that misunderstandings between cultures can have deadly results. Europeans found native people to be inconsistent with their images of society and considered them savages. Native people, on the other hand, found the newcomers to be overbearing, demanding, and disrespectful. The resulting conflicts represented the earliest manifestations of the culture clash that continues unresolved despite the passage of half a millennium. Today's battlefields, however, extend to classrooms, and the casualties are descendants of those who first greeted the ships that brought disease, hunger, and conquering armies.

In general, European-American efforts to assimilate native people throughout 500 years of European presence in North America have not been successful. American Indian people continue to value their cultures, but attempts by well-meaning groups to reform education in general have mostly ignored the cultural validation necessary for American Indian children to succeed in American schools. As a result, these youngsters continue to be classified as less likely to succeed in American schools than their European-American counterparts. American Indian youngsters figuratively and literally are embattled as they attempt to negotiate their ways through American public schools. They still must fend off efforts aimed at acculturation, and they must endure racial slurring in classrooms and textbooks.

This review of efforts to acculturate American Indian people through education is organized in three major sections. The first section reviews historic education activities, including a description of the Choctaw Nation's efforts to reform itself. The second section discusses the role of the federal government in the operation of schools for American Indians. The chapter concludes with a discussion of the potential resolutions that contemporary American Indian people themselves are demonstrating and proposing to reform American Indian education.

HISTORIC CULTURAL INTERFACES

Colonial Educational Efforts

The earliest significant interfaces between American Indian cultures and European-American education did not occur until early in the eighteenth century. The actions of the Congregationalists in New England and the Franciscans in the southwest provide two examples of the imposition of European cultures on the original inhabitants of North America.

In the southwest, the Franciscan priests were mission builders. The Pope of the Roman Catholic Church defined their objective as the conversion of Indians to the Christian faith. The resourcefulness of the priests, however, enabled them to find Indians useful for nonreligious purposes as well. For example, one finds frequent references to Indians who accompanied the mission-building priests and performed the manual labor required in construction as "servants." Rarely, however, were these workers, those the Pope thought worthy of Christianity, allowed inside the missions they constructed (Forrest, 1929; Naylor & Polzer, 1986). The Franciscans were content to "teach" the Indians with whom they had contact, only what was deemed necessary for minimal participation in worship services and for serving the comfort of the Franciscans. In other places, those called servants might have been called slaves.

In the Protestant northeast, the relationships were somewhat different. Indians did not build missions for the missionaries, but they were exhorted to accept Christianity just the same and abandon their own beliefs. Szasz (1990) has described the treatment of a Mohegan named Samson Occum, who became an instrument of Christian missionaries. Occum was educated by missionaries and became a licensed minister who was enlisted to take the Christian message to other northeastern Indians. According to Szasz, he served as a cultural broker between the Mohegans and other Indians of the northeast and the incipient English population.

The primary motive of the missionaries for offering the opportunity to learn European culture appeared to be an honest effort to Christianize. However, the ministers who "sponsored" Occum abused the relationship by using him for fund-raising purposes and by failing to acknowledge the value of his leadership or his talents as a preacher and writer. For his efforts as a Presbyterian minister and school master, Occum's total pay for 12 years equaled the amount paid to three English ministers for *one* year.

Institutions of Higher Education

Benefactors of such institutions as Harvard, William and Mary, and Dartmouth apparently desired to extend educational opportunity to American Indians. Harvard, in 1650, accepted the Indian College from the Society for the Propagation of the Gospel Among the Heathen, agreeing to educate 25 students a year. William and Mary also had an Indian College as part of its original mission, but there is little evidence that either institution ever carried out this aspect of its purpose.

Moors Indian Charity School, which eventually became a part of Dartmouth, was founded in Lebanon, Connecticut (McClure & Parish, 1811/1972). It survived the French-Indian War and in 1764 found itself with 30 students, half of whom were Indians. In 1770, Moors Indian Charity School was relocated near Hanover, New Hampshire, and the Christian association that oversaw it was disbanded in favor of the Dartmouth Board of Trustees. However, the Dartmouth Board of Trustees declined responsibility, arguing that Moors was a separate entity. Despite the Boards's refusal, the Moors Indian Charity School was subsumed by Dartmouth, although the Indian emphasis gradually faded from the decision-making process. The Harvard, William and Mary, and Dartmouth efforts were not the only activities aimed at the "higher" education of this country's original inhabitants, but they are notable because of the stature these institutions have attained.

Ministers' and Politicians' Motives

Eleazar Wheelock (Occum's teacher and a driving force behind Indian education) thought it would be more humane to Christianize and acculturate American Indians than to exterminate them. This view also was expressed later by Thomas Jefferson, who, while rationalizing the acquisition of land, wrote, "The ultimate point of rest and happiness for them [American Indians] is to let our settlements and theirs meet and blend together, to intermix, and become one people" (to Colonel Hawkins, February 18, 1803, in Washington, 1856).

Both ministers and politicians demonstrated concern for the education of the American Indian people, but for different reasons. Neither Wheelock the evangelist nor Jefferson the politician gave any indication that they had any understanding of the Indian cultures they encountered. Neither seemed to consider the possibility that their actions were in conflict with cultures that had endured and met the needs of American Indian people for many generations. Rather, the missionaries and politicians of the late eighteenth and early nineteenth centuries dealt with the original inhabitants as groups devoid of culture and religion. In fact, American Indian nations already were effectively transmitting their accumulated knowledge from one generation to the next in ways that served their economic, political, and social needs. Wheelock and others like him did not comprehend this. The civilization of those who did not meet the civilizer's criteria was said by Wheelock's biographers to be a slow process.

It is the work of ages. To enlighten the wild hunter of the forest with a knowledge of the arts and sciences, to inspire him with a taste for the refine-

ments of civilized society, and the practice and enjoyments of true religion,
has always been attended with great discouragements. (McClure & Parish,
1811/1972, p. 86)

This was partially designed to exclude what they must have considered a
disappointing record of educating those they considered to be without
religion and culture.

The Development of American Indian Educational Systems

Although the well-meaning educational efforts of Wheelock and other
missionaries did not have significant success in the acculturation of American Indians, some missionary efforts—especially those of the American
Board of Commissioners for Foreign Missions (ABCFM)—did eventually
provide a foundation for the development of systems of public schooling
in some American Indian groups prior to educational developments by
the American states (Strong, 1910). One significant example is the work of
ABCFM missionaries with the Choctaws.

The Choctaws, one of the largest nations in the southeastern portion
of North America, were a well-organized and sedentary people who had
developed an advanced level of agriculture. As interaction with Europeans
increased, the Choctaw leader, Pushmataha, concluded that the most effective method of dealing with the Europeans was to send Choctaw children to schools in which they could learn the ways of their new adversar-
ies. Thus educated, when these children became leaders, they would be
better prepared to cope with European-Americans (Noley, 1979). This
conclusion resulted in the dedication of the entire annuities of both the
1816 Treaty of Fort St. Stephens and the 1820 Treaty of Doaks Stand to
education (Bradshears, 1820; Kappler, 1904). The latter treaty also allowed for the sale of 54 sections of land, with the proceeds to be applied
to the support of Choctaw schools.

The Choctaws invited European-Americans to send teachers among
them for the purpose of establishing schools during the second decade of
the nineteenth century (Noley, 1979). Cyrus Kingsbury and his colleagues,
operating under ABCFM auspices, helped the Choctaws establish the foundation of what became a sophisticated system of public schooling that
clearly was more useful to its society than its counterparts in other parts of
North America. After about 10 years, the Choctaws began to establish
schools without missionary assistance, schools that provided opportunities
for adult learning as well as instruction for children. The missionaries
saw the potential competition of these schools and were critical of them,
suggesting that it was impractical to operate schools where the language

of instruction was Choctaw. The continued development of these schools was blunted by the removal treaty of 1830,[2] but the seed was sown for the development of schools that maintained Choctaw culture and language as well as providing for an understanding of the alien culture.

The missionaries attempted to inculcate Choctaws, as well as other southeastern Indians, with tenets of the Christian religion. In doing so, however, they also taught other aspects of their lives, it being their conviction, as it was Wheelock's, that Choctaws had no religion or culture. This misconception appears to have been the driving force behind the missionary zeal to "civilize" them. The missionaries did not allow for differing concepts of life and living and ignored every indication that they were interacting with people who had developed highly organized and complex societies. This view prevailed well into the twentieth century. Although they objected to Choctaw-only instruction, the missionaries *did* understand the value of bilingual education. They decided that if they were to succeed in teaching Choctaws, they first had to offer instruction in the Choctaw language. For this reason, some actually became proficient in Choctaw and translated religious documents, publishing them to be used as textbooks.

Kingsbury and his colleagues established schools throughout the old Choctaw nation in the state of Mississippi during the 1820s. They vigorously opposed the U.S. government plan to remove Choctaws to Indian Territory, or what is now Oklahoma. Upon removal of the Choctaws, the missionaries of the ABCFM demonstrated their loyalty by going to Indian Territory with the Choctaws and continuing their educational and evangelistic endeavors. Their educational work was in cooperation with other efforts sponsored by the Choctaw government.

During this time, when American educational leaders such as Horace Mann and others were struggling to establish public schools in the United States, the Choctaws, and their northern neighbors, the Cherokees, accomplished this task following their removal to Indian Territory. The Choctaws (in 1842) and the Cherokees (in 1838) passed legislation establishing workable systems of free schools before nearly all of the states.

Seven boarding schools, three for boys and four for girls, initially were established by Choctaw legislation, with the administration of each contracted to different missionary societies. In 1848, in addition to the boarding schools, the Choctaws began establishing neighborhood schools to make basic education available to all Choctaw children. All educational initiatives of the Choctaw Nation were supported totally from revenue derived from investments, treaty provisions, and incidental government income such as licensing (Noley, 1979).

Two important concepts utilized in the Choctaw Nation during the

1820s—bilingual education and Indian control of schools serving Indian children—continue to create discussion and controversy today. The missionaries of the ABCFM modeled bilingual education even as their counterparts in other societies dismissed the idea as being useless. Indeed, opposition to the value of this instructional necessity continues to be strident and vitriolic in some quarters.

Indian control, the second important concept modeled by the nineteenth-century Choctaws, has been implemented to a small degree in modern times. The Rough Rock Demonstration School, opened in the late 1960s, was the first contemporary school to be operated by an Indian nation (Roessel, 1977). Following the passage of the 1975 Indian Self-Determination and Education Assistance Act (88 Stat. 2203), other Indian nations began to contract with the federal government for the operation of schools. The challenge of these schools for American Indian educators is to better meet the needs of Indian children by making policy and curriculum decisions that recognize and respect Indian cultures. Schools governed by the majority have mostly failed to recognize individual and group differences and have tended to create policies reflecting majority interests.

THE FEDERAL ROLE AND TWENTIETH-CENTURY REFORMS

The Development of Federal Schools

Federal government responsibility for the education of American Indians was grounded in promises made in 108 treaties between the United States and various Indian nations. Unfortunately, the federal government has not met its obligations well. A 1969 report called government actions a national disgrace and national tragedy (U.S. Senate, 1969).

The most notorious of the United States efforts to provide education for American Indians was the Off-Reservation Boarding Schools (ORBS) of the Bureau of Indian Affairs (BIA). The model for these schools is popularly believed to have been the Carlisle Indian School in Pennsylvania, best known for its football teams led by the great athlete Jim Thorpe (Wheeler, 1979). Although Thorpe brought considerable attention to Carlisle, its other history was less positive.

Captain Henry Pratt, who became a "friend" of Indians when he was assigned to care for them when they were held captive by the United States in Florida in the mid-1870s, eventually escorted some of them to Hampton Institute in Virginia, where they received vocational training. Hampton was an institution established for African-Americans, leading

Pratt to envision a similar school for American Indians. Eventually, he found officials who agreed with him, and he was allowed to open a school in an abandoned military post in Carlisle, Pennsylvania (Heuman, 1965).

Pratt toured the northern plains to recruit students, sometimes threatening Indian parents and coercing them to send their children to Carlisle. Pratt operated his school in strict military style. His philosophy of "kill the Indian, save the child" was intended to rid the children of all vestiges of their cultures through strict military discipline and a non-Indian perspective on life. The children were required to exchange their tribal clothing for contemporary non-Indian clothing, and the boys had their hair cut. "Before" and "after" photographs were taken to demonstrate a "positive" contrast.

Like the missionaries, Pratt could see no value in the preservation, much less the promotion, of American Indian cultures, and his level of success, like theirs, was minimal. Students who left Carlisle hoping to join American society found acceptance elusive. They frequently went back to the reservation, where they found that, due to their long absences, they also were strangers. Some children succumbed to diseases and were buried on the grounds of Carlisle. Resting in that graveyard are children who died far from relatives, who probably never knew the circumstances of their children's death. It is one of the saddest places in North America.

Other ORBS were established across the United States. These schools, operated by the BIA, were similar to Carlisle in their methods of military-like discipline and their efforts to "kill" the Indian. The BIA long has been criticized for its shoddy operation of schools, yet several of these schools have celebrated centennials in recent years — 100 years of failure.

Conditions at the ORBS became notorious and were studied in a major government review of the Administration of Indian Affairs (Meriam, 1928). This study provided information regarding the shortcomings of these schools. It charged that the manner in which Indian children were made to work violated child labor laws in most jurisdictions. The study also criticized the methods of military discipline, describing how students were moved in formation from dormitory to classroom to dormitory. It criticized the curriculum and the quality of staff preparation, and it criticized the act of removing children, especially small ones, from their homes, parents, and other relatives for long periods of time, sometimes forever.

The importance of the study was that, for the first time since the early 1820s (Morse, 1822), the federal government attempted to assess the impact of its support of educational programs for American Indians. The criticism in this report contributed to the attention given Indian affairs in general, and education in particular, in the years before World War II.

The Progressives and Their Minority Agenda

Persons involved in the intellectual discourse surrounding progressivism became important actors in demands for reform in American Indian education that followed the 1928 publication of the Meriam Report. For example, both Horace Mann and John Dewey have been characterized as being deeply sensitive to the need for social integration. Dewey is said to have pressed "insistently" for the sort of common schooling that would bring the various creeds and ethnic and class backgrounds into "little embryonic communities." This is in keeping with the often presumed egalitarianism of Thomas Jefferson, who recognized the value of a public system of education, and Horace Mann, who is recognized as the champion of the common school movement. But, in fact, the thinking of Dewey and Mann may go beyond simple democratic inclinations.

A movement toward a "common culture" (see, for example, Dewey, 1900) should mean that all groups would sacrifice a part of their cultures in order to meet all others at some point at which new norms would be established. What has occurred, however, is that small groups have been compelled to discard many aspects of their cultures in order to conform to a European-American mainstream. It is hard to imagine that Dewey intended a lopsided situation where one dominant culture imposes a greater burden of assimilation on all other cultures. Schools clearly have been the instruments of assimilation in the twentieth century, and this is what American Indian people have nearly unanimously rejected. Cremin (1980) concluded that the common school thrives best where there is a reasonable homogeneity of race, class, and religion within the school population, and Goodlad (1984) asserted that "schools reflect the surrounding social and economic order." He wrote:

> If the school is to be anything other than a perpetrator of whatever exists in the society, states and local school districts must set—if they have a mind to—school policies that to some degree transcend and minimize the role of the classroom as reproducer of the culture. (p. 161)

This is a radical suggestion in today's conservatism. It respects the heterogeneity of cultures and conditions and seems to suggest that new norms are desirable, similar to Dewey's notion of a "common culture." In any event, it is a more realistic view of the status quo in the 1990s.

At the same time that the progressives were philosophizing about a common culture, African-Americans, American Indians, Hispanics, and others were being denied access to the benefits of public schools. In the case of American Indians, for example, there was limited access to public schooling due to the reluctance of some states to recognize their responsibilities to Indians as citizens. In addition, although in some cases schools were *available* to American Indian children, they were not *accessible* due to differences in language.

Will Carson Ryan, the progressive who became head of BIA education during the Hoover administration and who was a member of the survey staff of the Meriam Report, established a new attitude in this agency. He promoted tolerance and a desire to understand the Indian population. When Ryan was succeeded by Willard Wolcott Beatty in 1932, the BIA had a second progressive educator. His administration was characterized by attempts to bring an understanding of Indian cultures to the government's schools.

Beatty, like Ryan, believed that decision making should be based on a knowledge of Indian cultures, not on the intuitive judgments of politicians and bureaucrats. Bilingual education, recognition of the importance of family, and other ideas began to find their ways into the BIA schools until, unfortunately, the onset of World War II ended the activities designed to be more culturally appropriate for American Indian students. The postwar conservatism of Congress was not friendly to diversity in America, and abuses reminiscent of earlier times once again became common.

Focus on Legislation

Congressional action requiring change in the administration and delivery of American Indian education began in the political climate of the Great Depression. The Johnson-O'Malley Act, passed in 1934 (48 Stat. 596), encouraged public schools to enroll American Indian children and offered, for the first time, a per capita inducement. This action appears to have followed a Meriam Report comment lauding the government's plan to transfer Indian children into the public school system. Four caveats were given, however, one of them being "that the federal authorities retain sufficient professional direction to make sure the needs of the Indians are met" (p. 415). The Johnson-O'Malley Act authorized the BIA to contract with states to provide education and other types of assistance. The act also allowed federal regulation of the implementation of the law, including the establishment of minimum standards for services.

The regulations produced for this law were poorly enforced. Abuse of the Johnson-O'Malley Act included the diversion of funds into the general school budgets, while Indian students, for whom the funds were earmarked, were ignored. Finally, after more than 3 decades, demands by various American Indian groups caused the government to redraft the regulations and monitor their enforcement.

Parents are now more involved in the administration of the Johnson-O'Malley Act by virtue of Parent Committees. The Parent Committees are authorized by federal regulation to decide how public schools may use the funds they receive for the benefit of Indian children. Although in some jurisdictions these committees are still ineffective, they are growing in strength. Among other things, they provide Indian parents with a training ground for participation in school governance through membership on boards of education.

World War II and the Korean Conflict exposed large numbers of American Indian people to life off the reservation and out of the rural areas where they previously lived. Following their return to civilian life, many of these former soldiers explored life in urban areas, taking advantage of the G.I. Bill for college and the BIA's Relocation Program for job training. Although these programs seem to have offered opportunities for American Indians, the poor management of the Relocation Program stranded some individuals in urban areas without training or jobs, possibly beginning enclaves of what commonly are called "urban Indians." Urban Indians were and may remain less able to access services in the same way as their relatives who chose to remain on the reservation, so that health, employment, and educational needs often go unmet.

In the latter part of the 1950s, the BIA began the far more successful Higher Education Grants Program, which provides educational support to federally recognized Indian college students nationwide. The program usually is the first financial aid contact made by students seeking funds to support their educational ambitions, although the amounts available are small and must be distributed to growing populations of college-going American Indian students. In fact, the numbers of applicants may soon outstrip the available funds. This is due partially to the decision of some tribes to allow tribal membership, and thus eligibility, to large numbers of individuals who have minuscule degrees of Indian blood.

The Indian Education Act of 1972 (86 Stat. 334–341) was intended to encourage the public schools to provide activities designed to meet the unique, culturally related educational needs of American Indian children. Like the Johnson-O'Malley Act, it required that a Parent Committee agree to the programs offered.

The Indian Education Act followed the publication of a widely publicized government study entitled *Indian Education: A National Tragedy — A National Challenge*, popularly known as the Kennedy Report (U.S. Senate, 1969). As in the Meriam Report, there were criticisms of the failure of federal policy, of national attitudes, and of education itself. A dominant policy of coercive assimilation was blamed for these failures, a theme

not unlike the criticism that surrounded the activities of the missionaries
of centuries past.

In 1975, the United States Congress passed the Indian Self-Determination and Education Assistance Act (as noted earlier). This act, among
other things, permitted American Indian nations to enter into contracts
with the federal government to perform services previously performed by
the Bureau of Indian Affairs or Indian Health Service. This has proven to
be useful for Indian nations that have the organizational structures to
assume these responsibilities.

RESOLUTIONS

Relationships between American Indians and European-Americans
have not improved in many respects during the present century. Some
may argue that changes have occurred to the extent that, instead of fighting against the U.S. Army as in the nineteenth century, now American
Indian men and women proudly serve in the American military forces.
However, not all Americans are aware that American Indian people have
been fighting on the side of the U.S. military since the Revolutionary
War. Indeed, there has been an American Indian general in most wars,
beginning with the Revolution. Unfortunately, the experience of many
Indian veterans has been that, while they were valued as soldiers, their
value as Americans when they returned from war was ignored.

Others might argue that changes have occurred to the extent that
American Indians are now full and equal citizens of the United States,
with all the implied rights and responsibilities. But American Indian people have consistently been treated as second-class citizens and now rank at
or near the bottom in nearly all indices used as measurements of socioeconomic status in the United States. Education is only one of these indices,
but it is perhaps the most important due to its potential for aiding in the
improvement of other categories.

Indian Control and Involvement

American Indian education, using nontraditional methods, thrived in
nineteenth century America, as exemplified by the successes of the Cherokee and Choctaw Nations. These Indian nations developed and implemented educational models that were successful; for example, the mean
educational attainment of the citizens of these nations exceeded that found
in the adjacent states of Kansas, Arkansas, and Texas.

Presently, American Indian education leaders believe that the performance of their children would improve markedly if they had the same opportunity to control education that the Choctaws and Cherokees had more than 100 years ago. It seems ironic that of the two models of Indian education that were implemented in the nineteenth century—the boarding schools developed by non-Indians for Indians and the academies and neighborhood schools developed by the Choctaws and Cherokees for their people—the one that prevailed for Indian people was the non-Indian model, and the one that prevailed for all other Americans was the Indian model.

If anything is clear about American Indian education, it is that Indian people must become equal partners in the decision-making processes that create the conditions within which American Indian children are educated. This means that where and to the extent possible, American Indians should take over the schools presently operated by the Bureau of Indian Affairs; and where their children either are not served or are inadequately served by local educational institutions, they should create other schools. It also means that American Indian people must take advantage of the rights of participation and involvement given them by the Johnson-O'Malley and Indian Education Acts and use these opportunities to guide and influence the curricula and programs offered by the public institutions their children attend.

American Indian parental involvement is critical to the future educational development of their children. Parents can monitor and control the assimilation processes that continue to occur in the schools to the detriment of individual self-esteem. Parents can review texts and other printed material used in schools to identify the racial slurring that continues to be found in the assignments of elementary and secondary school students. And parents must become proactive and serve on boards of education in institutions where their children are distinct minorities, for these are the schools where they are most "at risk."

In many instances, federally mandated Parent Committees have served to perform the roles intended by the legislation. They have used their authority to improve regular educational programs and, also to develop after-school and summer educational activities ranging from basic skills development and "latchkey" programs to enrichment programs for high-achieving students. These committees also have worked to recognize the efforts and accomplishments made by Indian children by honoring them in special ceremonies as a means of reinforcing positive behavior.

Tribal organizations also can reinforce parent involvement and student achievement in a variety of ways. They can sponsor honoring activities for high school graduates (as is done by the contemporary Choctaw and Cherokee Nations) and provide financial support for postsecondary educational pursuits. Parent Committees and tribal organizations working together can promote activities that show elementary and junior high school students that (1) opportunities really do exist upon high school graduation and (2) there are many people who are interested in them as individuals. Parent Committees, which honor achievement and participation by students in these grades, demonstrate to students that someone cares and that they are valued. This is an activity now engaged in by many American Indian Parent Committees in all parts of the United States, and, although there is no research that demonstrates the impact, the responses of students and their parents clearly are positive and encouraging.

Of course, early recruitment of students by both universities and career representatives should accompany these efforts of tribal organizations and Parent Committees. For example, at the Cherokee Nation several years ago, the education department began sponsoring a "career" day for junior high school students. This event has since grown into an annual affair that attracts representatives from a variety of professions and institutional representatives from local as well as state and national institutions of higher education; it serves to underscore the positive prospects of high school success for Indian students.

Project Prime at Arizona State University recognizes the value of early identification and takes the Cherokee Nation model a step further. The students identified are assessed for their academic weaknesses and given the opportunity to improve their skills so that by the time they are ready to choose a university, they have become strong candidates for admission. Project Prime also works with the parents of these youngsters, giving them the confidence not only that their children are college material but also that they as parents can help their children get there. This recognizes the importance of family in American Indian communities — that is, that the success of one member of the family is a success for all.

Cultural Validation

American Indian children must have the opportunity to grow to adulthood with the understanding that they are worthwhile individuals who are equal to all other Americans. They must believe that they are respected for their Indianness as they respect others for their individual worth. They must believe that they are valued in American society in general and thus are able to achieve in any way they choose according to their individual talents. Parents cannot accomplish all this on their own.

They have the right to expect the cooperation of the institutions of higher education that train the professionals who staff the schools most of their children attend.

American society has a responsibility to serve all Americans equally, a mandate that is loaded with implications. This does not mean that non-Indian teachers should become modern missionaries imposing their values on Indian children. What it means is that elementary and secondary schools must strive to employ as teachers and administrators American Indians who are qualified for these positions. The modeling that occurs when American Indians are seen playing significant roles in schools validates both the presence of Indian students and the institution itself. Teacher training institutions must seek out and recruit these Indian people, providing them with the technical skills required of individuals who teach in America's schools, without denying them the opportunity to maintain and use their cultural heritage.

Institutions for teacher education should also seek to prepare non-Indian teachers of Indian youngsters to serve the unique needs of these children and their cultures. Too frequently, teachers are prepared to serve only a non-Indian population, and consequently, Indian students are left with instructors who have no knowledge of, or concern for, their educational and individual needs. This creates an inequality, precisely because teachers *are* knowledgeable about the educational and individual needs of *non-Indian* students.

Teacher education might better serve American Indian populations through the development and delivery of "on-site" programs. Many teacher aides hired under the auspices of federal programs are both capable of and interested in becoming certified teachers. Unfortunately, many of these teacher aides may be the sole support for their families or have some other valid reason that makes regular attendance at a university not feasible. As a practical matter, then, "on-site" teacher education for American Indian communities appears to be the most promising method for increasing the number of American Indian teachers. Although at least a small amount of work probably should be achieved on campus, most of the actual learning experience could be given either at the school where the teacher aides are employed or in another location near their homes. Teacher aides could be given some credit for their classroom experiences at the same time as they attend both lower and upper division classes.

Certain structural adjustments must be made for the sake of cultural validation on university campuses as well as in elementary and secondary schools. American Indian students at all levels have the right to expect that the intellectual and emotional demands they bring to the institution have the same chance of being met as those of majority students. Where opportunities are present for reinforcing values attributed to American middle-class culture—such as are embodied in curricula that focus on Euro-centric histories, traditions, and so on—similar opportunities should be available for Indian students. Minority students who do not have the opportunity to have their existences validated are students who do not have an equal opportunity to grow intellectually and emotionally. Therein lies a major shortcoming of university support for all minority students (Noley, 1991).

Universities and public schools are obligated to respect and protect the cultural integrity of their American Indian students just as they do for the majority. At the university level, this can be provided through duplication of academic programming, such as in the implementation of tutoring programs designed specifically for American Indian students. In addition, curricula should be examined for their ability to provide equal validation for all American-based cultures. Finally, since social opportunities are important for validating cultural perspectives, encouragement must be given by campus officials for the extra-academic activities sponsored by Indian clubs and campus cultural centers.

At the precollege levels, it is especially important to recognize that children who are subjected to attacks on their cultural integrity personalize those assaults and do not understand that they result from intolerance and ignorance. When these attacks come in the guise of learning, students become confused and seek to reject what they consider personal affronts to their dignity. Elementary and secondary schools that find ways to honor American Indian cultures in addition to screening text materials for offensiveness are institutions that are offering education on an equal basis to their students. Screening text materials for offensiveness is not the same as censoring; the literature *already* has been screened for its offensiveness to the majority population. It is necessary to perform the same task for the benefit of American Indian children and other American minorities.

Research and Development

One frustration of examining the education of American Indian people is that frequently, in large data sets, they are combined with other small groups in the "other" category, even when the subject of the data collection is minority populations. Even when data specifically for American Indians are presented, they may be unreliable due to the varying methods of defining just who can be categorized as American Indian. Because some tribes allow anyone who can trace their heritage to an Indian ancestor to be enrolled as a full member, and others require a high degree of Indian blood to claim membership, a person with a small degree of Indian blood can be enrolled in one tribe, while another with a higher degree cannot obtain membership in another tribe. However, tribes do have the right to determine their membership, so researchers are advised to be aware of the differences so their judgments may be tempered where necessary.

There are several specific research needs to be met that relate to the status and progress of American Indians in our schools. For example, there is growing but still inadequate literature on American Indian school dropouts. A series of specific studies should be commissioned focusing on tribal groups and geographically bound groups. Means of conducting ongoing dropout studies are available due to public school participation in federal programs, but tribes and the appropriate federal agencies need to place a priority on research. The appropriate agencies are the Indian Education Programs of the U.S. Department of Education, and the Office of Indian Education in the Bureau of Indian Affairs, U.S. Department of the Interior.

At the postsecondary level, there also are opportunities for research focusing on success or persistence. Tribes contracting for the administration of the Higher Education Grants Program are at least potential custodians of a considerable amount of data on college-going American Indian students. This is another area in which there is a small but growing body of literature, mostly dissertation research, but enough to have some utility for those charged with the responsibility for retention.

A key to the continued development of the research capability of tribes is the creation of tribal partnerships with universities. Research institutions that work with state and local governments should consider that tribes also may seek to sponsor research and development activities. At the same time, tribal governments should establish priorities and the mechanics for partnerships with universities and for the development of their own basic research initiatives.

Ideas and Activities

Certain programs and activities have provided opportunities for educational development to Indian people, but the extent to which commonly accepted educational methods are useful with American Indian children is sometimes questionable. Understanding this, various American Indian educators have identified approaches that appear to be more useful in serving their children. Many prominent American Indian educators (see, for example, Swisher & Deyhle, 1989) support the view that American Indian children have unique learning styles that should be understood and accommodated by teachers. Other American Indian educators have found that "holistic" approaches are successful, while still others are enamored with theories of hemispheric dominance.

American Indian educators take practical approaches to solving educational problems. They tend to identify specific problems and attack them directly. For example, the problem of drug and alcohol abuse has become an educational priority due to the impact it has on children in schools. Curricula to combat this problem, developed by tribes and educational institutions, have had varying degrees of success, but they represent important contributions.

Teen pregnancy has been the cause of unknown numbers of dropouts. A program developed at the Cherokee Nation, modeled after another serving a different population, gave pregnant girls a place to continue their education at the same time they were given prenatal attention. The young mothers could remain in the center after their babies were born to learn techniques of child care in addition to math and science. Some mothers stayed in the alternative schooling situation until they graduated.

In boarding schools, students come from a wide variety of backgrounds and often find themselves in academic trouble because of poor preparation or because the regular classroom is insufficiently stimulating. A "Saturday Academy," developed at Sequoyah High School, supported the additional needs of both extraordinarily talented students as well as those who needed help just to keep pace with the rest of the class. A variety of innovative classes were given on Saturday mornings; other activities included visits to university campuses, historical sites, and industrial facilities. A "ropes-challenge" course, for example, was constructed to aid in the development of self-confidence and to teach the value of cooperation and tutoring. In addition, innovative faculty developed a design class wherein students had the opportunity to learn about robotics in one year and to design, build, launch, and recover rockets during another. Other faculty found imaginative ways to help lower-achieving students grasp basic skills, and social skills training and other confidence-building exercises were provided as part of the instructional routine.

These are examples of the kinds of direct approaches to problem resolution that are simple in appearance, simple in their implementation, but complex in concept, such as the "ropes-challenge" course, which can successfully address serious problems related to trust and cooperative behavior. However, one must not be satisfied that these sorts of activities are answers to the serious problems of American Indian education. These are not long-term solutions; rather, they are direct approaches designed to "stop the bleeding," while imaginative educators take the time to address the longer-term needs of American Indian children. The educational problems of American Indians, created over a period of 500 years and characterized by unequal interrelationships, will require a combination of both short- and longer-term strategies to be effectively ameliorated.

NOTES

1. Tuscalusa was the Miko (leader) of the Mabilian Indians, a group belonging to the Muskogean language family and related closely to the Choctaws.
2. The Treaty of Dancing Rabbit Creek, signed by leaders of the Choctaw Nation in 1830, provided for the removal of Choctaws from their original homes in what is now Mississippi to land in what is now Oklahoma.

REFERENCES

Bourne, E. G. (Ed.). (1922). *Narratives of the career of Hernando de Soto* (Vols. 1-2). New York: Allerton Book.

Bradshears, E. (1820, March 30). Letter to Rev. Cyrus Kingsbury. *The Missionary Herald, 16*, 368–369.

Cremin, L. A. (1980). *American education*. New York: Harper & Row.

Dewey, J. (1900). *The school and society*. Chicago: University of Chicago Press.

Forrest, E. R. (1929). *Missions and pueblos of the southwest*. Cleveland: Arthur H. Clark.

Goodlad, J. I. (1984). *A place called school*. New York: McGraw-Hill.

Hauptman, L. M., & Wherry, J. D. (Ed.). (1990). *The Pequots in southern New England: The fall and rise of an American Indian nation*. Norman: University of Oklahoma Press.

Heuman, W. (1965). *The Indians of Carlisle*. New York: G. P. Putnam's Sons.

Kappler, C. J. (Ed.). (1904). *Indian affairs: Laws and treaties* (Vol. II). Washington, DC: U.S. Government Printing Office.

McClure, D., & Parish, E. (1972). *Memoirs of the Rev. Eleazar Wheelock*. New York: Arno Press. (Original work published in 1811)

Meriam, L. (Ed.). (1928). *The problem of Indian administration*. Baltimore, MD: John Hopkins Press.

Morse, J. (1822). *A report to the Secretary of the United States on Indian affairs*. Washington, DC: Davis and Force.

Naylor, T. H., & Polzer, C. W. (1986). *The presidio and militia on the northern frontier of New Spain, 1570–1700*. Tucson: University of Arizona Press.

Noley, G. B. (1979). *The history of education in the Choctaw Nation from precolonial times to 1830*. Unpublished doctoral dissertation, Pennsylvania State University, University Park.

Noley, G. B. (1991). Fear, higher education and change. *Thought and Action, 7*, 105–114.

Roessel, R. A. (1977). *Navajo education in action: The Rough Rock Demonstration School*. Chinle, AZ: Navajo Curriculum Center, The Rough Rock Demonstration School.

Strong, W. E. (1910). *The story of the American board*. Boston: Pilgrim Press.

Swisher, K., & Deyhle, D. (1989). The styles of learning are different but the teaching is just the same: Suggestions for teachers of American Indian youth [Special issue]. *Journal of American Indian Education*, 1–14.

Szasz, M. C. (1990, October). *Cultural broker: Link between Indian and white worlds*. Paper presented at the annual meeting of the Western History Association, Tacoma, WA.

U.S. Senate. (1969). *Indian education: A national tragedy — a national challenge* (Senate Report No. 91-501). Washington, DC: U.S. Government Printing Office.

Washington, H. A. (Ed.). (1856). *The writings of Thomas Jefferson* (Vol. IV). New York: J. C. Ricker.

Wheeler, R. W. (1979). *Jim Thorpe: World's greatest athlete*. Norman: Oklahoma University Press.

CHAPTER 5

"Look Me in the Eye"

A Hispanic Cultural Perspective on School Reform

RAFAEL VALDIVIESO AND SIOBHAN NICOLAU

> "The parents never come to school and they don't teach respect in the home. Why, the children won't even look me in the eye when I talk to them."
> *Texas Teacher*
> "Respect is the most important thing is what I tell my kids. Don't make trouble, don't ask questions, and look down when the teacher talks to you."
> *Latino Parent*

Being undereducated is undoubtedly the single biggest obstacle to the overall social and economic assimilation of Hispanics in the United States. Educational attainment is the indicator that most dramatically illustrates the lack of parity between Hispanic and Anglo populations. For example, in 1991, 90% of white 25- to 29-year-olds were high school graduates, compared with only 56% of Hispanics (Alsalam, Ogle, Rogers, & Smith, 1992, p. 62). Although the low education attainment figures of Hispanic young adults reflect in part the large-scale immigration of Hispanics, many of whom arrive as youths with little education, they also attest to the problems of Hispanics who are educated in U.S. schools. The Hispanic adults most likely to have school-aged children are in the 24 to 34 age bracket. In 1990, about 40% of this group had not completed high school and were over three times as likely not to have done so as other Americans (U.S. Bureau of the Census, 1992). Even among those who were high school graduates, many graduated without the skills required to secure employment in a stable sector of the economy (for example, see National

Education Goals Panel, 1992, p. 28, and Valdivieso, 1986a, pp. 6–8). Thus a majority of Hispanics in the 25 to 34 age group are meeting adult responsibilities with inadequate educations.

Research has revealed that parental level of education — regardless of whether the parents are native born or immigrant — is the most powerful predictor of how well a child will do in school. That being so, the prognosis is clear and dismal. The children of a majority of this nation's Hispanics aged 25 to 34 — immigrant and native born — are at risk of being trapped in the cycle of poverty unless they are enrolled in effective schools that are sensitive to their culture and traditions, recognize their needs, and reach out to work with their families (Nieto, 1992; Valdivieso, 1986b).

UNDERSTANDING THE COMPLEXITY OF
THE CULTURAL BACKGROUND

Who is Latino/Hispanic?

Individuals do not readily self-identify as "Hispanic" or "Latino." The vast majority generally think of themselves in relation to the country from which they or their ancestors came (Skerry, 1992). In a television interview, for example, Bill Moyers asked Ernie Cortez, a MacArthur Foundation "genius" award winner and community organizer, what it was like to be a Hispanic in the United States. Cortez answered to the effect that he wasn't sure what it was like to be a Hispanic because, although he had been a Mexican-American all his life, he had been a Hispanic only a few years. Arturo Villar, former publisher of *Vista Magazine*, points out that he had to emigrate from Cuba to become a Hispanic. Hispanics exist only here in the United States.

In fact, the term *Hispanic* was created by the federal bureaucracy as a means of labeling a category that included several groups. The term *Latino* derives from Latin America, a term devised to distinguish Spanish- and Portuguese-colonized American lands from those American lands colonized by Northern Europeans. The first widespread use of *Latin*, apart from the geographical designation, denoted certain kinds of music, as in the phrase "a Latin beat." Only recently has *Latino* been proposed as an alternative to *Hispanic*, largely by proponents of Hispanic unity movements.

Latino/Hispanic leaders have discussed the benefits of unity for decades. However, strong Latino/Hispanic coalitions designed to broaden the base of support for or against policies and practices that affect the diverse Latino/Hispanic communities have taken shape only over the course of the past 20 years. The selection of an "umbrella" word accept-able to all members of these coalitions has often strained the cause of "unity." *Latino* is the term of choice in California and the New York, Chicago, and Miami metropolitan areas; Texas and other locales still pre-fer *Hispanic*. Some unity spokespersons have avoided the Hispanic/Latino debate by using "La Raza," a word that originally referred to peoples of Mexican heritage.

Labels aside, what are Hispanics? Western Hemisphere Hispanics are a cultural blend resulting from the expansion of the Spanish empire in the fifteenth and sixteenth centuries. Their diverse origins include New World civilizations from Aztecs and Incas to Apaches and Zapotecs; African slaves; Spanish explorers, governors, soldiers, and servants — and their women — and the English and French who competed with the Spanish for a piece of the New World. U.S. Hispanics are united by a common Spanish language and a heritage that contains aspects of Indian, African, and Spanish cultural and religious values. But U.S. Hispanics are divided by geography, country of origin, race, class, traditional group differences, and the time and circumstances of their entry into the United States.

White, black, brown, and red — both native born and immigrant — Hispanics are the fastest growing U.S. minority according to the U.S. Census. Their numbers — 22.4 million in 1991 — are expected to double in 30 years and triple in 60. The Hispanic birthrate is higher than that of the general population, and it is estimated that legal immigration will con-tinue at the present rate of close to 300,000 a year. As a consequence of this natural increase and immigration, it is estimated that within 20 years Hispanics will become the nation's largest minority.

Hispanics are the most urbanized population in the United States, and they are highly concentrated geographically. About 76% live in five states: California (33%), Texas (21%), New York (11%), Florida (6%), and Illinois (5%). About 65% reside in only 13 key markets: Los Angeles, New York, Miami, the San Francisco Bay Area, Chicago, Houston, San Antonio, El Paso, San Diego, Dallas, McAllen, Phoenix, and Denver. In these areas, their children — immigrant and native born — are becoming the predominant number or majority of the school-aged population.

Immigrant Versus Native Born

Americans by fiat. For most Hispanics, entry into the United States has been voluntary and has implied an acceptance of the unspoken obligation of the immigrant and the immigrant's descendants to adapt — not assimi-late — to their host country. However, an estimated quarter of our native-born Hispanic U.S. citizens owe their presence to the U.S. policy of Manifest Destiny, a policy of conquest. Both the Southwest and Puerto Rico were settled by the Spanish in the late 1500s — before the Pilgrims landed on Plymouth Rock. These territories were ceded to the United States in peace treaties more than 300 years later, and the individuals living in them — native language, culture, and all — became involuntary inhabitants of the United States. This fact has implications for how the country deals with questions of the language and culture of these individuals and their descendants. In the Hispanic arena it especially affects Puerto Ricans, 3.5 million of whom are U.S. citizens residing on an island whose first and official language is Spanish.

Immigrants. The United States is a young nation all of whose population, with the exception of the American Indians, came from somewhere else. Central to our national mythology is a celebration of "the melting pot" in which it is claimed that we all did — or we all should — blend into farina with no lumps. Another aspect of the mythology is the dearly held notion that we are oblivious to class distinctions. In fact, immigrants have selectively blended into the melting pot, and it is class — closely tied to education level and race — that preserves the lumps in the farina.

The United States formally admits 700,000 newcomers a year; adding those who arrive informally probably raises the total to one million. Historically, that is not unprecedented. According to Gary Rubin (1992) in a recent report of the American Jewish Committee, flows roughly equaled that level six times between 1905 and 1914. At that time, the U.S. population totaled 100 million compared with the present 250 million, so in some respects the impact then was even greater. At the turn of the century, foreign-born individuals constituted 12% to 14% of the nation's population. Today they make up 6% to 7%. But there are some differences. At the turn of the nineteenth century, the U.S. economy was creating its infrastructure and identity. Today's immigrants, near the turn of the twentieth century, must find a place in an established system that is becoming ever more technologically sophisticated. The internal U.S. frontiers are gone.

A second difference from the early 1900s is that the current immigrant population is highly diverse. Immigration at the turn of the nineteenth century was almost entirely European and white. By contrast, just over a tenth of today's new arrivals have European roots. Forty percent now come from Asia and 40% from Latin America. And greater diversity is reflected within the categories. For example, a decade ago Hispanic immigration could have been summed up as being largely Mexican and Cuban. Today, although Mexico continues to be dominant, significant flows come from the Dominican Republic, the Central American Republics, Colombia, Peru, Ecuador, and Venezuela. A third difference is that most European immigrants — before the advent of affordable air travel — came to the new world to stay. Advances in travel and the proximity of the Latin-American countries offer the possibility of more temporary and cyclical immigration. Although the motivations of Latin immigrants are as diverse as the countries that send them, the majority who enter the United States are low-skilled individuals who hope to improve their futures and those of their children. Some come to stay. Others come to work, send back money to their families, and dream of returning to their native lands. Still others are cyclical workers who cross the border seasonally to fill jobs.

Presently, at least 43 % of all Hispanics are immigrants (Farnsworth Riche, 1991). Hispanic immigrants, like other groups, mostly settle in locations where there are others of their background, to provide a base of support while they learn how to cope with the new culture. As a result, the impact of immigration is recognized and strongly felt on the local level and especially by the public schools which are expected to transition children from Spanish to English, integrate the new students into regular classes, give them the skills they need to succeed in the United States, and often provide English classes for their parents and other adults as well.

Refugees. International and U.S. laws designate as a refugee anyone outside his or her own country having "a well-founded fear of being persecuted for reasons of race, religion, nationality, membership in a particular social group, or political opinion." Although that is very straightforward, the U.N. High Commissioner for Refugees published a 90-page book explaining how to apply this definition.

The United States has taken in well over a million refugees since the mid-1970s, far more than any other nation. Still, all nations practice selective policies on refugee admission, and until recently that translated into the United States giving preference to those escaping communism. Although some Central American refugees have been admitted in recent years, by far the largest group of Hispanic refugees have been those fleeing Castro's Cuba.

Refugees or exiles tend to have different mind-sets than most immigrants. A primary focus of a large proportion of refugees is how and when they can return home, even when that does not seem to be a practical option in the near term. Often they are actively involved in international activities designed to change regimes and make that possible. Like immigrants, they settle in designated areas. However, they tend more than immigrants to dedicate themselves to ensuring that their children maintain the home culture and the language, because they believe that they must be ready for "the return." On the other hand, their children, educated here, tend to identify with "here," not the "there" they never knew. Most are culturally strong, but they do not relate the culture to the homeland in the way their parents do.

The native born. There are native-born Hispanics whose families have been here since the arrival of Spanish settlers in the sixteenth century. Some of them, along with the children of third-, fourth-, fifth-, and sixth-generation Hispanics, are thoroughly blended into the farina. Little remains of their "Hispanidad" beyond the surnames, and sometimes even these have been changed or the pronunciation has been anglicized. But others, by choice or by the isolation that geography and poverty can impose, maintain aspects of cultural identification and practice.

The three factors that most affect native-born Hispanics and those who emigrate to the United States as young children are the popular youth culture, income level, and school. The pervasive U.S. youth culture, supported and promoted by television, tends to push all young people into a tribal conformity that does not seem to draw upon the strengths or traditional values of any of the melting pot cultures. Poverty tends to narrow options and trap individuals in physical and mental stasis; it can affect family formation, and it can limit the amount of time adults can spend with children. Finally, school is the factor that has the potential to balance the negative influences of the other two. Education can open doors and increase options for both families and their children, when and if schools are given resources and are helped to be sensitive to the cultures and needs of the families they are serving. As a start, schools must become familiar with the diverse histories and the collective experiences of the Hispanic groups, as outlined below.

Thumbnail Histories

Mexican-Americans. In 1990, the Census indicated that 14 million Mexican/Mexican Americans or Chicanos (a self-affirming term popular among young people in the late 1960s and early 1970s) lived in the United States. They represented 63% of the U.S. Hispanic population, half of whom were concentrated in two states, California and Texas. The median age of the group was 24.3 years; the median family income was $19,968, considerably below the white median family income of $35,975. As a group, Mexican-Americans are difficult to categorize. The large population ranges from recent arrivals to descendants of families who lived in what is now the United States in the late 1500s. The category of U.S. Hispanics of Mexican ancestry includes the highest percentage of individuals who are native born and were raised in the United States.

The first Spanish settlements were concentrated in northern New Mexico and southern Colorado, at the end of the Spanish Crown's Santa Fe Trail. In the 1820s when Spain's colonies broke away and established new nations, Mexico encompassed much of what is now the southwestern United States, and Mexicans were a mixture — cultural and physical — of Spanish and Native-American peoples. When half of Mexico's territory was annexed by the United States in the 1840s, the rights of the Spanish residents in the new U.S. territories were guaranteed by treaty. But those rights were unprotected, and the majority of the original families in New Mexico and Colorado lost their holdings. Most isolated themselves in small villages, maintained Spanish culture and language, and survived for over a century as a poor rural majority. Until World War I, they were relatively cut off from Anglo society and from other Hispanics as well.

The bulk of the Mexican immigration to California, Arizona, and Texas occurred after 1847, as waves of low-skilled, predominantly Indian-heritage Mexicans fled poverty and political oppression. The immigrants became the underclass of the Southwest — the often exploited labor force for agriculture, industry, and service. Severe discrimination, including Jim Crow laws and political disenfranchisement, caused them to withdraw into their barrios. Despite overt prejudice and discriminatory practices, prior to World War II Mexicans were unofficially allowed — and often encouraged — to enter the United States to fill labor needs. But policy fluctuated with the rises and falls of the U.S. economy. For example, in the 1930s when jobs were scarce, Mexicans were declared illegals and deported in great numbers, citizens and noncitizens alike. In response, Mexicans and Mexican-Americans adopted survival skills — most endeavored to be as inconspicuous as possible.

Major change occurred after World War II. Many Mexican-Americans served the United States well on the battlefields and home fronts. When the war was over, they took advantage of both the skills they had learned in service and in the factories and the benefits of the G.I. Bill. They began to improve their lives economically, socially, and politically. National, regional, and local organizations seeking equality, justice, and protection began to emerge. And Mexicans moved from rural areas to the cities. By 1980, the Census showed that the majority of Mexican-Americans were urban residents, and many were migrating to the industrial cities of the Midwest. A solid middle class began to take root. At the same time, the "push/pull" factors maintained immigration from Mexico at high levels. When the U.S. economy was expanding, this immigration was welcome; Mexicans filled jobs U.S. citizens did not want. In periods of economic decline, Mexican immigration was blamed for hard times, and Mexicans were accused of taking jobs from deserving U.S. citizens.

But in good and bad times, the flows of youthful migrants continued, the numbers swelled, and, by 1990, urban schools in the states of high concentration—California, Texas, and Arizona—saw their Hispanic student enrollments burgeoning.

Puerto Ricans. In 1991, there were 3.5 million Puerto Ricans residing on the Island. The 2,651,815 living in the continental United States represented 11% of the continental Hispanic population. Puerto Ricans are young; the median age is 26.7 years. In the United States, New York City has been the center of Puerto Rican settlement since the early 1900s, and mainland Puerto Ricans are the most metropolitan of all Hispanic groups, with settlements in the major cities of New Jersey, Florida, Illinois, and California. In 1990, the median family income on the Island of Puerto Rico was $9,988; the median family income for Puerto Ricans living on the mainland was $18,000. As these dollar figures indicate, regardless of where Puerto Ricans reside, an alarming proportion of the population is poor. Puerto Rican disadvantage is rooted in both nature's distribution of resources and the policies and practices of the two nations that have claimed Puerto Rico—Spain and the United States.

Spain quickly exhausted Puerto Rico's meager gold mines and shifted its attention to the wealth of Peru and Mexico. Thereafter, Puerto Rico languished as a relatively ignored military outpost that protected the Spanish shipping lanes. The indigenous Indian population was all but obliterated by disease, conflict, and overwork, and African slaves were introduced by the Spanish, first to work the mines and later the sugar industry. The Island was a passive victim in wars between the great colonial powers, and in 1898—following the Spanish-American War—both Puerto Rico and Cuba were annexed by the United States.

Puerto Ricans were granted U.S. citizenship in 1917, and some improvements in health care and education resulted from the U.S. connection, but dramatic changes did not take place until the initiation of Operation Bootstrap, a joint Puerto Rican/U.S. development strategy based on outside investment, technology transfers, and tax incentives. From the 1940s to the 1960s, Operation Bootstrap went a long way toward modernizing Puerto Rico. Industries were established, and the amount of housing and the number of schools and health care facilities were increased; the service sector was expanded, jobs were created, incomes rose, and Puerto Rico became a showcase. In the 1970s, Operation Bootstrap found itself in grave trouble, due in part to recession on the mainland. Unemployment increased, the Island's debt soared, and transfer payments from the United States rose by more than 750% within a decade. Even when Operation Bootstrap was booming, however, Puerto Rico could not support its grow-

ing population, and despite official denials, it was generally recognized
that the health of the economy required the out-migration of 50,000 persons each year.

Emigration to the mainland—principally New York—began at a relatively slow pace in the early 1900s and increased dramatically after World
War II, peaking at 74,000 in 1953. The flows decrease and decline in
direct relation to the economies of the Island and the mainland. And a
large part of the migration has always been cyclical. While recent migration has included significant numbers of professionals, most Puerto Rican
migrants have been poor and unskilled and have experienced major cultural shock upon arrival on the mainland. The Island is characterized by
a community-centered life, by reliance on extended families and support
networks of relatives and friends, by a system that provides respect and
care for the elderly, and by vast amounts of sunlight and profusions of
flowers, even in the barrios of the poor. The mainland reality most face
in urban centers of the Northeast and Midwest could hardly be more
different.

Most Puerto Ricans do not come to the mainland with intent to stay.
They want to make some money and go home, or they want to spend
their working years earning better wages and then retire to Puerto Rico.
Some do, but many remain. They, and most particularly their stateside-
born children, become "Americanized." Their culture is not quite the
same as that of the Island. They like to visit, but many, particularly the
young, are not comfortable living there, and the Island residents are not
always comfortable with them. Sometimes "Neyoricans," as the returnees
are called, suffer discrimination on the Island. Young people find themselves rejected by two worlds; they are too "American" to be fully accepted
on the Island and too "Puerto Rican" to be fully accepted on the mainland.
Themselves the product of a racially mixed society, many Puerto Ricans
confront white prejudice in the States and find themselves unaccepted by
or competing with members of black communities. Sometimes they suffer
discrimination at the hands of other Hispanics, a discrimination rooted in
class, race, and an old scale of privilege and status that Spain conferred
upon its colonies.

In the 1950s and 1960s, most Puerto Rican migrants found the jobs
they were seeking and became the backbone of specific industries such as
the needle trades. They clustered in relatively stable low-income neighborhoods. But in the 1970s, Puerto Ricans in New York were dealt severe
economic blows. A recession took hold, the garment industry exited New
York, skills-training programs were reduced, and heavy immigration
flows of documented and undocumented Asians and other immigrant
groups—including significant numbers of Dominicans—increased compe-

tition for a diminishing number of jobs. Puerto Rican women, who had enjoyed the highest rate of female labor force participation in the United States, suddenly found themselves without employment. Young men could not make a living. Family formation suffered, and the rate of Puerto Rican welfare dependency increased, as did the number of female-headed Puerto Rican households. In the 1980s the flow of other Hispanic groups to New York accelerated. By 1990, New York's "first Hispanics" found themselves pushed out of their position of dominance; "other" Hispanics represented a little over half of the New York Hispanic population, and some of the others were moving up the economic ladder faster than Puerto Ricans, largely because they had higher levels of education.

Cubans. Most of the 1,055,000 persons of Cuban background living in the United States are relatively new arrivals. They represent 5% of the U.S. Hispanic population. Compared with other Hispanic groups, the Cuban population is older — the median age is 39.3 years — and they have higher levels of educational attainment. This translates into higher income levels — the median family income is $26,858 — and higher levels of business ownership.

Cuba enjoyed unique and preferred status under Spanish rule. The island was Spain's "Pearl of the Antilles," and it served as the administrative center of much of the New World Empire. The history of Cuban migration into the United States is unique because — from its inception in the late nineteenth century — most Cubans entered the United States as refugees, not immigrants. The first wave, which settled in the Florida Keys, Tampa, and New York City, were refugees from the 1868–1895 Cuban Wars of Independence. In 1898, after the Spanish-American War, the United States annexed Cuba. Shortly thereafter, when Cuba was granted independence, another flow of political refugees sought asylum. In 1900 there were 100,000 Cubans living in the United States, most of them having fled their homeland for political reasons.

Cubans fleeing the oppression of the Batista regime arrived in the 1940s and 1950s, but the major migration (600,000) occurred in the early 1960s as a result of the Cuban revolution. It is estimated that a third of these political refugees — most of them from Havana — came from upper- and middle-class professional and business backgrounds. They relocated in Florida, New Jersey, New York, Illinois, and California, assisted by a federal relocation program. They rapidly transferred their skills and built an economic infrastructure that allowed them to maintain their culture and to deal as peers with the majority community. At the same time, they were able to provide employment opportunities for many of the Cuban workers who had migrated with them. Their notable economic success contributed to the transformation of Miami into a commercial and financial center for Latin America.

In the spring of 1980, the Cuban government announced that Cuban citizens wishing to leave the country could seek asylum at the Peruvian Embassy in Havana; over 10,000 did so, until access ended, and then the government opened the port of Mariel for emigrants who wanted to go to the United States. U.S. Cubans began a Mariel/Key West boat lift of 200 boats of all kinds, and between June and September 1980, another 125,000 Cubans entered the United States. Fifty percent of the Mariel refugees had family members here. The others were predominantly young males — a small percentage of whom had been in prison and who caused well-publicized problems that alienated both the Anglo and the Cuban communities. Moreover, the new refugees had been raised under socialism. They had heavy adjustment needs, and there were few programs to address them. Those who did not have family connections were adrift; it took a decade for them to overcome their initial problems.

Most of the Cubans who fled Castro expected that they would return to Cuba. They did not mentally unpack or seek U.S. citizenship in large numbers until the end of the Carter administration. However, the children of the refugees, most of whom are now young adults, do not dream of returning to reside in a place they never knew. Although they live a culture that is deeply Cuban and tend to be fully bilingual, they are rooted here. These young Cuban adults enjoy higher than average educational levels.

Central and South Americans. The 1990 Census reveals that Central and South Americans represent 13.7% of the U.S. Hispanic population: 520,151 from the Dominican Republic, 1,323,830 from Central America, and 1,035,602 from South America. Until 1980, Central and South Americans and other Hispanics who were not Mexican, Puerto Rican, or Cuban were lumped into a catch-all category titled "Other." In 1980, it was discovered that "Other" ranked second among the major Hispanic groups, and Census created two categories — "Central and South Americans" and "Others."

Central and South Americans can be divided into at least three groups. The first group consists of highly skilled Latin-American immigrants, who tend to be young, college-educated, and often trained in specialty areas (e.g., engineering, law). They come to the United States seeking opportunity. The second group, a refugee professional class, is well-trained and was once employed in universities or government. They are impelled to leave their native countries due to a change in political leadership. The third group consists of Central and South American economic refugees, often from small towns in rural El Salvador, Guatemala, Nicaragua, and South American countries, who come to the United States seeking work and/or opportunity to better their lives. They were caught in the cross fire — often literally — of rival political factions in their countries. Their educational levels are lower, and they are generally poorer. Should they find steady work, it probably will be in the service occupations. When they cannot find work, their lives are a constant struggle for survival. Their lot is further complicated when they are undocumented.

The Dominican population is concentrated in New York and New Jersey, and it includes individuals from all the categories described above. The Colombian population is centered on the East Coast, from New York to Florida. Central American economic refugees tend to cluster in the southwestern centers, Houston and Los Angeles, for example, but they are found in the East as well. New York's Latino population has become remarkably diverse since the early 1980s, and during the same time period the Washington, DC area experienced incredible growth of Latinos from all parts of Central and South America.

Other Hispanics. Other Hispanics fall into four general categories: Hispanos in the Southwest, mixed Hispanics, part Hispanics, and the Spanish. Together, they account for 6.9% of the U.S. Hispanic population.

Hispanos are long-term residents (five or more generations) of the Southwest, especially New Mexico, whose origins are the Spanish settlers. Hispanos have maintained an identity that distinguishes them from other Mexican-origin people in the Southwest. They speak a distinctive Spanish, and the majority are bilingual. Those who do not migrate out continue to lead rural lives, and they have had the advantage of being the majority population in small towns where they have wielded political control.

Mixed Hispanics are the offspring of marriages between members of different Hispanic groups, and most live in major metropolitan centers where there is greater opportunity for contact among groups. Part Hispanics are the children of out-marriage — a Hispanic and a non-Hispanic. As a rule, the parents of the Hispanic who out-marries have lived in the United States for a long time or are well-educated immigrants from Central or South America. Part Hispanics are found throughout the United States. They generally have few language or acculturation problems.

Finally, the Spanish are individuals or descendants of individuals who immigrated to the United States directly from Spain without stopping to colonize or settle in Latin America. The flow has been small but steady since the middle of the nineteenth century, and it has represented a mix of older persons who are craftspeople, small businesspeople, and professionals.

Poverty and Educational Achievement

As our wide-angle view of "Hispanidad" illustrates, Latino groups differ in some important characteristics, and there are considerable differences in social class, origin, race, and education status. The migration histories of the various groups are not the same, and they reside in different parts of the country. Nonetheless, what does characterize all the major groups, with the exception of the Cubans, albeit in varying intensities, are high levels of poverty and low levels of educational achievement.

In 1990, census data revealed that 38% of Hispanic children lived in families with incomes below the official poverty line. When one looks at the median incomes of Hispanic men ($14,141) and Hispanic women ($10,099), it becomes clear that many more families — even when both partners work — are heavily represented among the working poor. In 1990, Hispanic married-couple income was only 69% of white married-couple income, even though Hispanic men have higher labor force participation rates than non-Hispanic men and the labor force participation of Hispanic women is increasing. The 1990 Census reported that a little over one-half of all Hispanic women were in the labor force.

As for educational achievement, most middle-class Hispanic children fare well to reasonably well in U.S. schools, largely because their parents — immigrant, refugee, or native born — know how to negotiate the education system. But alarming numbers of lower-class Hispanic children do not fare well in U.S. schools. Hispanics experience some of the highest rates of school failure, both in terms of those who fail to graduate from high school and those who graduate but with limited skills. They drop out almost three times more often than white students, and one and one-half times more often than black students. Almost half the Hispanics who remain in school can be considered at risk of dropping out because of their below-average grades, and even among high school graduates, Hispanics are less likely to attend college than are either white or black graduates.

For most children, their attitude toward school, as well as their sense of themselves as intellectual beings, is established by a good start. Too many Hispanic poor children experience shaky starts, and a considerable part of the problem can be attributed to the gulf between schools' expectations of parents' roles and parents' understanding of their responsibilities vis-a-vis the formal schooling of their children.

WHAT ARE THE DIFFERENCES IN EXPECTATIONS?

Most low-income Hispanic parents want their children to succeed in school. But most low-income, newly arrived Hispanic parents, and many low-income Hispanics born in the United States as well, do not know that the expectations of American schools are different from the expectations of schools in their countries of origin or in their parents' countries of origin. As a consequence, many poor Hispanic youngsters come into the classroom unprepared to tackle schoolwork because their parents have not known how to provide them with the social, linguistic, and cognitive skills U.S. teachers expect (Fillmore, 1990; Nicolau & Ramos, 1990).

In Latin-American countries, the role of parent and the role of school in relation to education are sharply delineated and divided: Parents have a serious duty to instill respect and proper behavior in their children; it is the school's job to instill knowledge. Most low-income parents are unaware of specific practices — such as talking and reading to children and encouraging their curiosity — that lay the foundation for academic skills. Many Hispanic children enter school not knowing their alphabet or numbers, not familiar with crayons or pencils, not telling time, and not exposed to books and the concept of reading.

In the United States less than 20% of Hispanic children enter school with any prekindergarten experience (Alsalam et al., 1992). Some Hispanic parents are reluctant to place preschoolers in institutional care: Small children are vulnerable, and the tradition is to keep them within the family. Still other poor parents who might consider preschool or day-care arrangements find that it is either unavailable or unaffordable. A considerable number of Hispanic youngsters enter school never having been out of their immediate neighborhoods, and many low-income Hispanic parents remain uninformed about the educational value of free out-of-school activities — such as trips to parks, zoos, museums, and libraries. Deeply concerned for the safety of their children, some Hispanic parents do not allow their children to go on field trips even when they are enrolled in school. Similarly, although most Hispanic parents understand that children should do their homework, few have been exposed to the idea that school-aged children should spend up to 20 hours a week engaged in other "constructive" home-learning activities, such as reading for fun, writing, pursuing hobbies, talking with adult family members, playing games in the family, or watching educational television (Clark, 1990).

Hispanic parents do take parenting very seriously, however. They work hard to teach their children essential social skills such as cooperation and loyalty, and they deliver them to school neat, well-disciplined, and respectful. These are all positive values greatly appreciated by teachers. Yet *respectful* in Hispanic culture often is expressed by not looking adults in the eye, not speaking to adults unless spoken to first, not volunteering answers, and not asking questions. Teachers unfamiliar with the culture can interpret this behavior as rudeness, withdrawal, or excessive shyness. In addition, frequent, casual conversation between adults and children

and reading to children are not the norm in many poor Hispanic households, and many poor Hispanic parents do not themselves have wide vo-
cabularies in Spanish or English. As a consequence, language delay is one
of the most serious obstacles — and often the most misunderstood obstacle — that many low-income Hispanic children must overcome when they
enter school. Many teachers assume that language delay is directly related
to families speaking Spanish in the home. They fail to notice that it can
manifest itself in English-speaking, Spanish-speaking, *and* bilingual children; they are not aware that many Hispanic children are conditioned to
be quiet around adults and therefore lack the interaction that develops
linguistic skills. Of course, monolingual Spanish-speaking children must
accelerate their overall linguistic development and learn a new language
in order to succeed in U.S. schools. The burden of that challenge is reflected in achievement histories. Children who enter school with a Spanish-language background tend to suffer higher levels of grade retention
than do their Hispanic peers who enter school with a working knowledge
of English.

When Hispanic children arrive in school without preschool experience
and lacking the basic skills that the school expects, and when Hispanic
parents tend to distance themselves from the school, teachers and administrators may become perplexed and frustrated. A significant number leap
to the conclusion that the parents don't care. In fact, most Hispanics
respect the school system deeply, but they tend to relate to it as most
Americans relate to doctors or lawyers or priests — with awe. In their view,
schools are in control, and teachers are the experts who are not to be
questioned. They do not feel that they have any role to play in the education process, and they do not think that they belong in school unless their
child has been causing trouble. In this case, their strong respect for schools
actually serves to restrict parents' teaching. It can, however, be harnessed
to strengthen educational performance. The key lies in bridging the gulf
(Nicolau & Ramos, 1990).

SCHOOL FAILURE

What Can Be Done About It?

Policy makers generally do not acknowledge either the extent or the
severity of Hispanic underachievement, nor have they developed policies
to address it. The Council of Great City Schools (1986), for example,
sampled its member systems and found that where such policies do exist,

they tend to be oriented toward and shaped by federal legislation and are focused on a minority of Hispanic children — such as those served in bilingual education classes. Not only can we say that many Hispanics have been adrift, floundering through school, their potential neglected, but we can also foresee further difficulties for these students if reforms beyond the reforms for excellence are not implemented. Many Hispanics are indeed potentially achieving students, but traditional school organization can interact negatively with the class and cultural differences of Hispanics.

The Early Years/Lack of Quality Preschool

Poor Hispanic children are among those who can most benefit from quality child care and preschool, but only a little over a quarter of the 3- and 4-year-olds are enrolled in preschool programs of any nature. Affordability and availability are factors that restrict Hispanic participation. But so too does the culture, which strongly holds that small children should be protected by trustworthy members of the extended family. A program in San Antonio and Houston that involves children and mothers together is one example of how the cultural gap can be bridged (Lewin, 1988).

While quality preschool and child care are not a panacea, they reach parents and children early, provide children with basics that can make their introduction to school a rewarding experience, and familiarize parents with the skills and behaviors that schools expect. Key to the success of these parent components is sensitivity to the parents' cultures and needs. The best of the parent programs respect the children's cultures, respect the families' parenting styles, and suggest only that the parents augment what they are already doing. They are programs of addition, not subtraction. We need more of them, and we need school personnel who are specially trained to deliver them, because experience has shown that the business-as-usual methods of parent involvement and orientation are not an effective way to reach Hispanic parents.

Elementary School Years

In school, a child is labeled, formally or informally, by the time he or she is seven. Children who enter school with limited English proficiency or underdeveloped verbal skills are often labeled "slow," no matter how bright they are. Less is expected of them than of their peers, and subtle messages about being "dumb" are clearly transmitted. When the parents aren't around, and when schools do not understand the families' culture, too often teachers simply lower their standards to what they think the students are capable of achieving. Many children are written off by the fourth grade, when schoolwork shifts from simply learning the basics into more sophisticated application of these skills. As reading becomes more content-oriented, poor children, many of whom have not been exposed to the same experiences as their middle-class peers, are handicapped. At this point, a child who has not mastered the basic skills is left behind, and if he or she has not been tracked earlier, tracking occurs now.

Foreign-born children are particularly likely to be left back in the mid-elementary school years. Often, in fact, they are placed a grade behind when they enter school, or they repeat kindergarten or first grade because they have not been able to master content when they lacked knowledge of English. An obvious solution is the teaching of content in the native language while the child masters English. Yet less than 25% of children with limited proficiency in English are in programs that teach English while regular courses are taught in the child's language (Baratz-Snowden & Duran, 1987). Schools also fail immigrant children and many native-born Hispanic children when no advisors, counselors, or parent outreach workers can communicate with them and their families to provide needed attention and one-on-one help.

Middle School/High School Years

The mentors and counselors Hispanic students lack in elementary school are absent in middle and high school as well. At many inner-city schools, a single guidance counselor may serve as many as 700 children. Few of these youngsters see Hispanic role models—teachers, principals, community leaders, officeholders—to emulate. Worst of all, perhaps, is that most of these young people have no exposure to "what might be," little or no knowledge of the multitude of occupations and professions that might engage them or of the detailed steps that they must take to succeed. Most Hispanics are sent pro forma down the "general track" that neither prepares them for college nor provides them with salable vocational skills.

Perhaps the factor that most affects the heavy exodus of Hispanics at the beginning of tenth grade, when 40% drop out, is that many are doing poorly and are already one or more years overage for their grade. There is little incentive for bearded tenth graders to remain in a situation that humiliates them on a daily basis, and few school systems have taken the initiative to move overage students—boys and girls—into learning environments that can upgrade their skills and instill self-esteem. Traditional in-school remediation strategies will not address the educational needs of these students.

What Do Hispanic Students Think?

Students, although most directly affected by school reform, are seldom asked what they think. The High School and Beyond survey, a longitudinal study sponsored by the federal government, did question students about their schools and teachers. About one-half of the Hispanics surveyed said that students in their schools often cut classes or did not attend class. More than one in five Hispanics said that students in their schools often refused to obey instructions and got into fights with one another. Five percent said that students often attacked or threatened to attack teachers.

Hispanic students rated as positive the following characteristics of their teachers (corresponding percentages in parentheses): enjoy their work (37%); are clear in their presentations (30%); treat everyone with respect (30%); are patient and understanding (26%); make you work hard so you'll learn (24%); and are witty and humorous (16%). Only about one-tenth of the students thought their teachers were interested in their lives outside of class—a sad commentary on the fragmented and anonymous nature of school life for both students and teachers.

RELATING SCHOOL REFORM TO THE NEEDS OF HISPANIC STUDENTS

The strengths and needs Hispanics bring to school should be understood and addressed by schools rather than ignored or used to justify lower expectations for what these students can accomplish. It is not special policies for Hispanics that are needed, but a working understanding of how background factors and conditions characterizing Hispanic students can be matched by school policies that are suitable for all kinds of students. Some guiding principles need to be applied with common sense and attention to local realities. These principles include creating a comprehensive sense of responsibility for the well-being of the school; demonstrating care and concern for every member of the school community; expecting academic excellence; grouping heterogeneously (and eliminating tracking); requiring involved, active learning; strengthening the counseling function; involving and educating parents; connecting school and work; immersing students in family and life planning; and providing opportunities for advancement upon high school graduation. Each of these principles is discussed below.

Responsibility for the Well-Being of the School

All students need to share responsibility for the social and material well-being of their school. This can begin in small ways in early elementary years and increase in scope at each grade level. Adolescents, in fact, should bear considerable responsibility for self-government, including the setting and monitoring of standards for student behavior and deportment. In the absence of a formal framework of student government, with positive incentives for student leaders and groups, an informal system usually evolves. Experience illustrates that informal systems spawn competing leadership and groups, including gangs, that can wreak havoc in and around a school. Student responsibilities must be meaningful and must include solving real problems and developing real opportunities to improve school life. Many private schools have long traditions of student involvement and responsibility. This active involvement by students in the well-being of their schools needs to replace the attempt of many traditional schools to instill a factory-like order of conformity and docility in students. These attributes of passivity are the very factors that the children of the working poor, including many Hispanics, have to overcome if they are to be socially and economically successful in America.

A Culture of Concern

Shared responsibility for the social well-being of a school is rooted in a culture of concern, which fosters bonds among students and between students and the school and promotes a strong sense of belonging. In this climate, students support each other in a variety of ways, including helping each other with schoolwork. Many elementary schools, for example, have introduced the practice of having children tutor each other across grades. Experience is that the young tutors benefit academically as much as their "tutees," according to the Valued Youth program in San Antonio and other cities. This principle taps and builds on the social cooperation that Hispanics are often taught at home, but which they often are not allowed to express positively in school.

A large student body can be a serious barrier to developing strong relationships among students and faculty alike; big schools alienate parents as well. Many cities have giant schools designed to produce economies of scale. In fact, they produce alienation on the parts of school personnel, parents, and students. However, as demonstrated in Harlem in New York, and in selected other sites, these large schools can be organized successfully into several mini-schools or "houses" under the same roof. A mini-school allows all parties (including parents) to relate to an identifiable entity; it allows teachers to know a small group of students better; and it encourages more interaction between students.

There are other ways that schools can be subdivided to promote achievement and belonging. For example, at a Catholic high school in Newark the student body is divided into groups, which remain together throughout the 4-year high school experience. Each group includes students with different abilities and interests, and these groups compete with each other in a variety of ways, including attendance, community service, academics, and sports. The program is based on competition and cooperation that together inspire an enthusiasm and a sense of group honor among team members, as well as personal devotion and regard for each other. Another example is provided by a community-based program, "Twelve-Together," that organizes peer-counseling groups of high- and low-risk ninth graders in Detroit high schools. The students in each group pledge to help each other through all 4 years of high school and reinforce group attendance, achievement, and, ultimately, graduation.

Expecting Academic Excellence

All students should achieve mastery of a core curriculum with academic content requirements in English, math, science, and social studies. The learning tasks should be defined and structured to make clear what the students are to accomplish. Absolute standards of excellence are not necessary, but all students should be encouraged to *strive* for academic excellence. Students who require more time and help to master any of the core curriculum subjects should be provided with peer and volunteer tutoring, after-school sessions, and intensive summer programs; taking more time to accomplish the task must not be seen as punishment, but as an opportunity. In middle and high school, the core curriculum should probably contain a vocational content requirement to prepare the students for the workplace. Colorado, for example, has initiated an Employability Skills Project aimed at developing basic entry-level job skills in all graduates.

Extra English language instruction is especially needed by students whose parents are poorly educated, and doubly needed by students who come from Spanish-speaking homes. Even after students learn enough English to be in regular classes, extra support is required for full mastery of English. Moreover, students who speak Spanish should be encouraged to read and write it well. It is a marketable skill that they should not lose.

Heterogeneous Groupings

By the time Hispanic children arrive in high school, less than a third are placed in academic or college preparatory programs; the remaining students typically are placed in general and vocational programs, with emphasis on the former. The problem is that general and vocational tracks do not prepare students for much of anything. In addition, in most public high schools, students who are bound for college immediately after graduation are considered "winners" and all other students are "losers" in one way or another. As a consequence, an environment is created in which teaching and counseling college-bound students has high status, while teaching students in the nonacademic tracks confers low status.

Schools without differentiated ability tracks allow students with varying academic abilities to interact with and accept one another. The high-achieving students gain acceptance and provide academic leadership for the other students. Other students excel in different ways, and their skills are respected. Friendships are made, and many opportunities to gain and confirm self-worth within the school context are available. Feelings of group solidarity and concern are strong in these schools. Unfortunately, although tracking has been criticized for years, few schools have examined how they could organize themselves and serve diverse needs without it.

Involved, Active Learning

Overly bureaucratic school systems, structured from the top down, "freeze" the problem-solving attitudes and capacities of both teachers and students. Some schools are organized to reinforce a factory-worker/assembly-line mentality, a sense of static harmony. Such an approach may have made sense in the past, when schools thought that it was their job to prepare an "industrial army" for work on the manufacturing assembly lines. But today, even modestly paying service jobs require a different set of skills: flexibility, human relations, communication, and problem solving.

The bulk of poor Hispanic parents are workers in the leftover blue-collar and low-skill service occupations that tend to reward obedience rather than initiative. Most of their children's teachers, especially in large urban systems, have little or no say in selecting textbooks or materials and little or no control over the conditions of their classrooms. How are Hispanic children to learn to be problem solvers who demonstrate flexibility and initiative, when they are surrounded by adults who are discouraged from displaying these skills and attitudes? The parents' employment patterns cannot be altered easily, but schools can change the way they deliver learning.

Schools must adopt instructional styles that allow students to be active learners through participation, deliberation, and reflection. Principals, teachers, and school communities need much more autonomy in setting specific goals and developing annual plans and budgets for their schools that meet legal requirements but relate education to the reality of the students' lives. Teachers need more latitude in how they are to accomplish their mission. And schools and the communities they serve must work together to develop mutually agreed upon and understood missions and "hows."

Strong Counseling

The counselor (and the counseling function in general) plays a crucial role — especially for Hispanics — in diminishing or inspiring educational and occupational ambitions. In addition to carrying unreasonably large case loads, in some schools with large Hispanic student populations the counselors on staff do not understand Hispanic cultures and/or cannot communicate in Spanish with their students' parents. This can be particularly damaging to the educational development and future careers of Hispanic students, because many Hispanic parents and students are not likely to understand, for example, how a succession of curriculum placements in vocational or general education can limit opportunities. To prevent such problems, counselors and teachers need to work with students to expand their visions of possible options in the adult working world. This is important for all Hispanic students, but most particularly for Hispanic girls. Some poor Hispanic families continue to steer daughters to early marriage, partly to ensure that they have a man to protect and support them, and partly because the education of girls who will become mothers and housewives is not viewed as a necessity.

Involving and Educating Parents

Hispanic parents must be made to feel welcome in the schools, and the schools must take responsibility for communicating with them, in Spanish if necessary. Hispanic parents, especially those with limited education and limited English proficiency, often report that they feel awkward in approaching teachers and often fear they will be misunderstood because of cultural characteristics unknown to school personnel. Parents with limited language skills in English, and often in Spanish too, report difficulties in reading school announcements and notes from teachers.

Perhaps the most important consideration in working with Hispanic parents is that Hispanic culture is a very "personal" culture, and the only way to reach Hispanic parents is through personal contact and the development of one-on-one relationships. For this reason, schools must adapt their approaches to the schedules and life-styles of their students' parents. When families cannot get to school, the school must reach out to them in their homes. Hiring part-time community liaison workers is an excellent way to reach out to parents, especially through home visits and community meetings. Professional staff should also be involved in reaching out; principals should consider serving on the boards of local community groups or writing columns for neighborhood newspapers. Activities that help build bridges and close the cultural "gulfs" include opportunities for parent volunteer work, the establishment of school "family rooms" to overcome the reluctance of parents to be in the school, and the scheduling of special classes for parents in subjects as diverse as nutrition, English, preventive health care, money matters, drugs, AIDS, abuse, things to do in the summer, or the generation gap.

Connecting School and Work

The connection between attending school and working requires close examination in the context of high school reform because it figures so prominently in the Hispanic students' world. Many Hispanic students, especially senior males, lead double lives as workers and students because they need to support themselves or contribute to the support of their families. High School and Beyond (HS&B) data, for example, reveal that Hispanic senior males averaged more hours of work per week (22) than other males. However, schools pay little attention to their students' employment needs, and few have any idea where or how long their students work. If school and work were integrated, a student's schoolwork and work for pay could dovetail to the benefit of both, with the result that dropout rates probably would be lowered. Some promising efforts at combining work and study have already been made. An Albuquerque high school, for example, offers evening classes that are part of the school's regular roster of classes. California offers a "continuing education" program for students over age 16 who are working; these students earn credit toward their high school diplomas on a part-time basis (Valdivieso, 1986a).

Family Life Planning

Hispanic youths often assume adult responsibilities sooner than other groups. We have seen this with a good portion of the dropouts. For example, at the time of the 1984 HS&B follow-up, nearly half the Hispanic female nongraduates in the sample were married and over one-third had children. This early assumption of adult roles also occurs with graduates, including those with good grades. Within 2 years of graduating from high school, about 22% of the Hispanic females and 11% of the males in the HS&B sample had married. Some Hispanic young adults, especially women, are caught early in a web of adult responsibilities that restricts further education or career advancement.

Schools need to immerse students in "life-options education," teaching young people to set goals not only for the kinds of families they want to have, but also for their own future education and employment. Education and instruction of this nature need to permeate the school environment. Sexuality education — sometimes controversial in the Hispanic community for cultural and religious reasons — can be treated as a component of life-options education, or more comprehensively as a separate program. In addition to providing anatomical information, these courses cover sexuality-related topics such as dating, peer pressure, establishing values, decision making about sexual behaviors, sexual abuse prevention, and the economic, health, and social consequences of adolescent pregnancy. As drugs and AIDS continue to invade poor communities, it is Hispanic and other poor children who are most at risk.

School-based health clinics are an excellent way to give adolescents convenient access to nutrition education, physical examinations, screenings, and help with drug and alcohol abuse. Such clinics also provide family planning and may dispense contraceptives. Although the latter services have engendered heated debate, they may be provided within the framework of holistic health care. The most innovative of the school-based health clinics offer services to the families of students as well, and some schools combine the health clinics with on-site day-care facilities for the children of teenage parents, so that the mothers can improve their knowledge of child care and return to class and stay in school.

Opportunities for Advancement

Youth at risk from working-class and poverty backgrounds need active encouragement, through a variety of incentives and supports, to stay in school. Many do not see that a diploma will confer any advantage. In fact, for many it does not; low-skilled graduates do not earn more money than dropouts when they both qualify for the same job as packing clerk at the supermarket.

Corporate America has begun to recognize the need for programs to make students want to graduate and aspire to postsecondary education, whether academic or vocational. A number of incentive programs are now in place, roughly based on the *I Have a Dream* model, that offer students who graduate with decent grades support for college or postsecondary training. Another example is the Boston Compact, a coalition of businesses and other private-sector interests, which has an arrangement with the Boston schools to improve students' achievement and work preparation in exchange for increased opportunities in employment and higher education. And slowly and carefully, the nation is looking at apprenticeship opportunities as a dignified alternative for the noncollege bound, an alternative that can offer a secure ladder to well-paid, skilled employment.

Hispanics at risk of school failure (like all such students) need more humane and cohesive school units that integrate a well-defined, academically rigorous curriculum with a sense of community, rooted in nurturance, self-discipline, and esteem. All students and faculty stand to benefit in such learning environments, and most educators agree. The real question central to school reform is not the *what*; it is the *how*.

REFERENCES

Alsalam, N., Ogle, L. T., Rogers, G. T., & Smith, T. M. (1992). *The condition of education 1992*. Washington, DC: National Center for Education Statistics, U.S. Department of Education.

Baratz-Snowden, J., & Duran, R. (1987). *The education progress of language-minority students: Findings from the 1983–84* NAEP *reading survey*. Princeton, NJ: Educational Testing Service.

Clark, R. M. (1990, Spring). Why disadvantaged students succeed: What happens outside school is critical. *Public Welfare*, pp. 17–23.

Council of Great City Schools. (1986, January). *Hispanic policy development in selected great city schools: Final report*. Unpublished, Washington, DC.

Farnsworth Riche, M. (1991, October). We're all minorities now. *American Demographics*, pp. 26–34.

Fillmore, L. W. (1990). Now or later? Issues related to the early education of minority children. In *Early childhood and family education: Analysis and recommendations of the Council of Chief State School Officers*. Orlando, FL: Harcourt Brace Jovanovich.

Lewin, T. (1988, March 8). Program in Texas helps Hispanic mothers discover their children and themselves. *New York Times*, p. 8.

National Education Goals Panel. (1992). *The national education goals report: Building a nation of learners*. Washington, DC: Author.

Nicolau, S., & Ramos, C. (1988). *Queridos padres*. Washington, DC: Hispanic Policy Development Project.

Nicolau, S., & Ramos, C. (1990). *Together is better: Building strong partnerships between schools and Hispanic parents*. Washington, DC: Hispanic Policy Development Project.

Nieto, S. (1992). *Affirming diversity: The sociopolitical context of multicultural education*. New York: Longman.

Rubin, G. (1992). *Are there too many people in the lifeboat? Immigration and the American dream*. New York: American Jewish Committee.

Skerry, P. (1992, Summer). E pluribus Hispanic? *Wilson Quarterly*.

U.S. Bureau of the Census. *The Hispanic population in the United States: March 1991*. Washington, DC: U.S. Government Printing Office.

U.S. Bureau of the Census. (1992). *Statistical abstract of the United States: 1992*. Washington, DC: Author.

Valdivieso, R. (1986a). *Must they wait another generation? Hispanics and secondary school reform*. New York: ERIC Clearinghouse on Urban Education, Teachers College.

Valdivieso, R. (1986b, Summer). Hispanics and schools: A new perspective. *Educational Horizons, 64*(4), 190–197.

CHAPTER 6

Harvesting Talent and Culture

African-American Children and Educational Reform

A. WADE BOYKIN

It has long been recognized that African-American children do not fare well in our nation's schools. This has raised sufficient concern over the years that several programmatic efforts have been launched to rectify this reality. By and large, various reform efforts have not appreciably altered the achievement status of African-American students. I have come to take the position that if we are genuinely sincere about ameliorating the academic difficulties of black children who are particularly placed at risk educationally, and, moreover, if we are serious about real educational reform in this country, we must be prepared to be more thorough in our understanding of the roots of the problems. There is a wise African proverb that goes, "If you don't know where you are going, then any road will take you there." That generally covers the efforts to enhance schooling in recent years. Indeed, effective educational reform for African-American children, perhaps for all children, must start from, must be predicated on, a searching understanding of the functions and purposes that public education, especially in urban settings, has served since its nominal inception in early twentieth-century America. This implies that altering the achievement status of African-American children may require the reformulation of the nature, function, and objectives of public schooling.

Public education was instituted during the early twentieth century in much the form that still exists today. It represented the culminating triumphs of a legacy of social, political, and economic interests that went back to the Revolutionary War era and was finally secured by the confluence of a constellation of political, economic, and social forces that fell into place in the years just prior to World War I (Kaestle, 1983; Spring, 1990; Tyack, 1974; Vallance, 1974). Mass public education, especially in urban settings, was set up to implement a particular mass acculturation function — an homogenization function if you will. Schools were set up to serve as bureaucratic institutions based on the prevailing corporate-industrial model that especially stressed efficiency of operation and quality control. They were set up to serve the human resource needs of an ascendingly industrialized society, such that the students so trained (or educated), with a few talented exceptions, would be willing (1) to be cogs in the large industrial wheel, (2) to accept low-status, principally unskilled factory work while still being good citizens, and (3) to work long hours on repetitive, tedious tasks that were largely unrelated to personal motives, interests, desires, or experiences (Carlson, 1982; Cornbleth, 1984; Spring, 1990; Tyack, 1974).

Since this educational model was based on the prevailing corporate-industrial prototype, it stood to reason that efficiency of system operation was a paramount concern. An efficient system, in turn, would be predicated on classification and assessment. Who secured or ensured this efficiency? Who were the quality control experts? Psychologists, with their newfangled "standardized" tests. Psychologists, who through their scientific and objective procedures, could determine the "problem" students that caused the system to function inefficiently (Tyack, 1974). They then could justify the removal of the inefficient elements for their repair, remediation, or permanent segregation. Almost by definition, psychologists were able to locate the "problems" of education in the individual students who potentially would undermine the organizational integrity of schools.

One of the chief consequences of these developments and functions is that talent assessment emerged as a chief preoccupation of public schooling. Talent assessment denotes that the search is to discern the relatively few who are talented enough to receive the benefits of more advanced and challenging education. It implies separating the wheat from the chaff, since the majority of not-so-talented pupils would be consigned to the unskilled labor pool anyway. Talent assessment is deemed necessary in a system that not only is predicated on efficiency and quality control, but that sees these as ends in and of themselves. Assessment in this regard also implies a focus on classification and sorting of pupils and is predicated on standardization of procedures. Obviously, this brand of talent assessment is also wedded to social control.

Relatedly, also emerging as a major reason for schooling was the serious pursuit of the homogenization of the population. Surely the pursuit of homogenization ipso facto led to the systematic suppression of genuine pluralistic expressions. The practices and procedures of schools were officially at odds with principles of multiculturalism. Suffice it to say that purposes and functions of schooling, as embodied, for example, in the pursuit of talent assessment and homogenization, have persisted as major pillars in the functions school serve at present. And it is functions like these that have scarcely been addressed in the various reform efforts and concerns for schooling in general or for the needs of African-American children in particular.

Now surely the agenda for education described above made some sense in America at the turn of the century, in light of the social, economic, and political realities of the time. But we must ask ourselves how well it applies today at the threshold of the twenty-first century. American society is becoming less reliant on heavy industrial manufacturing. Some call this a postindustrial era. The labor market is no longer dominated by low-wage factory work. The service sector is becoming the chief source of employment. Moreover, as technology becomes more sophisticated and as the economic, social, and even ethical demands of our society become more complex, the level of intellectual and social sophistication demanded of our students has substantially increased. The entry-level skills required for participation in the labor market are becoming increasingly sophisticated, and America must now also compete economically with nations that are more truly racially and culturally homogeneous — nations that because of their greater homogeneity can more readily marshal coordinated efforts involving their business, schooling, and political communities to articulate national priorities and commitments.

These changes and concerns for global competition must be understood against the reality that we have a latent pluralism in America that has always been here, but has been historically ignored in the construction of our educational system. We have domestic cultural groups who have been here for centuries and who may not have voluntarily come here to seek the good life. We have groups whose relationship to the American social order has always been problematic; whose schooling remains problematic; whose schooling difficulties have never been successfully resolved. Surely, African-Americans fall squarely in this category. Yet the realities of the very near future are such that children from these "problematic" groups will form the lion's share of this country's labor pool. They will be the ones who must occupy the increasingly sophisticated skilled positions. They are the ones this country will have to rely on socially, politically, ethically, and economically. Yet they are the ones that continue to fall under the label of being educationally "at risk." This poses an exceptionally demanding educational challenge for America. If our society is truly up to the task, it must find ways to turn this reality of pluralism and diversity into a national strength. Since homogenization of these groups has not worked, other than to provide a convenient excuse for their dis-education, we must shift to a more profound embracement of multicultur-alism.

In short, then, I advocate that we shift our focus educationally in at least two major ways. First, we must shift from a preoccupation with talent assessment and its trappings and move toward a commitment to talent development. Talent development connotes a concern with generat-ing broad-based, pervasive academic (broadly defined) competence among our students. Second, we must move away from an obsession with social homogenization and social control to a system predicated on cultural and racial diversity. It is not enough to simply gesture that there will be a focus on talent development. Indeed, it is tantamount to window dressing to express a commitment to talent development and continue to hold the same assumptions that undergird talent assessment. It is not enough to lay claim to multiculturalism but continue the structural, curricular, and cultural commitments to social homogenization and mainstream accultur-ation. This, in spite of the best of stated intentions, will prove ineffective. To make a genuine shift to talent development will require a fundamental change in the very ways we conceptualize the psychological processes attendant to learning/cognition and motivation and, in turn, how we conceptualize the individual. It will also require that we challenge the very nature of the knowledge that is transmitted in our schools as well as the modes of transmission. Moreover, we must come to grips with the profoundly cultural fabric of American education. Culture inheres at the deep-structure level, and is so profoundly pervasive that it is taken for granted and viewed by some as forming the basis, paradoxically, for a "hidden curriculum" (e.g., Cornbleth, 1984; Vallance, 1974). Multicul-tural reform must be pitched at this deep-structure level.

In all, then, this chapter will include two major sections. There will be a discussion of "traditional" and alternative assumptions for psychologi-cal and pedagogical processes. The former, it will be argued, underlie the present-day focus on talent assessment. The latter are more aligned with a focus on talent development. As will be seen, an essential focus on the concept of *context* will be entertained. The second section will make the case for cultural deep structure. I join the advocates for the incorporation of the Afro-cultural ethos into the pedagogical process. I insist that it be done at the deep-structure level; that the incorporation be into the mar-row of the way schooling is done and in terms of the values and contexts that inhere in the process of schooling.

ON PSYCHOLOGICAL AND PEDAGOGICAL ASSUMPTIONS

Pedagogical and instructional practices are built upon explicit and implicit theories and presuppositions about learning, cognition, and motivation.

Traditional Assumptions

The main assumptions that have traditionally undergirded pedagogy over the years have been quite consistent with a talent-assessment approach to schooling. For one, there is the notion that thinking (if it exists at all as a phenomenon) occurs wholly inside the head, and that it is ultimately possible to understand thinking processes in purely abstract forms quite apart from any concrete points of reference (Greeno, 1989; Rogoff, 1990; Shweder, 1990). A second, widely held assumption is that the quality of thinking and/or of learning processes is necessarily consistent in people and across situations (Gergen, 1990; Greeno, 1989; Rogoff, 1990). A third assumption is that the course of learning, or the development of thinking skills, follows a direct input–output, cumulative, building-block process (Freire, 1970; Greeno, 1989; Sleeter & Grant, 1991). Other framing assumptions focus more on motivational processes. There has been an abiding commitment, for example, to the promotion of internal and external forms of motivation (Boykin, 1977; Sleeter & Grant, 1991). Motivation is seen as internal, that is, residing inside the person. One is either motivated or unmotivated. If one is not internally motivated, then the recourse is to employ external sources of motivation. That is, one can be induced to perform through the various devices and processes attendant to rewards, reinforcements, external incentives, punishments, threats, and the like.

These various assumptions have clear-cut implications for what is construed to pass for knowledge in formal educational settings. Everhart (1983) has captured it quite well in his conception of *reified knowledge*. Reified knowledge is that which is prepackaged, decontextualized, and abstracted. It is knowledge that is linked principally to "static" information, information requiring a passive, absorbing recipient. These conceptions also converge with a prevailing notion of *bifurcated individualism*, which has been spawned and even nurtured in traditional academic settings (Carlson, 1982). This is the notion that individuals come to separate their personal meanings, interests, and enjoyment from their work experience. Of course, this feeds right into the notion of talent assessment. Only the comparatively "talented" few will find sufficient incentives to do well in such a system. Only the "best" students will be internally motivated or wise enough to respond to the external incentives that are provided.

Of course, classical psychometric assessment is also linked to the assumptions of talent assessment. The concern is to discern who are the smart ones and who are the not-so-smart ones, and our assessment devices are designed to go inside pupils' heads (in an objective and standardized fashion) and make a withdrawal of the accumulated (or even "inherent") reified knowledge in order to draw the proper intellectual conclusions.

Alternative Assumptions

In contrast, there are now emerging what I will call an alternative set of *operative assumptions* for the subjects of cognition, learning, and motivation. These assumptions are ones that can provide an appropriate psychological infrastructure for a talent-development approach to schooling practices. Now, as the term implies, the attempt here is to develop academic talent in as many students as possible. The focus is on fostering pervasive intellectual development. Until incontrovertibly proven otherwise, the position is that any given child can learn developmentally appropriate content and skills; can acquire the knowledge base we *challenge* them with; and should be encouraged and *stimulated* to strive continuously for intellectual (and socioemotional and ethical) growth in all facets of school-relevant activity. These alternative operative assumptions, which are described below, are associated with recent conceptions offered by a host of scholars from different areas. Consider, for example, the work of Vygotsky and neo-Vygotsky scholars (Rogoff, 1990; Vygotsky, 1962; Wertsch, 1985); of cross-cultural psychologists (Goodnow, 1990); of recent philosophically oriented critics of psychological constructs and explanations (Gergen, 1978, 1990; Riegel, 1979; Shweder, 1990); and of heterodox cognitive and motivation psychologists (Csikszentmihayli, 1990; Greeno, 1989; Walker, 1980). Alternative assumptions are evident in the conceptions of psychologists from domestic cultural groups (e.g., Akbar, 1985; Jones, 1979; Nobles, 1991; Ramirez & Castenada, 1974; Sue, 1991).

One major alternative assumption is that thinking is largely contextualized (Greeno, 1989; Rogoff, 1990; Shweder, 1990). That is to say, it is fundamentally and typically linked to specific situations. Thus, it is not conceived as occurring in a vacuum or independent of time, place, and circumstance.

A second assumption is that thinking is not a neutrally executed activity. People think not in neutral terms but according to or in terms of personal frames of reference. They invoke, as Greeno (1989) says, "personal epistemologies." People think from certain vantage points, value orientations, frames of reference, and theories of reality, born out of prior experiences (see, for example, Akbar, 1985; Gergen, 1978; Rogoff, 1990; Spence, 1985). Moreover, personal epistemologies are imbued in contexts. People construe and construct contexts in terms of their prevailing explicit or implicit personal epistemologies; contexts are inevitably value-laden.

A third assumption is captured in the notion that Greeno (1989) refers to as "conceptual competence." By this is meant that, due to prior experiences, individuals will have (even) implicit intuitions about some knowledge or skill domain even if it cannot be readily articulated in specific and concrete ways. People will have informal understanding of phenomena that, with the proper learning environment or with the guidance of more knowledgeable others, can become formal understanding. Thus, children do not and should not be assumed to enter learning situations cold, even if their knowledge is in rudimentary form or their lenses for viewing the learning experience are divergent from the teacher's.

Finally, in the domain of motivation, there is increasing recognition that the internal/external dichotomy does not exhaust all possibilities. There is a third brand, called *intrinsic motivation.* Intrinsic motivation is that which inheres, that which resides, within the interaction of a person and his or her environment (Boykin, 1977; Hunt, 1965; Walker, 1980). It is tied to the stimulation value of the interactional context and/or to its personal significance. As such, it is tied to such factors as the interestingness, novelty, salience, and meaning of the interaction for a given individual. The locus of the motivation is neither in the environment nor in the individual, but in the person–environment interaction in and of itself.

I argue this package of assumptions yields a different type of knowledge production. Everhart (1983), for one, has referred to it as re-generative knowledge. This is knowledge that is constructed in real contexts by individuals attempting to negotiate their everyday lives. It is knowledge that is not imposed on people but is created through social interactions, through negotiated participation, and through active transactions with people, places, things, and circumstances. Furthermore, the implication is that the learner is an active being who is prone to critical thinking and (even nascent) metacognitive understanding of the predicaments in which he or she is placed or places him- or herself.

Following from these assumptions, the individual is surely not bifurcated; instead, he or she is *integrated.* If the educational environment is sensitive to the contexts of learning and thinking; if it is elicitous of learning and thinking; if it recognizes the importance of children's personal lenses; if it is mindful of providing learning situations that are personally meaningful, stimulating, and engaging; if it is encouraging of learning in the form of active and critical knowledge production; and if it is embedded in a web of social interrelationships, then *integrated individuals* will be nurtured. Integrated individuals will not see schoolwork as inevitably tedious and unfulfilling, nor will they be driven to stand alone, inspired exclusively by self-interest. In contrast, they will work in partnership with others in the learning environment to develop their talents for the twenty-first century.

Critique

Public schooling has been and is now typically conducted in synchrony with traditional assumptions about learning, thinking, and motivation. This has exacerbated the educational problems of all too many African-American children. More specifically, when many black children do not perform adequately in school, it is often presumed that they are uninterested in learning, that they are unmotivated, that they have learning problems in the form of deficiencies inside their heads per se. They are deemed not bright enough, and the assessment devices bear out these claims. Since pedagogical *contexts* are exempt from scrutiny, the search ensues for factors in these students' out-of-school experiences that would lead to their academic predicament.

Is it not possible, however, from a talent-development standpoint that we have failed to provide educational contexts that sufficiently trigger the intellectual engagement of these children, that draw sufficiently on their existing competencies, and that sufficiently activate intrinsic motivation? A more hopeful scenario would include these educational contexts that allow for the expression of values, personal experiences, and frames of reference — in short, behavioral repertoires that would yield greater responsiveness and receptiveness. All this implies culture. It is in the concept of culture that the matters of values, personal frames, epistemologies, and experiences come together. For this reason, the key to fostering talent development in African-American children may lie in providing them with culturally sensitive, culturally appropriate educational contexts.

CULTURAL DEEP STRUCTURE AND THE SCHOOLING OF AFRICAN-AMERICAN CHILDREN

It is becoming increasingly fashionable to bring issues of culture to bear on educational analyses. Indeed, multiculturalism is a term enjoying considerable currency. Yet in such analyses, it is often overlooked that matters of culture reside in the very marrow of the schooling process.

They pervade virtually all facets of the schooling enterprise. In a phrase, if we are to comprehend the role of culture in education, we must access culture at the level of *deep structure*. We must recognize that cultural phenomena already form the substrate of schooling. Cultural matters are at the heart of the socialization function schools were set up to address in the first place. So when there is now talk of incorporating the culture of various ethnic minorities into schooling, we cannot operate as though this will be done vis-a-vis a pre-existing, culturally neutral educational context. In addition, we must appreciate that the move toward multiculturalism must go substantially beyond adding dark faces to textbooks, additional holidays on the calendar, greater sensitivity to odd or different forms of expression, and even providing new history lessons or information on the contributions of minority groups. So what then will be required?

Culture Defined

A starting point is to first grapple with a working conception of culture. Clearly, culture can have a myriad of definitions and connotations. Indeed, there are many legitimate forms. I submit that for the present purpose the proper focus should be on what I choose to call *fundamental culture*. This form has to do with how a given reference group codifies reality, creating a corresponding three-tiered, interlocking system of beliefs, values, and behavioral expressions (Boykin, 1983). These behavioral expressions may be in the form of particular receptiveness or responsiveness to appropriately culture-laden contexts.

For several years now, scholars have illuminated the "hidden curriculum" operative in schools that forms the prevailing cultural substrate for existing schooling practices and priorities (Spring, 1990; Tyack, 1974; Vallance, 1974). This hidden curriculum has served the homogenization and mainstream socialization functions of the public schools. As Vallance (1974) has stated, for example, this curriculum became hidden only because its functions became so effective and so pervasively accepted that it could be taken for granted, allowing the practices, routines, postures, and structures associated with it to be identified as the proper ways to educate. As a result, the cultural medium of schooling now operates in a hegemonic fashion (Apple, 1979) and serves, as Delpit (1988) asserts, as a veritable "culture of power" in our nation's schools. The rules of this culture of power go unarticulated. Some children come to school with the knowledge of these rules based on their out-of-school experiences. Other children will be prepared to be receptive to or at least not to be resistant to these rules. Still other children, however, will come to school with a different set of cultural rules, and they will be penalized for not knowing or for appearing to be resistant to the culture of power.

What are some of the specific manifestations of this culture of power? Silverstein and Krate (1975) give us some insight when they claim that schools especially treasure strong impulse control, the elevation of reason over emotion, and the inclination to funnel effort into tasks that are unrelated to personal motives, wants, and goals. Gay (1975) has offered still other factors. These include movement restriction and a task, rather than people, orientation. Several have pointed to an emphasis on "rugged" individualism and interpersonal competition (Gay, 1975; Katz, 1985; Spence, 1985). Katz (1985) has spoken of an emphasis on delayed gratification; rigid adherence to clock time, with time viewed as a commodity; an emphasis on "destiny control"; and the linking of individual status to possessions, whether physical, material, or intellectual. These kinds of factors form the very fabric of education as it traditionally has been conceived and practiced. They form the matrix of the behavioral expectations that teachers and other school personnel have of students, even when they are not fully conscious that these are central objectives of schooling. These form the landscape on which pedagogy is carried out. They often are treated as prerequisites to learning. They, in the form of behavioral expressions, are what a good student should act like, be like, value. They constitute the elements of the cultural deep structure of schooling. They are manifestations of the Anglo-Euro-American cultural ethos.

When children are ordered to do their own work, arrive at their own individual answers, and work only with their own materials, they are being sent cultural messages. When children come to believe that getting up and moving about the classroom is inappropriate, they are being sent powerful cultural messages. When children come to confine their "learning" to consistently bracketed time periods, when they are consistently prompted to tell what they know and not how they feel, when they are led to believe that they are completely responsible for their own success and failure, when they are required to consistently put forth considerable effort for effort's sake on tedious and personally irrelevant tasks, and when these things are accomplished in a routinized, almost matter-of-fact kind of way and all of this is reinforced in terms of the themes presented in texts and worksheets, then children are pervasively having cultural lessons imposed on them.

To be sure, children do have a responsibility to master the social and task-related skills teachers expect from them and to negotiate the interpersonal demands placed upon them by peers and adults (Taylor, 1991). But when factors like emotional containment and delay of gratification are seen not as culturally valued expressions, but rather as signs of "social maturity" (Alexander & Entwisle, 1988), and when children are penalized for not knowing that such elements are part of the behavioral rules (or because they may display alternative expressions), then such children are put at a needless disadvantage, especially when the press is to pursue talent development.

On the other hand, a growing chorus of scholars in recent years has called for cultural analyses in accounting for psychological and educational phenomena (e.g., Rogoff, 1990; Spence, 1985; Tharp, 1989). A central theme in this regard for many is the concept of "intersubjectivity." Rogoff (1990) defines this as "a shared focus and purpose between children and their more skilled partners and their challenging and exploring peers" (p. 8). As Gergen (1990) argues, intersubjectivity is predicated on mutual understanding, or an understanding of each other's understanding. All this implies that being "on the same cultural page" is essential to successful intersubjectivity. The educational implications are that teachers are more effective teachers and learners are more effective learners when intersubjectivity has been firmly established, when it is reasonably operative. When participants are on different cultural pages, intersubjectivity is undermined, possibly along with the learning of the relevant lesson.

Incorporating the Afro-Cultural Ethos

A logical next step in the line of arguments presented is that there should be promotion of more culturally compatible learning contexts for children who are traditionally placed at risk by traditional schooling practices and learning contexts. Systematic efforts to incorporate more relevant cultural factors for certain domestic groups have produced meaningful results (Tharp, 1989). It would seem to follow that efforts of this sort on behalf of African-American children should be encouraged as well. Indeed, many have advocated this position in recent years. Consider the works and positions of Delpit (1988), Gay (1975, 1988), Irvine (1990), Taylor (1991), and Willis (1989), among many others.

In distilling my own and the aforementioned positions and fashioning them into the themes of the present chapter, I submit that by building on distinctive black cultural capital, we can, among other things, create better intersubjectivity, we can access intrinsic motivation, and we can provide opportunities for the exercise of certain cognitive skills practiced in out-of-school settings. The contexts of pedagogy, if not of schooling, for African-American children should reflect Afro-cultural expression. I submit that genuine educational effectiveness will be the result for black children and youth if the infusion of Afro-cultural expression occurs at the deep-structure level of schooling.

To be sure, this Afro-cultural ethos is not shared by all African-Americans to the same degree. Certain aspects of it may be more evidently embraced or realized for some, while other facets may be more represented in the lives of others. In general, it is likely to be more manifest in those African-Americans who are most disconnected or disenfranchised from the current mainstream of American life. Yet, the ethos does find significant expression among the majority of African-Americans. Moreover, this ethos does not exhaust all of the experiences of African-American people. Elsewhere, I and others (Boykin, 1983, 1986; Boykin & Ellison, in press; Cole, 1970; Jones, 1979) have described three distinct realms of social experience that inform the lives of African-Americans in this country. There are the *mainstream experience* and the *minority experience*, and there is also the *Afro-cultural experience*, which captures the fundamental cultural integrity of African-Americans and represents the continuation of a legacy from Africa that is at least 5,000 years old—a legacy of such prepotency that it has been maintained, in various forms, throughout the African diaspora. Now, one should not glean, simplemindedly, from this that black culture is what black people do, or that Afro-cultural expression represents racial determinism. This kind of thinking breeds overgeneralization and racial stereotyping. Instead, what should be understood is that aspects of Afro-cultural expression are, on a probabilistic basis, linked to accessibility, availability, familiarity, primacy of experiences, and role modeling, which in turn lead to individuals' orientation toward the ethos or various aspects of it and the degree of susceptibility to, receptiveness to, and pervasiveness of Afro-cultural conditioning.

What is the concrete substance of this Afro-cultural ethos? Drawing on my own previous work (Boykin, 1977, 1979) and the works of others (e.g., Dixon, 1976; Jones, 1979; Levine, 1977; Nobles, 1991; White, 1970; Young, 1970, 1974), I have distilled nine dimensions of this ethos that find manifestation in the lives of African-Americans (Boykin, 1983, 1986). These dimensions are

1. *Spirituality* — This connotes an acceptance of a nonmaterial higher force that pervades all of life's affairs.
2. *Harmony* — This implies that one's functioning is inextricably linked to nature's order and one should be synchronized with this order.
3. *Movement* — This connotes a premium placed on the interwoven amalgamation of movement, (poly)rhythm, dance, and percussion embodied in the musical beat.

4. *Verve* — This connotes a particular receptiveness to relatively high levels of sensate (i.e., intensity and variability of) stimulation.
5. *Affect* — This implies the centrality of affective information and emotional expressiveness and the equal and integrated importance of thoughts and feelings.
6. *Expressive individualism* — This denotes the uniqueness of personal expression, personal style, and genuineness of self-expression.
7. *Communalism* — This implies a commitment to the fundamental interdependence of people and to the importance of social bonds, relationships, and the transcendence of the group.
8. *Orality* — This connotes the centrality of oral/aural modes of communication for conveying full meaning and the cultivation of speaking as a performance.
9. *Social time perspective* — This denotes a commitment to a social construction of time as personified by an event orientation.

In considering these dimensions, it should (again) be kept in mind that there will be diversity in how strongly any or all of them are expressed, embraced, or positively regarded.

I believe that there are three logically distinct pedagogical issues to consider in this cultural deep-structure analysis. These are the issues of Afro-cultural *integrity*, Afro-cultural *continuity*, and mainstream cultural *fluency*. Presently, there is little regard in schools for the integrity of the Afro-cultural experience. This has implications for teacher (or other school personnel) attitudes and expectations with regard to children who display Afro-cultural expression. For example, these children's displays are likely to be viewed in pejorative terms, and teachers' expectations for these children often may not be particularly positive. At the same time, while these children may not be able to articulate their ethos, they are likely to perceive efforts to undermine it as personal attacks to be actively resisted. This, of course, can lead to an "us versus them" mentality and create contests of power in classroom settings.

In contrast, when children's Afro-cultural expression is seen as having integrity and coherence, as making sense in these children's lives and representing a central component of these children's legitimate frames of reference, positive educational consequences may result. Behavioral-control time can give way to academic time, and barriers to seeing the academic potential in these children will be substantially lowered. Indeed, the possibility of forging educational partnerships between teachers and students can be increased.

With regard to continuity, when no effort is made to incorporate the Afro-cultural ethos into the contexts of pedagogy, certain problematic circumstances can arise. For one, there will not be outlets for the expression of existing conceptual competencies that have been developed independently of formal school settings. Further, the skills that have been developed will be practiced in other than school settings — for example, on street corners, on basketball courts, in peer settings, and maybe in antisocial, or gang, activities. A lack of Afro-cultural incorporation can also be motivationally debilitating. Opportunities to tap into intrinsic motivation in particular will be missed. Moreover, children may be reluctant to engage in certain educational activities because of their violation of cultural norms, even if these norms are only implicitly understood. When efforts to infuse the Afro-cultural ethos are made, however, certain potential benefits are likely to result. First, there will be increased likelihood that existing and emerging skills and competencies will be displayed and used in formal school settings. Second, there will be greater opportunity for active academic task engagement and more practice of relevant intellectual skills in school contexts. Third, it is feasible that school as an institution will connect with other aspects of students' social ecology; school can become, perhaps, an outlet for the positive, proactive, and constructive renditions of Afro-cultural expression.

The reality-demands of the major institutions of our society dictate that, for the foreseeable future, mainstream cultural socialization will remain part of the schooling agenda. Children *can* be taught to become more fluent in the dominant overarching culture, but this should not mean they must internalize the mainstream culture per se. The mainstream socialization function should be made explicit to children and be devoid of efforts to dishonor any existing cultural frames of reference children bring with them. In this way, the functional value of learning how to operate effectively within the confines of mainstream culture will be better appreciated, and the pickup of relevant mainstream cultural skills should be more successfully accomplished.

Supportive Research

While I believe that the conceptual scenario just delineated is plausible and coherent, it surely requires empirical support. Over the years, I and my associates have been involved in an empirical research program that attempts to serve this end. We have tried to be increasingly responsive to the alternative set of framing assumptions and conceptions about motivation and cognition that undergird a talent development orientation. We have tried to contribute greater conceptual clarity and understanding to parameters and processes attendant to the intersection of culture, cognition, motivation, and context. We have attempted to gain a proactive, empirical handle on Afro-cultural expression and to discern benefits that may result from incorporating Afro-cultural expression into learning and performance contexts. Ours has been a basic research program, but one aimed at addressing the real and pressing academic problems of extant African-American children.

We recently completed an investigation, for example, that speaks directly to the issue of the personal epistemologies that children bring with them into learning contexts (Boykin, Marryshow, & Albury, 1992). We sought to examine the perceptions of schoolchildren toward high-achieving peers. This issue has received noted attention in recent years, inspired by the claim that black children reject high-achieving peers because these peers are perceived as "acting white" (Fordham, 1988; Fordham & Ogbu, 1986). We reasoned that, given the presence of the mainstream cultural deep structure in which schooling is typically embedded, many black children may not be rejecting high achievement per se but only the contexts that high achievement traditionally has been bound to and the cultural values yoked to this achievement. Thus we reasoned that if high achievement was linked to different, more culturally compatible contexts, then the perceptions of black students might be more favorable.

In our study (Boykin, Marryshow, & Albury, 1992), we presented fourth- and fifth-grade, low-income black and white children with four hypothetical learning context scenarios. Each scenario depicted a different high-achieving student that the children in the study were instructed to view as a classmate. One student-example achieved through individualistic striving, that is, in working alone and keeping materials to himself. Another of our high achievers had earned her status through interpersonal competition, or trying to outshine classmates. A third high achiever exhibited his accomplishments through cooperative/communal means (i.e., through sharing and interdependent group work). Finally, the fourth student-example achieved in a context characterized by a high level of verve; that is, in the midst of several ongoing activities and with much variation in subject matter and learning/teaching methods at any one time. The first two approaches were drawn from the mainstream cultural ethos, while the latter two were consistent with the Afro-cultural ethos. Each child was presented with all four high-achiever orientations and asked a set of four questions about his or her social acceptance of the child depicted in each scenario. Our findings revealed that the black children who were tested clearly rejected the high achievers depicted in the mainstream cultural learning scenarios but fully embraced those who succeeded via Afro-cultural expression. In contrast, the white children tested were substantially more accepting of high achievers portrayed in the contexts of mainstream cultural ethos than were the black children.

Other research of ours has addressed whether allowing for Afro-cultural expression in learning and task contexts facilitates performance. Several investigations have examined the possible effects on student learning of increased variability in task presentation (e.g., Boykin, 1979, 1982). This manipulation is taken as an operationalization of the verve dimension. While all the studies have produced consistent findings, perhaps the most illuminating one is that of Tuck and Boykin (1989). In this study, we assessed the performance of a sample of low-income black and white fourth and sixth graders across four distinctly different types of problem-solving tasks. The tasks were presented under two conditions. In one, five examples of each of the four task types were presented in a blocked sequential format, such that all five examples of a type of task were presented together. In the second condition, the four task types (or the 20 task-examples in all) were presented in a random sequential fashion, without regard to type. The former condition was considered to be less varied, while the latter was a more varied presentation format. We also assessed the children's perceptions of the stimulation levels of their homes, asking questions such as the amount of time music was played or television was on, the amount of loud talking and active games that routinely occurred in the home environment, and so on. We also asked each child about the level of stimulation variability he or she preferred. Finally, ratings were obtained from the children's homeroom teachers that described their academic standing and levels of classroom motivation, and scores on a standardized reading achievement measure were also collected for each child.

Results revealed that the homes of the black children were rated higher in stimulation level and that the black children exhibited preferences for greater stimulation variability than did their white counterparts. At the same time, classroom teachers rated the white children higher on the average in classroom academic achievement levels and in levels of classroom motivation. Even though these children were drawn from the same classes, the distributions of achievement and motivation ratings for the two groups scarcely overlapped. There was physical integration, but in terms of classroom performance, segregation remained quite high. White children also scored higher on the standardized achievement test.

Results also revealed a race-by-treatment interaction with the task performance data. Under the relatively constant format condition, the white children significantly outperformed the black children, while under the more varied format condition, the two groups did not differ; both the white and black children performed significantly better in the varied than in the constant format condition. However, the increment in performance that accompanied the change to the more varied treatment was substantially greater for the black children. In addition, perception of the extent of home stimulation was negatively related to performance on the academic indicators for black children; that is, the higher the rated home stimulation level, the lower these children were rated in classroom achievement and motivation and the lower their reading scores were. On the other hand, home stimulation for black students was positively related to preference for stimulation variability and performance under the varied format condition; that is, the greater the home stimulation, the higher the stimulation variability level preferred and the higher level of performance achieved under the varied format. Variability preference also was found to be positively related to varied task performance. These latter findings, taken together, are noteworthy. They suggest that receptiveness to variability and performance responsiveness to variability is seemingly cultivated in the home environment for black children. In its simplest form, is culture not what is cultivated?

In a recent doctoral dissertation, Albury (1993) investigated the effects of group versus individual learning conditions on vocabulary test performance of low-income, fourth-grade black and white children. After an initial pretest to ascertain word knowledge, children were assigned to one of four different learning conditions.

1. *Individual Criterion* — Three children working at the same table were given separate study materials and told that any one of them achieving 18 (out of 25 possible) correct answers on a posttest would receive a reward.

2. *Interpersonal Competition* — Three children at the same table were given separate materials and told whichever one of them received the highest score on the second test would receive a reward.

3. *Group Competition* — Three participants at the same table were given one set of materials among them and told they were competing against other groups to receive a reward.

4. *Communal* — Three persons at a table were given one set of materials and, rather than being offered the opportunity to earn a reward, were encouraged to work together and were told of the importance of sharing and helping each other for the good of the group.

In each condition, participants were allotted 20 minutes' study time. In each learning session, the three children were of the same race, but mixed in gender. The first two were individual study conditions deemed consistent with traditional educational practice and mainstream culture. Group competition was drawn from the prototypical cooperative learning paradigm advanced by Slavin and his associates (Slavin, 1983). The fourth was an operationalization of a dimension of the Afro-cultural ethos. Specifically, when children are operating with a sense of communalism, then a reward inducement or the lure of competition should not be necessary to inspire learning.

Results revealed that the white children's learning gains were at their highest in the two individual study conditions and at their lowest in the communal condition. In contrast, black children's gains were at their highest under the communal condition, next highest under the group competition, and at their lowest under the individual criterion condition. While the white children substantially outperformed their black counterparts in the second testing, which followed the individual criterion learning condition, the black children significantly outperformed their white counterparts when the second, or post-, testing followed the communal study condition. Indeed, the black children under the communal condition produced the highest second-test performance and highest learning gains of any group under any conditions in the entire study. Additional findings also of interest revealed that black children expressed greater liking for the group study conditions than did the white children, whereas the white children expressed greater preference for the individual study conditions than did the black children. Black children also displayed greater interpersonal liking for their study mates than did the white children in the communal condition and reported utilizing more sophisticated learning strategies in the communal condition than did their white counterparts. In the individual study conditions, however, the white children reported more sophisticated strategies.

In other research (Allen & Boykin, 1991; Boykin & Allen, 1988), it has been demonstrated that when rhythmic music is present, along with opportunities for coordinating it with movement expression, enhanced performance on a simple pairing task was recorded for low-income, first- and second-grade black children, while the same treatment proved detrimental to the learning of similarly aged white children. Yet when black and white children's learning was compared under a condition where music and movement opportunities were not afforded, white children showed superior performance. Black children also expressed strong (personal) preferences for learning under a rhythmic music/movement condition (Allen, 1987).

Implications for Education

We would be the first to indicate that there are limitations associated with the work we have done. We recognize that until more work is done, caution should be attached to any conclusions drawn. More refined studies are needed that operationalize key variables in different ways. In addition, different tasks requiring different cognitive and motivational levels must be defined, and students of various ages and backgrounds must be involved. Yet in spite of the limitations, we are confident that certain points stressed in this chapter have been illuminated and reinforced by our work to date. Indeed many of our major findings seem quite consistent with themes advanced herein.

In the perception of high achievers' work, the notion of personal lenses or epistemologies is surely implicated. In examining the several studies that have attempted to operationalize learning and performance contexts capitalizing on Afro-cultural expression, it seems that certain "culturally facilitating contexts" seem to trigger competencies, skills, and performances unrevealed in other contexts. Moreover, black students expressed greater preferences and liking for the contexts more consistent with the Afro-cultural ethos, and performance advantages were obtained without the employment of external reward inducements. These results suggest that intrinsic motivational processes likely were activated.

Taken together, the evidence suggests the operation in our work of what amounts to *prescriptive pedagogy* (Boykin, 1983; Allen & Boykin, 1992). By this term is meant the fashioning of particular experimental task and learning conditions, contexts, and scenarios that are prescriptions for effective and facilitative instructional approaches for African-American children in classroom settings.

It remains important that the claims just made be properly qualified as we draw specific implications for classroom practice. Nothing in the arguments and inferences drawn from our results should lead one to suggest that black children cannot learn or will not perform in the absence of contexts that allow for Afro-cultural expression or that are imbued with characteristics of the Afro-cultural ethos. At the same time, these arguments and inferences do suggest that the contexts in question appear to be cognitively and motivationally facilitating for black children, and this is useful information for those who choose to take a talent-development approach to schooling. Additional comments, pedagogical implications, and qualifiers remain in order, however.

The focus for teachers should be on maximizing those opportunities when a particular Afro-cultural factor can work to facilitate learning, although teachers must also be attentive to those situations where such factors may be inappropriate. Black children, for their part, should learn to become discriminating in the use of their cultural capital. They must be taught a "sense of audience" (Goodnow, 1990); that is, they must learn to discern the time and the place for use of certain expressions and that not every academic instance will be occasion for expression of the Afro-cultural ethos. Yet another type of implication is that different kinds of pedagogical arrangements may be necessary to ensure academic success for all children. More specifically, in order to make academic success more generally pervasive, the talent-development classroom may not fit the classical pedagogical configuration. Indeed, multiple group activities, each with its own distinctive defining context, may be going on simultaneously in the same classroom. Children may be presented with lesson information and corresponding instructions and then prompted, if not actually taught, to practice the requisite cognitive skills individually or collectively, all the while infusing the learning situation with familiar cultural markers and practice techniques. For example, when doing prescribed seatwork, one child may choose to work all of the problems of one type of subject matter before going on to another type, while another child would be allowed to skip among the problems from different subject matters in the course of time. Similarly, one child may work his or her lesson while listening to music via headphones, while another may not, and some children may elect to work in communal groups, while others may elect to compete against other teams of students.

In sum, the economic, social, and general living demands of the twenty-first century are likely to necessitate all children becoming more multiculturally fluent. As we move toward a more service-oriented society in particular, the cultivation of speaking as a performance and the importance of affective expressiveness and sensitivity may grow in importance. In the same vein, as work life becomes increasingly fast-paced, being able to shift focus among several different tasks simultaneously may become quite adaptive, and music could come to serve therapeutic functions on the job. Finally, as this society and even the world become more interdependent, a healthy sense of genuine communalism may prove advantageous.

CONCLUDING STATEMENTS

Proactive educational reform for African-American children must be understood against the backdrop of historical, psychological, and cultural forces and factors that have shaped much of the character of present-day American education. Against this backdrop, an appeal is made to embrace (1) the assumptions and objectives of a talent-development approach to schooling and (2) deep-structure multiculturalism. With these as a foundation, we call for the greater utilization of more culturally responsive pedagogy via the incorporation of the Afro-cultural ethos into classroom approaches. An empirical research program and results so far obtained from that program support this call and have begun to identify specific practices that can enhance the school performance of black children and youth. It is our hope that the conceptual analyses and findings provide a sense of the challenges, complexities, perplexities, pitfalls, and promises that will accompany genuine educational reform for African-American children, if not for all children, as we stand at the gateway to the twenty-first century.

REFERENCES

Akbar, N. (1985). Our destiny: Authors of a scientific revolution. In H. McAdoo & J. McAdoo (Eds.), *Black children* (pp. 17–31). Beverly Hills: Sage.

Albury, A. (1993). *Social orientations, learning conditions and learning outcomes among low-income black and white grade school children.* Unpublished doctoral dissertation, Howard University, Washington, DC.

Alexander, K., & Entwisle, D. (1988). Achievement in the first 2 years of school: Patterns and processes. *Monographs of the Society for Research in Child Development, 53*(2, Serial No. 218).

Allen, B. (1987). *Differential effects of low and high sensate stimulation and movement affordance on the learning of black and white working class children.* Unpublished doctoral dissertation, Howard University, Washington, DC.

Allen, B., & Boykin, A. W. (1991). The influence of contextual factors on Afro-American and Euro-American children's performance: Effects of movement opportunity and music. *International Journal of Psychology, 26,* 373–387.

Allen, B., & Boykin, A. W. (1992). African-American children and the educational process: Alleviating cultural discontinuity through prescriptive pedagogy. *School Psychology Review, 21,* 586–596.

Apple, M. (1979). *Ideology and curriculum.* London: Routledge & Kegan Paul.

Boykin, A. W. (1977). Experimental psychology from a black perspective: Issues and examples. *Journal of Black Psychology, 3,* 29–49.

Boykin, A. W. (1979). Psychological/behavioral verve: Some theoretical explorations and empirical manifestations. In A. W. Boykin, A. J. Franklin, & J. F. Yates (Eds.), *Research directions of black psychologists* (pp. 351–367). New York: Russell Sage.

Boykin, A. W. (1982). Task variability and the performance of black and white schoolchildren: Vervistic explorations. *Journal of Black Studies, 12,* 469–485.

Boykin, A. W. (1983). The academic performance of Afro-American children. In J. Spence (Ed.), *Achievement and achievement motives* (pp. 321–371). San Francisco: W. Freeman.

Boykin, A. W. (1986). The triple quandary and the schooling of Afro-American children. In U. Neisser (Ed.), *The school achievement of minority children* (pp. 57–92). Hillsdale, NJ: Lawrence Erlbaum.

Boykin, A. W., & Allen, B. (1988). Rhythmic-movement facilitated learning in working-class Afro-American children. *Journal of Genetic Psychology, 149,* 335–347.

Boykin, A. W., & Ellison, C. (in press). The multiple ecologies of black youth socialization: An Afrographic analysis. In R. Taylor (Ed.), *Black youth.* Newbury Park, CA: Sage.

Boykin, A. W., Marryshow, D., & Albury, A. (1992). *High achievement in cul-*

tural context: The views of some black and white low-income schoolchildren. Unpublished manuscript, Howard University, Washington, DC.

Carlson, D. (1982). "Updating" individualism and the work ethic: Corporate logic in the classroom. *Curriculum Inquiry, 12,* 125–160.

Cole, J. (1970). Black culture: Negro, black and nigger. *Black Scholar, 1,* 40–43.

Cornbleth, C. (1984). Beyond the hidden curriculum. *Journal of Curriculum Studies, 16,* 29–36.

Csikszentmihalyi, M. (1990). Literacy and intrinsic motivation. *Daedalus, 119,* 115–140.

Delpit, L. (1988). The silenced dialogue: Power and pedagogy in educating other people's children. *Harvard Educational Review, 58,* 280–298.

Dixon, V. (1976). Worldviews and research methodology. In L. King, V. Dixon, & W. Nobles (Eds.), *African philosophy: Assumptions and paradigms for research on black populations* (pp. 54–101). Los Angeles: Fanon Center Publications.

Everhart, R. (1983). *Reading, writing and resistance.* Boston: Routledge & Kegan Paul.

Fordham, S. (1988). Racelessness as a factor in black students' school success: Pragmatic strategy or pyrrhic victory? *Harvard Educational Review, 58,* 54–84.

Fordham, S., & Ogbu, J. (1986). Black students' school success: Coping with the burden of "acting white." *Urban Review, 18,* 176–206.

Freire, P. (1970). *Pedagogy of the oppressed.* New York: Seabury Press.

Gay, G. (1975). Cultural differences important in the education of black children. *Momentum, 2,* 30–33.

Gay, G. (1988). Designing relevant curricula for diverse learners. *Education and Urban Society, 20,* 322–340.

Gergen, K. (1978). Toward generative theory. *Journal of Personality and Social Psychology, 36,* 1344–1360.

Gergen, K. (1990). Social understanding and the inscription of self. In J. Stigler, R. Shweder, & G. Herdt (Eds.), *Cultural psychology* (pp. 569–606). New York: Cambridge University Press.

Goodnow, J. (1990). The socialization of cognition: What's involved. In J. Stigler, R. Shweder, & G. Herdt (Eds.), *Cultural psychology* (pp. 259–286). New York: Cambridge University Press.

Greeno, J. (1989). A perspective on thinking. *American Psychologist, 44,* 134–141.

Hunt, J. M. (1965). Intrinsic motivation and its role in psychological development. In D. Levine (Ed.), *Nebraska symposium on motivation* (pp. 189–282). Lincoln: University of Nebraska Press.

Irvine, J. (1990). *Black children and school failure: Policies, practices and prescriptions.* New York: Greenwood Press.

Jones, J. (1979). Conceptual and strategic issues in the relationship of black psychology to American social science. In A. W. Boykin, A. J. Franklin, & J. F. Yates (Eds.), *Research directions of black psychologists* (pp. 390–432). New York: Russell Sage.

Kaestle, P. (1983). *Pillars of the republic: Common schools and American society.* New York: Hill and Wang.

Katz, J. (1985). The sociopolitical nature of counseling. *Counseling Psychologist, 13,* 615–624.

Levine, L. (1977). *Black culture and black consciousness.* New York: Oxford University Press.

Nobles, W. (1991). African philosophy: Foundations for a black psychology. In R. Jones (Ed.), *Black psychology* (3rd ed., pp. 47–63). Hampton, VA: Cobb and Henry.

Ramirez, M., & Castenada, A. (1974). *Cultural democracy: Bicognitive development and education.* New York: Academic Press.

Riegel, K. (1979). *Foundations of dialectical psychology.* New York: Academic Press.

Rogoff, B. (1990). *Apprenticeship in thinking.* New York: Oxford University Press.

Shweder, R. (1990). Cultural psychology: What is it? In J. Stigler, R. Shweder, & G. Herdt (Eds.), *Cultural psychology* (pp. 1–43). New York: Cambridge University Press.

Silverstein, B., & Krate, R. (1975). *Children of the dark ghetto.* New York: Praeger.

Slavin, R. E. (1983). *Cooperative learning.* New York: Longman.

Sleeter, C., & Grant, C. (1991). Mapping terrains of power: Student cultural knowledge vs. classroom knowledge. In C. Sleeter (Ed.), *Empowerment through multicultural education* (pp. 49–67). Albany: State University of New York Press.

Spence, J. (1985). Achievement American style: The rewards and costs of individualism. *American Psychologist, 40,* 1285–1295.

Spring, J. (1990). *The American school 1642–1990* (2nd ed.). New York: Longman.

Sue, S. (1991). Ethnicity and culture in psychological research and practice. In J. Goodchilds (Ed.), *Psychological perspectives on human diversity in America* (pp. 51–85). Washington, DC: APA Publications.

Taylor, A. (1991). Social competence and the early school transition. *Education and Urban Society, 24,* 15–26.

Tharp, R. (1989). Psychocultural variables and constants: Effects on teaching and learning in schools. *American Psychologist, 44,* 349–359.

Tuck, K., & Boykin, A. W. (1989). Verve effects: The relationship of task performance to stimulus preference and variability in low-income black and white children. In A. Harrison (Ed.), *The eleventh conference on empirical research in black psychology* (pp. 84–95). Washington, DC: NIMH Publications.

Tyack, D. (1974). *The one best system.* Cambridge, MA: Harvard University Press.

Vallance, E. (1974). Hiding the hidden curriculum. *Curriculum Theory Network, 4,* 5–21.

Vygotsky, L. (1962). *Thought and language.* Cambridge, MA: MIT Press.

Walker, E. (1980). *Psychological complexity and preference.* Monterey, CA: Brooks-Cole.

Wertsch, J. (1985). *Vygotsky and the social formation of mind.* Cambridge, MA: Harvard University Press.

White, J. (1970, September). Toward a black psychology. *Ebony, 25,* pp. 44–45, 48–50, 52.

Willis, M. (1989). Learning styles of African-American children: A review of the literature and interventions. *Journal of Black Psychology, 16,* 47–65.

Young, V. (1970). Family and childhood in a southern Negro community. *American Anthropologist, 72,* 269–288.

Young, V. (1974). A Black American socialization pattern. *American Ethnologist, 1,* 405–413.

Part III

REFORMS IN PROCESS: FROM THE SCHOOL TO THE SYSTEM

The five chapters in this part are both informative and instructive about the nature of reform efforts. In describing specific reform initiatives at various levels, they tell us what is currently going on in cities and towns across the United States; in addition, they tell us about why reforms were attempted and how the efforts came to be in their present forms.

In Chapter 7 Russell Rumberger and Katherine Larson describe a one-school project aimed at promoting learning and retention among Hispanic middle school students. Michelle Fine, in Chapter 8, relates experiences and accomplishments of efforts made to create more intimate and more challenging learning environments in urban secondary schools. In Chapter 9 Joseph Grannis provides an overview of a citywide dropout prevention initiative, noting just how the dynamics of implementation and evaluation may work in contexts that are also politically charged. Alfred Hess, in Chapter 10, recounts the challenges and early returns from the move to reform governance and administrative practices in all Chicago schools, thereby providing additional insights into the interplay of political and systemic frames of reference.

Chapter 11 moves the lens away from the big cities and reminds us that the majority of poor children and youth attend rural schools. Alan DeYoung describes the historical, demographic, and social and economic trends that have shaped the schools and systems in our rural areas, and he takes us inside one system to examine how school staff and the community at large are attempting to improve student experiences. Far from being unrelated to the other chapters in the part, this one underscores many of the similarities in conditions, circumstances, and challenges that face our nation's schools.

CHAPTER 7

Keeping High-Risk Chicano Students in School

Lessons from a Los Angeles Middle School Dropout Prevention Program

RUSSELL W. RUMBERGER AND KATHERINE A. LARSON

One of the major challenges facing American education is reducing the number of students who fail to graduate from high school. The urgency of this challenge was recognized by the president and the nation's governors when they adopted the goal of increasing the high school graduation rate to 90% by the year 2000 as one of the six National Goals of Education. A related objective is to eliminate the gap in high school graduation rates between minority and nonminority students (U.S. Department of Education, 1990, pp. 4–5).

The urgency to reduce dropout rates is predicated on two concerns. The first is economic. Dropouts experience higher rates of unemployment, receive lower earnings, and are more likely than high school graduates to require social services over their entire lifetimes (Rumberger, 1987; Stern, Paik, Catterall, & Nakata, 1989). In short, dropouts are costly. One year's cohort of dropouts from Los Angeles city schools was estimated to cost $3.2 billion in lost earnings and more than $400 million in social services (Catterall, 1987, Tables 3 and 4). The social costs of failing to complete

The project reported in this chapter is being supported by grants from the U.S. Department of Education, Office of Special Education Programs; the University of California Presidential Grants for School Improvement; and the University of California Linguistic Minority Research Project.

high school could rise in the future as the demands for low-skilled labor are reduced.

The second reason for an urgent response to the dropout problem is demographic. Demographic changes in the United States are increasing the number of persons who traditionally are more likely to drop out of school: minorities, poor children, and children living in single-family households (Natriello, McDill, & Pallas, 1990).

The dropout issue is a particular concern for Hispanics. Hispanics have the highest dropout rate among the major ethnic groups in the United States. In 1989, the percent of high school dropouts among persons 16 to 24 years old was 33% for Hispanics, 14% for blacks, and 12% for Caucasians (U.S. National Center for Education Statistics, 1991, Table 97). The Hispanic population is also expected to grow faster than any other major ethnic group. Between 1985 and 2020, the number of Caucasian youth between the ages 18 to 24 is expected to *decline* by 25%, while the number of Hispanic youth will *increase* by 65% (Rumberger, 1990, Table 2). Thus, based on current dropout rates, the total number of young dropouts could actually *increase* over the next 35 years. These trends are not lost on employers, who are now among the most vocal proponents of educational reform to improve school success for Hispanic and other minority populations (e.g., Committee for Economic Development, 1987).

Although a wide variety of programs and policies have been initiated at the national, state, and local levels to help students finish school, few specifically target Hispanic youngsters. Of the almost 500 school or community-based dropout programs nationwide surveyed by the U.S. General Accounting Office (GAO) in 1986, only 26 served primarily Hispanic youth (U.S. GAO, 1987, p. 27). Clearly, more programs are needed that target this population. The need is especially urgent in California, where Hispanics represented 34% of students in 1990 and will constitute 58% of all new students projected to enter the state's educational system over the next 10 years (California Department of Finance, 1991).

Research literature indicates that Hispanic dropouts display many of the same characteristics as other dropouts: low academic achievement, a dislike for school, discipline problems, and low educational aspirations (Rumberger, 1991). Yet there are some important differences. First, Hispanics are more likely to attend large urban schools with high concentrations of poor, minority students. In such settings, dropping out is more the rule than the exception. Second, Hispanics are more likely to drop out *before* reaching high school. National data show that almost 50% of Hispanic males who left school between October 1984 and 1985 dropped out before the ninth grade (U.S. Bureau of the Census, 1988, Table 7). Thus, dropout prevention for Hispanic students needs to focus on their middle school years.

Efforts to address the Hispanic dropout problem must also be sensitive to the vast differences in the Hispanic population, as is appropriately described in Chapter 5 of this volume. Hispanic generally refers to persons of Mexican, Puerto Rican, Cuban, Central or South American, or other Spanish culture or origin, regardless of race. Along a variety of educational and economic indicators, the differences among Hispanic subgroups are actually greater than differences between Hispanic and non-Hispanic populations. For instance, in 1988, differences in dropout rates between Cuban- and Mexican-origin populations were greater than differences in dropout rates between Hispanic and non-Hispanic populations (U.S. Bureau of the Census, 1988, Table 1). Therefore, attention to subgroup differences is warranted as well as attention to major ethnic group differences.

Mexican-Americans, or Chicanos, represent two-thirds of the Hispanic population in the United States, by far the largest of the Hispanic subgroups. Chicanos represent an even larger proportion of the Hispanic population in Texas and California. Moreover, they generally have the lowest socioeconomic status and the lowest level of educational attainment of all the Hispanic subgroups (U.S. Bureau of the Census, 1988). Thus the educational and economic circumstances of Chicanos warrant particular attention by researchers and policy makers. Of course, Chicanos themselves are a diverse group who differ in such ways as language use, immigration status, and their own ethnic identities.

This chapter describes the initial implementation and outcomes of a Chicano dropout prevention program in a large, urban junior high school in Los Angeles. Three features make this program unique. First, it focuses on the highest-risk Chicano students, including special education students, in the school. Second, it represents a comprehensive cluster of interventions, based on research evidence, that address different spheres of influence on a student's life and school performance. Third, the program is being conducted using a rigorous research and evaluation design, involving true random assignment between treatment and control groups and an extensive evaluation of costs and effectiveness.

DESCRIPTION OF THE ALAS PROGRAM

Program Components

ALAS — Achievement for Latinos through Academic Success — translates to "wings" in Spanish. The program is being implemented with both school-site and university staff. Three on-site counselors have experience in individual and family counseling. The majority of the staff speak Spanish;

others use translators in communicating with parents. The program consists of a series of specific intervention strategies that, as described below, simultaneously address some of the most critical factors operating within *four spheres of influence* on student achievement: *students, teachers,* the *school,* and *parents.*

Students' social and task-related behavior. Social and task-related behavior has been consistently reported as problematic for low-achieving youth. School behavior problems contribute directly to low grades and dropping out (Kavale, Alper, & Purcell, 1981), and they are also the problems that most disturb teachers and school staff. For example, in a recent study of Hispanic junior high school students, the 500 students most at risk of failure in school had four times the rate of classroom expulsions as other students and generated nearly 25,000 disciplinary contacts during seventh and eighth grades (Larson, 1989a, 1989b).

To improve students' social and task-related behavior, the ALAS program incorporates a social, metacognitive problem-solving training program previously found to significantly reduce truancy and misbehavior incidents and improve school work habits and academic grades among high-risk Hispanic junior high school students (Larson, 1989a). This program was also found to significantly reduce misbehavior and improve prosocial behavior among emotionally disturbed and learning-disturbed incarcerated delinquents and to increase school and work days and reduce gang involvement, drug use, and crime among chronic delinquents (Larson, 1989c). This problem-solving approach teaches students to apply skills to problems in various contexts (e.g., familial or academic).

Teacher feedback. A basic principle of behavior change is specific and frequent feedback to the performer. The traditional feedback system in secondary schools is report card grades every 10 weeks. Many schools provide interim "progress reports" every 5 weeks. However, low-achieving students, particularly Chicano students and their parents, require feedback and progress reports much more frequently than this. Larson (1989a), for example, found that the lowest-achieving junior high school students were not able to accurately predict their 5-week school grades without interim feedback reports from teachers, and Delgado-Gaitan (1988) reports that Hispanic parents were angry when the school did *not* notify them of their adolescents' poor school performance. For these reasons, the ALAS program provides daily, weekly, or bimonthly teacher feedback reports to students *and* their parents, depending on student need. Students can thus use this teacher feedback for focusing thinking and decision making during problem-solving maintenance training.

School attendance monitoring. Prior research shows consistently that dropouts have poor school attendance prior to dropping out (e.g., Ekstrom, Goertz, Pollack, & Rock, 1986). In many large middle and secondary schools, however, attendance is not closely monitored, and students quickly get the message that school staff don't really care whether they are in school. The ALAS program, in contrast, provides *hot-seat attendance monitoring*, which is school monitoring of period-by-period attendance. In addition, parents are contacted daily about student truancy or extended absence, and students are required to make up missed time and are provided with *positive* adult contacts, communicating a personal interest in their attendance. These specific strategies grow out of the findings of several studies (e.g., Clark, 1987).

Efforts to increase the students' affiliation with school. Several studies have found that dropouts are more likely than other students to report being alienated from school, feeling that schools and teachers don't care about them, not having an adult at school to turn to for help, and not participating in extracurricular events (e.g., Wehlage & Rutter, 1986). Ethnic and racial minorities in general and Hispanic students in particular are even less likely than other students to report a sense of membership or bonding to school (Delgado-Gaitan, 1988; Ogbu, 1989). In response, the ALAS program provides both student–student and adult–student bonding activities. A number of extracurricular activities are provided for students to stimulate bonding with other students. In addition, the ALAS staff function as adult advocates for student participants, which helps develop adult–student bonding.

Parent participation and monitoring. Parental values and attitudes play an important role in students' academic achievement, and parental monitoring of students' behavior, in particular, may have a positive impact on grades and homework completion. Lower-class parents, however, are likely to attend fewer school events, make fewer complaints to the principal, and enroll their children less often in summer school than are middle-class parents, and Hispanic parents interact significantly less than non-Hispanic parents with teachers and school personnel. This is not because these parents don't value education, but rather because Hispanic parents often may be confused about the roles they are expected to play in their children's education or they may lack the confidence and skills to interact with teachers and other school staff (Casas & Furlong, 1986). The fifth and final component of the ALAS program, then, is to train parents in two skills: (1) parent–child problem solving and (2) parent participation in school and literacy activities. The parent–child problem-solving training consists of weekly problem-solving "tutorials" that provide suggestions for improving the child's school behavior. In addition, parents receive instruction in *how* and *when* to participate in school activities, to contact teachers and administrators, and to monitor their child's school performance. Communication with parents is done in writing for those parents who can read either Spanish or English, and orally otherwise.

Program Setting

The ALAS program is being implemented in a large junior high school (grades 7–9) in the Los Angeles Unified School District. The school enrolls 2,000 students, 94% of whom are Hispanic, nearly all of them Chicano. Average student performance is at the twenty-fifth percentile rank on the California Test of Basic Skills (CTBS), making it one of the 25 lowest academically achieving schools in the district. Absenteeism averages 25% for seventh and eighth graders, and although middle schools are not required to keep dropout statistics, the school principal recently reported that up to 50% of the students may never reach high school. In addition, the California State Department of Education (1989) reports that 61% of the students' parents did not graduate from high school, and 75% speak only Spanish in the home. The setting for this project is somewhat better illustrated, however, by the findings from an informal survey of 130 incoming seventh graders conducted by one of the teachers in the school in the summer of 1991. Partial results, shown in Table 7.1, suggest that many students live in a world surrounded by crime, gangs, and the constant threat of death. Unfortunately, these student reports are confirmed by recent statistics that show an average of almost one teenager a day died violently (most from guns) in the County of Los Angeles in 1990 (Berger, 1991).

Program Participants

This project targets three different populations of seventh-grade Hispanic students: (1) the highest-risk group, consisting of the bottom 25% of regular education entering students and two groups of special education students, (2) learning-disabled students, and (3) emotionally disturbed students. Definition of the highest-risk group was based on a five-item teacher rating that identified (1) need for supervision, (2) level of motivation, (3) academic potential, (4) social interaction skill, and (5) teachability. This scale was previously used to measure student characteristics related to teacher decision making (e.g., Shavelson, Cadwell, & Izu, 1977) and to predict special education referral at both the elementary and secon-

TABLE 7.1 Partial results of seventh–grade student survey administered summer 1991*

Survey Items	Percentage Responding Affirmatively	
	Boys (n = 68)	Girls (n = 62)
Drink alcohol regularly (1–2 times weekly)	16%	3%
Are currently failing a class	50%	34%
Have had two or more physical fights since school began	51%	27%
Have had trouble with police (stopped or arrested 2 times past year)	33%	21%
Have stolen something from a store (2 times in past year)	60%	61%
Have good friends who are in gangs	65%	63%
Have ever thought about suicide	40%	50%
Have ever attempted suicide	25%	22%
Have a close relative in jail	39%	63%
Have had anyone close die violently	45%	34%
Think they are a good person	78%	92%

*School is on a year-round schedule, with 3/4 of the students starting school in July.

dary levels (e.g., Gerber & Semmel, 1984). In an earlier study of 350 students from 13 sixth-grade Hispanic classrooms that used this instrument, Larson (1989a) found 30% of students were initially classified in the highest-risk category and that these students were functioning on average at the seventeenth percentile rank on national norms of the CTBS. Two-and-one-half years later, these teacher ratings predicted 73% of the variance in eighth-grade *classroom expulsions*, 80% of the variance in *truancy*, and 50% of the variance in *grade point average*.

Subjects identified for ALAS as high risk were selected from among those students who entered the school in the fall of 1990 from 11 feeder elementary schools. All sixth-grade students in those schools (approximately 625 students from 23 classrooms) were assessed by their classroom teachers the previous spring. For each classroom, the classroom mean and standard deviation on each of the five scale items were calculated. Every student within a given classroom was assigned a "troublesome" score, which is the total number of rating scale items on which he or she was one standard deviation below the classroom mean (troublesome scores ranged from 0 to 5). Students were targeted as highest risk if they were at least one standard deviation above their classroom mean on the troublesome score. Approximately 25% to 30% of the students from each classroom were targeted as highest risk using this method, and, of these, 60% were male. All other students were targeted as lower risk. Of the 159 highest-risk students who entered the school as seventh graders, 57 were excluded from consideration because they were served only in limited English proficiency classrooms and could not be provided the intervention as designed. Of the remaining 102 students, 90 were randomly assigned to high-risk control and high-risk treatment groups, with gender equated in both groups. In addition to these students, the ALAS program worked with all seventh-grade special education students (both learning disabled and severely emotionally disturbed) in the years 1990 and 1991; control groups in this case consisted of all seventh-grade students in the years 1992 and 1993. Students in both the high-risk and special education treatment groups began their intervention as seventh-graders and are projected to continue to be monitored by the program through the completion of tenth grade. Control students will be followed during this same time frame. Students from either group who leave the school will be followed, unless they move out of the state.

Research Design

The ALAS program is being conducted in a true experimental fashion, with students randomly assigned to treatment and control groups, to ensure that observed differences between treatment and control groups can be attributed solely to the intervention rather than to other factors. The experiment is designed to assess the impact of the program on a variety of outcome measures and to assess the costs and cost-effectiveness of the intervention.

Outcome measures. Information is being collected on a variety of student outcomes related to school performance and dropout. These measures include school attendance, school grades, teacher ratings of cooperation and work habits, self-esteem, self-efficacy for school/classroom activities, locus of control, depression, stress, parental involvement in school activities, student perceptions of school climate, student perceptions of teachers, student job and educational expectations, student participation in extra-curricular activities and community, student attitudes about ethnicity and use of the Spanish language, student involvement in school-related tasks/ activities, student/parent decision-making styles, and English language proficiency/usage. The data are being collected from a variety of scores, including school records, standardized tests, teacher and staff ratings of students, and a student survey about parenting practices designed and refined by Dornbusch and colleagues that has been shown to predict school performance and dropout behavior (Dornbusch, Ritter, Leiderman, Roberts, & Fraleigh, 1987).

Assessment of program effectiveness. Program effectiveness is being assessed in three steps. First, we generate descriptive information on the characteristics and performance of the highest-risk Hispanic youth control group and compare their experiences with those of other Hispanic students in the school, district, state, and nation, based on published sources, to assess similarities and differences. These comparisons capture the representativeness of the general population from which ALAS participants were drawn. Second, we compare the treatment and control groups across the various independent variable domains discussed above. This step determines the efficacy of the treatment intervention. Third, we estimate multivariate models to predict attendance, school performance, and attrition based on various student characteristics, as well as by group membership (highest risk versus lower risk).

Cost and cost-effectiveness. The third component of the research involves a cost-effectiveness evaluation of the intervention. We assess the total costs involved in implementing the program by employing an "ingredients" method that determines all resources (personnel, facilities, materials, etc.) used in the intervention, who contributes them, and their monetary values, and then derive separate estimates for each intervention strategy. We ascertain the cost-effectiveness of the overall intervention by computing a ratio of effects to costs. For example, if the overall intervention reduces the number of dropouts in the treatment group versus the control group by a certain number, then the cost-effectiveness of the intervention would be the total number of dropouts "prevented" divided by the total costs of the intervention, yielding a figure showing the cost for each dropout prevented.

PROGRAM ASSUMPTIONS AND CULTURAL BOUNDARIES

The ALAS program was not designed to reform the organization, curriculum, or instruction in schools. Rather, it was designed to enhance the traditional urban middle and secondary school experiences of a group of high-risk Hispanic students outside of their regular classroom activities. This approach was based on the assumption that traditional school programs simply needed augmenting—both with additional resources and with expertise. Almost 2 years into the project, these assumptions were found to have proved false. Contrary to our initial expectations, many of our efforts served not simply to supplement existing school services with additional resources, but rather to mitigate and remediate the negative and damaging effects of the traditional school program and culture on Chicano students' learning and attitudes toward school.

As a consequence of this negative reality, ALAS project activities have been expanded to include advocacy and brokerage functions over and beyond our original plans. All activities have required project staff to develop methods for crossing *three cultural boundaries*: school culture, student culture, and Chicano culture. Below we briefly share some preliminary insights about implementing our project in terms of these three cultures.

School Culture

School culture is real and entrenched. Problems arise when outsiders, whose intent it is to reform existing educational practices, serve neither to perpetuate nor at times even to support the existing culture as it is defined and promoted by teachers and administrators. This is the case when our ALAS staff function primarily as brokers and advocates for children and their families.

Conflict with the school culture is most pronounced when ALAS staff attempt to negotiate, individualize, and soften school policies and practices for students and families, especially for students who are colliding with the existing school culture. As a result of our attempts, which are sometimes less than graceful, to cross the school culture boundary, we have derived several principles that help bridge the chasm between insiders and outsiders.

We have found that to keep insider skepticism and ill will at bay, it is critical that we work at the school in a consistent fashion. Historically, academics, university-based researchers, and others involved in educational research have remained apart from schools, and, as a consequence, practitioners may understandably be skeptical, resistant, and even resentful when solutions from "the ivory tower" are proposed. Only by being involved with the day-to-day realities of the school is credibility for the project goals maintained so that ALAS research staff can more effectively negotiate the school culture as outsiders. We have learned three principles in negotiating the school culture.

Attend to individual adult needs. "Little things" do hurt our relations with school staff and, as a consequence, we have learned to make extraordinary effort to attend to the details of our activities that directly impact school personnel, especially teachers. For example, aggravating teachers or other school staff is unfortunately easy to do, yet extremely counterproductive in terms of negative public relations and withdrawal of support for substantive issues. We have learned that we can more easily change "big" things about the school culture as we recognize and address the unique needs and idiosyncratic practices of individual staff members. Similarly, we have come to realize that support for our efforts is built through personal interaction. Consequently, ALAS staff spend a great deal of time in conferences with individual school staff.

Be aware of covert resistance. It was only after a year-and-a-half in the school that we realized the most frequent and harshest criticism from teachers was not stated directly to us or expressed in notes of disgruntlement sent to our office. Instead, most teachers chose to air complaints about ALAS in the teachers' lounge or lunchroom. This was also the forum used by a few teachers who felt particularly threatened by our reform efforts. Since the teachers who might disagree with the complaint or negative inference about ALAS did not speak out or disagree publicly with their colleagues (schools typically offer little or no administrative support for teachers to speak up or criticize colleagues) we were forced to take an active role in implementing an informal information campaign to counter the spreading of disinformation, negativity, and resistance.

Use teachers as advisors. Since the inception of the project, a dozen teachers within the school have identified themselves as supporters of the ALAS program. Their knowledge and goodwill as insiders have been invaluable. We have used these teachers as advisors on how to implement a project activity, as liaisons between the project and school staff, and as sounding boards on how to address a complaint about the program.

Student Culture

Crossing the borders of student culture has been another primary challenge of project staff. Working with students directly is such a significant aspect of our effort that, in one sense, it could be said that ALAS staff spend most of their time building relationships with students. Even during many of the interactions that are directed toward insiders and parents, the primary intent is to build a stronger bond between students and ALAS staff by enhancing the school and family system for them. These activities also build stronger bonds between students and parents and between students and educators.

In our attempts to cross student culture boundaries, we have derived four principles that describe how our project attempts to structure student–adult relationships and thereby increase student affiliation, instill hope, and promote empowerment.

Be accountable for students' growth and progress. This principle is primary and drives the remaining three principles. Our dedication to the concept of holding ourselves responsible for student performance is reflected in our use of the word *intervention* to describe our efforts. Webster defines intervene as "to come in between by way of modification." We hold ourselves accountable for coming in between and modifying effectively the interface of disadvantaged youth with academic learning. It is our mission and the way we find and define professional success. Consequently, we interpret poor student performance as *our* failure and an indicator that we must recast our approach with a particular child and/or parent. This does not mean that the student or parent is not asked to change or to assume responsibility for his or her performance. Quite the contrary. It simply means that we must change our approach so that the student and parent *can* change in order to be held accountable and function optimally within an institutional learning environment.

Having staff hold themselves accountable for student performance automatically sustains motivation to be creative and to deliver maximum effort. It also requires an ongoing assessment of student performance and frequent feedback. We check marker variables compulsively on a weekly and even daily basis — that is, we check attendance, tardies, truancies, student behavior, classroom behavior, notes home, and so on. We monitor, monitor, monitor students and change our behavior based on feedback.

Accept students as they are. In order to be accountable for change or performance, it is essential to embrace the reality that most urban students are not middle-class Anglos. Surprisingly, most adults in schools with high proportions of minority children living in poverty appear to respond to the students as if they *were* middle-class Anglos. For example, in our school, assignments are given with little acknowledgment of or accommodation to the facts that few of our students have calculators, rulers, magazines, or newspapers in their homes to aid homework; few of the parents know English and therefore they cannot help with homework, and few of the parents read or write Spanish and therefore do not read school bulletins or letters sent to their home.

Students must be accepted and valued for who they are and for what skills and assets they bring to the school task. For example, Juan sleeps in a different house every night. Whether he should have been able to or not, Juan simply could not keep track of his school materials and was frequently sent out of classes for having no supplies. Our solution was to personalize the environment for Juan — have extra supplies for him and have him keep important schoolwork in our office. (School lockers in this case are not a viable solution because break-in, theft, and vandalism are rampant.) Once one accepts students' needs and their life circumstances unconditionally and stops blaming them for their background or their life-style, then it is a small and inevitable step to recognizing the third principle of creating an effective child–adult relationship.

Attend to students' many needs and their complex situations. Our students are not only economically needy, but often psychologically needy as well. Many are fragile. Compassion must flavor the behavior of educators who work with them. Whether it is resignation on the parts of many adults in schools or a sense of being overwhelmed, there is an all too frequent sense of indifference or uncaring toward children who are suffering.

High-risk Chicano students in particular may require a great deal of assistance. One-third of ALAS students require daily monitoring of their school performance in order to experience success in following through on their responsibilities. About 25% of these students carry teacher feedback forms with them throughout their school day so that their behavior and assignments can be recorded by each of their teachers and monitored daily by ALAS staff. This feedback is used to communicate nightly with parents. Given current school resources and the organizational structure, school staff cannot be expected to provide this degree of monitoring. Perhaps more important, we have found that to solve students' school problems often requires attending to their home or family problems, such as welfare, legal matters, medical problems, or siblings. Again, we can certainly expect school staff to be empathic and to demonstrate emotional and psychological support for students; however, given current resources, they cannot be expected to provide the necessary social work services that high-risk students need. Attending to the whole child as a high-need and highly complex individual forces one to adopt a fourth principle for creating effective adult–child relationships within the school environment: be flexible and individualize.

Alter and individualize procedures and policies. Flexibility requires that our staff take the time to really listen to individual students. High-risk students often have difficulty identifying a problem and expressing clearly what they need to have happen to succeed in school. A significant task of the listening adult is to filter the confusion, frustration, and often anger of the student and to determine whether the student or the system, or both, need to adjust in order for the student to succeed. Flexibility and individualization are the key to successfully working with high-risk students, and we have found that it is impossible to succeed with these most difficult-to-teach students if the school context is not tailored to their individual psychological needs and skills. Flexibility permits personalization of the educational experience for students.

We have found that success often requires only minor adjustments of school-wide procedures. We refer to this as tinkering with the system. However, as presently structured, large middle and secondary schools are rarely malleable to even minor adjustments in policies or procedures for individual students. Student advocacy serves primarily to "free up" and personalize the system for each student. The degree to which an institution must respond flexibly varies with each student. For this reason, ALAS staff do not require students to justify individual preferences or to justify why the system should be changed for them. If it is possible and practical to change the system, we make every effort to get the system to accommodate individual preferences of students. We regard this as simply a form of nurturing.

Importantly, this type of nurturing must extend beyond preferences to accommodating student needs. More specifically, to meet the learning needs of a particular student, ALAS staff will change or attempt to change prevailing policy (e.g., arranging a student's schedule so that he or she is taking classes on more than a single grade level with teachers from several different track, or calendar year, schedules). To succeed with the 25% or 30% most difficult-to-teach students will always require adults to "tweak" the school system to meet students' individual needs.

Chicano Culture

The final boundary that we must cross to succeed with our students concerns Chicano culture. Differences between Chicano culture and the culture of typical American schools can lead to poor performance in school (Trueba & Delgado-Gaitan, 1988). To help educational practitioners bridge the boundary of Chicano culture and facilitate school performance in highest-risk Chicano youth, we have derived two operational principles.

Communicate with parents verbally. Home–school communication is vital to student achievement, and our project is founded on the assumption that Chicano parents, like most parents, care about how their children are doing in school and want to be informed. Yet, from the outset, our substantial efforts at sending home notes (in Spanish and English) were unsuccessful. When queried, parents would tell us they either had not seen our weekly note or did not respond to the communiqué as requested because of a basic reticence to confront school officials. The problem was not incorrect addresses. Rather, parents cited a number of reasons for not receiving the written information: (1) mail is lost within the home because many people open mail, including children who often function as brokers between their parents and the mainstream society; (2) mail is opened by older siblings who have taken on the role of parent and who will often, without informing the parent, use their own judgment to admonish or praise younger siblings about school performance; (3) mail does not get opened for 2 or 3 weeks after being received because for many low-income, immigrant families, mail frequently represents negative events such as legal notices, immigration inquiries, and bills.

It is somewhat unclear to us whether these types of hindrances to school–home communication are common to low-income immigrant families in general or just to low-income Chicano families. In any case, we have abandoned this approach and replaced it with direct contact, either in person or by telephone. Talking to parents directly has been demanding — it requires Spanish-language skills or translators to be available before 7:00 a.m. and after 10:00 p.m. and on weekends, and, in the case of the 10% of our families that have no telephone, it requires home visits to make contact. The payoffs from talking to parents directly have been tremendous, however. After just a few direct contacts from ALAS counselors, parents who were not yet "connected" to the ALAS project after a year of receiving notes at home have become strong allies and cooperative partners in designing interventions to help their children succeed in school. The most crucial result of parents dialoguing directly with ALAS counselors appears to be the parents' opportunity to assess and ultimately confirm the commitment, caring, and concern of the ALAS counselors for their children. Most of the parents of ALAS students say that they feel greatly unempowered when facing school personnel and that previous interactions with school personnel have developed much mistrust, fear, and alienation toward the educational system. Our direct contact with parents has become crucial in establishing a bond and sense of trust between the ALAS family members and counselors.

Help parents be more directive in their adolescent's life. Some preliminary research suggests that parents of school dropouts have either a more laissez-faire or more authoritarian style of parenting, rather than a more moderate approach (Rumberger, Ghatak, Poulos, Ritter, & Dornbusch, 1990). We have found that our Chicano parents are, as a rule, quite laissez-faire when it comes to setting boundaries for their adolescent sons, but quite authoritarian in setting boundaries for their daughters. Boys were frequently truant from school, wore gang-related clothes, hung out on the street, and received poor grades in school, with little or no consequences from parents. On the other hand, girls were under strict parental control when it came to social behavior such as dress and going out; however, they did not receive specific parental intervention for school absenteeism or poor school grades.

For most of the parents of ALAS students, this parenting style was not effective in successfully guiding their adolescent into a culture that was substantially different from the one in which they had been raised. Their children were not succeeding in school, had been involved with the police, and were teetering on the brink of gang involvement. Parents readily expressed concern and dissatisfaction with how their children were performing and were very open to being helped to apply different methods of guiding their offspring. ALAS counselors have taken an active role in encouraging, training, and supporting parents to give specific punishments and rewards when their adolescent does or does not meet agreed upon behavior standards.

PRELIMINARY OUTCOMES

The ALAS project is designed to work with youngsters during 3 years of junior high school. To date, we have been working in one school for almost 2 years, and a final evaluation of the project is more than a year away. We have, however, collected a variety of qualitative and quantitative data that provide the basis for a preliminary evaluation of the project. These data suggest that ALAS is successful in improving attrition, attendance, and grades for the highest-risk Chicano students participating in the project. In addition, we have documented changes to specific children to illustrate the transformation that has taken place.

Attrition

The data indicate that students in the ALAS program are much more likely to be enrolled in school than a comparable group who are not receiving ALAS services. Of the original two 45-student cohorts, 41 from the ALAS (treatment) group were still in school as of April of their eighth-grade year, compared with 33 from the non-ALAS (control) group. At this point, we have not identified how many of the school-leavers are enrolled in another school and how many have actually dropped out. The large differences in the two groups suggest much higher dropout rates for the control group.

One common reason difficult-to-teach middle school students leave school is administrative transfers, often referred to by school staff as "opportunity transfers" or by students as getting "kicked out." We have come to realize that ALAS students are at continuous risk of being administratively transferred because of their behavior, their "attitude," or their poor attendance.

Attendance

ALAS students have made significant progress in improving their attendance. Although first-semester data do not show large differences in average attendance between ALAS and non-ALAS students, they do show great differences in the extent of chronic absences. Only 5% of the ALAS students were absent more than 30 days in the first semester of eighth grade, compared with 21% of the control students. In some cases, ALAS staff were able to make remarkable changes in student behavior. Joe is one such case.

Joe, a seventh grader, stayed home from school more often than he went. Joe's mother was extremely young. She had him when she was a seventh grader attending the same middle school that Joe was dropping out of. We didn't learn this, however, until nearly the end of Joe's seventh-grade year. At that point we were told by his aunt, with whom he lived periodically, that his excessive absences (we contact families every day a student is absent) were the result of severe asthma. We were in the process of getting Joe home teaching when his mother showed up and "confessed" that Joe did not have asthma and that he simply refused to go to school.

After his mother's visit, we began picking Joe up for school. In doing this, we uncovered the complications that kept Joe from school. Joe, his mother, and three younger siblings slept in one of three relatives' houses. Which house was apparently decided spontaneously; often we would be told to pick him up at one place only to find that he hadn't slept there after all. Picking Joe up improved his attendance, but he was still absent 2 days a week. We then discovered that his sister, a year younger, was not going to school either and that the 5-year-old had not been enrolled in kindergarten because the mother had not gotten the proper inoculations. It became clear that to get Joe to school regularly, we would have to facilitate the whole family attending school. This included the mother, who had just been cut off from public assistance because she did not attend job training regularly. Through coaching the mother, delivering

TABLE 7.2 Academic outcomes for high-risk students, grade 8, semester 1

	Percentage Failed	
	---	---
Courses	Control Group ($n = 45$)	Treatment Group ($n = 45$)
English	45%	29%
Math	59%	37%
History	24%	18%
Science	24%	22%

all the children to school (the mother had no transportation), and helping the mother re-enroll in job training, we have been able to get Joe to school 90% of the time in the past 6 months.

Grades

The high-risk population that ALAS targets are students who are extremely poor performers. Our intervention, which does not focus on academics directly, is expected to increase the number of classes that students are able to pass. Preliminary data suggest we are making some improvement in this area (see Table 7.2). Future data will also examine changes in work habits and cooperation that students exhibit in their classes.

We can also point to success with particular students, as in the case of Oscar. When we first met Oscar as a seventh grader, he stood clearly apart from the other ALAS students because he was such a dependent child. Oscar was so emotionally needy that he literally clung to the arms and hands of ALAS staff. His face exuded sadness, and indeed Oscar had a very sad life. Neglected and rejected as a child, by seventh grade Oscar had lived in four step-family and grandparent configurations. According to Oscar, he had been turned out from each family because he was just too loud, too noisy, too naughty — just too hard to take care of. In the previous year Oscar had moved in with his father (whom he hadn't lived with since age 2) and a stepmother. After receiving his first report card of all fails except for PE, we put Oscar on a daily teacher feedback report. He was very resistant and expressed concern when we informed him that his father would receive daily notes at home. We requested a parent conference and set up with the father a specific home reward and penalty system for Oscar's school behavior. Daily feedback from teachers permitted ALAS staff to monitor Oscar's classwork completion and homework. We rewarded him for performance and withdrew attention when he failed to complete schoolwork. Through support and problem-solving counseling, Oscar learned to cope independently with school and peer problems. ALAS counselors also helped him come to grips with family problems and feelings of rejection. One day, near the end of seventh grade, Oscar entered the ALAS office and spontaneously announced to all present that he had discovered something. When asked what it was, Oscar responded that he had discovered that he wasn't a D person and that he wasn't a D student! Oscar is now finishing the eighth grade. He still needs daily notes sent home. And, as with most teenagers, adults have to keep on his case about homework. However, he is no longer a clinger and has "taken charge" of several younger students whom he says need help. His grades are not high, but he is passing all of his classes and even mentions now and then that he plans to go to college. Oscar was recently elected to student body office as the ninth-grade artist!

Costs

We have gathered some preliminary data on the time and resources being spent on the project. The project is currently funded at about $200,000 a year, including not only intervention costs, but also the costs of conducting the research and of evaluation of the project and auxiliary activities. Most of the intervention or program costs are related to personnel, particularly project staff who work at the school daily.

In order to get some idea of the amount and use of personnel time for actually running the ALAS program, project personnel periodically are required to keep detailed time-use records. These records are helpful in determining which activities require the most time from project staff. Ultimately, they will be used to determine which of the project activities are the most costly. A tabulation of staff time for one week in the second year of the project is shown in Table 7.3. The data indicate that ALAS staff spend much of their time directly on intervention activities — problem-solving training, attendance monitoring, and preparing progress reports. Although student bonding, in isolation, appears to occupy a small amount of staff time, as the previous discussion pointed out, most of the contact ALAS staff have with students promotes bonding.

The data indicate that project staff spend almost 150 hours a week on intervention activities. This averages out to a bit more than one hour a week per student at an average cost of less than $15. Over a 35-week school year, the cost per student would be about $500. These costs are partially offset by additional revenues — currently about $25 per student a day — that school districts receive due to improved student attendance. Of

TABLE 7.3 ALAS **program: Preliminary time and cost analysis**

	Average Per Week		
Program Activities	Hours	Percentage	Cost
Problem solving training	29.1	19.7%	$397.80
Attendance monitoring	17.1	11.6	127.33
Progress reports	32.2	21.8	258.73
Parent contacts	12.8	8.7	154.51
Student bonding	2.5	1.7	32.22
Intervention meetings	18.0	12.2	255.90
Intervention supervision	10.0	6.8	263.80
Project administration	25.8	17.5	290.55
TOTAL	147.5	100%	$1,780.84
Per student ($n = 123$)			$14.48

course, these figures do not include other direct and contributed resources for the project, which will be analyzed when the final cost evaluation is conducted. But they do suggest that significant resources are needed to even begin to address the needs of the most disadvantaged students who attend urban schools. Yet these costs are easy to justify economically when compared with the large social costs associated with dropouts (Rumberger, 1987).

SUMMARY AND CONCLUSIONS

In 1913, Helen Todd, a factory inspector in Chicago, systematically questioned 500 children of immigrants about working and going to school: Would they choose to continue working long hours in the sweatshops, or would they choose to go to school if they did not have to work? Four hundred and twelve children told her that they preferred factory labor to the monotony, humiliation, and even sheer cruelty that they experienced in school (Kliebard, 1986).

Eighty years later, the high dropout rates among Mexican-American children suggest that many children of immigrants still find schools to be joyless places. Far too many of today's schools literally drive Chicano youths into the streets, or into dead-end jobs, or into welfare lines—just as in 1913.

The middle school in which our project takes place is not atypical of urban schools attended by many poor, Latino youngsters. And like other schools, it is too often a place of little learning, much rejection, and sense-less cruelty. The ALAS project is attempting to counter this environment for the most problematic and lowest-achieving youngsters in the school. Although originally designed to focus on problem solving, monitoring, and training, ALAS staff persons have expanded their intervention and become more involved in support and advocacy for students and their families. In doing so, we have developed a series of principles to help cross three cultural boundaries that exist in the school: school culture, student culture, and Chicano culture. Some preliminary data suggest we are help-ing our students to successfully address the negative school culture that they experience and to remain in school. Yet our goals of helping these children remain formidable. As other reformers have pointed out, even major attempts to reform schools are not always able to change the things that matter most — a positive school culture that supports children and promotes their learning.

REFERENCES

Berger, L. (1991, August 22). Boy, 13, mingling with members of gang shot. *Los Angeles Times*, pp. B1, B10.

California Department of Finance. (1991). School enrollment projections. Mimeo.

California State Department of Education. (1989). *Performance report for California schools: 1989*. Sacramento: Author.

Casas, J., & Furlong, M. (1986). *Santa Barbara student success story: A final report*. (Available from the Santa Barbara School Districts, Santa Barbara, CA)

Catterall, J. S. (1987, November). On the social costs of dropping out of school. *High School Journal, 71*, 19–30.

Clark, T. A. (1987). Preventing school dropouts What can be done? *CBC Quarterly, 7*(4), 1–8.

Committee for Economic Development. (1987). *Children in need: Investment strategies for the educationally disadvantaged*. New York: Author.

Delgado-Gaitan, C. (1988). Sociocultural adjustment to school and academic achievement. *Journal of Early Adolescence, 8*(1), 63–82.

Dornbusch, S. M., Ritter, P. L., Leiderman, P. H., Roberts, D. F., & Fraleigh, M. J. (1987). The relation of parenting style to adolescent school performance. *Child Development, 58*, 1244–1257.

Ekstrom, R. B., Goertz, M. E., Pollack, J. M., & Rock, D. A. (1986). Who drops out of high school and why? Findings from a national study. *Teachers College Record, 87*(3), 356–373.

Gerber, M. M., & Semmel, M. I. (1984). Teacher as imperfect test: Reconceptualizing the referral process. *Educational Psychologist, 19*(3), 137–147.

Kavale, K., Alper, A., & Purcell, L. (1981). Behavior disorders, reading disorders and teacher perceptions. *The Exceptional Child, 28*, 114–118.

Kliebard, H. (1986). *The struggle for the American curriculum: 1893–1958*. Boston: Routledge & Kegan Paul.

Larson, K. A. (1989a, March). *Early secondary school adjustment for at-risk and highest-risk students.* Paper presented at the annual meeting of the American Educational Research Association, San Francisco.

Larson, K. A. (1989b). Problem solving training for enhancing school achievement in high-risk young adolescents. *Remedial and Special Education, 10*(5), 32–43.

Larson, K. A. (1989c). Youthful offender's success on parole: The efficacy of teaching social problem solving skills. In S. Duguid (Ed.), *Yearbook of correctional education.* Burnaby, BC, Canada: Simon Fraser University and the Correctional Education Association.

Natriello, G., McDill, E. L., & Pallas, A. M. (1990). *Schooling disadvantaged children: Racing against catastrophe.* New York: Teachers College Press.

Ogbu, J. U. (1989). The individual in collective adaptation: A framework for focusing on academic underperformance and dropping out among involuntary minorities. In L. Weis, E. Farrar, & H. G. Petrie (Eds.), *Dropouts from school: Issues, dilemmas, and solutions.* Albany: State University of New York Press.

Rumberger, R. W. (1987). High school dropouts: A review of issues and evidence. *Review of Educational Research, 57*(2), 101–121.

Rumberger, R. W. (1990). Second chance for high school dropouts: The costs and benefits of dropout recovery programs in the United States. In D. Inbar (Ed.), *Second chance in education: An interdisciplinary and international perspective* (pp. 227–250). Philadelphia: Falmer Press.

Rumberger, R. W. (1991). Chicano dropouts: A review of research and policy issues. In R. Valencia (Ed.), *Chicano school failure and success* (pp. 64–89). New York: Falmer Press.

Rumberger, R. W., Ghatak, R., Poulos, G., Ritter, P. L., & Dornbusch, S. M. (1990). Family influences on dropout behavior in one California high school. *Sociology of Education, 63,* 283–299.

Shavelson, R., Cadwell, J., & Izu, T. (1977). Teachers' sensitivity to the reliability of information in making pedagogical decisions. *American Educational Research Journal, 14,* 83–97.

Stern, D., Paik, I., Catterall, J. S., & Nakata, Y. (1989). Labor market experience of teenagers with and without high school diplomas. *Economics of Education Review, 8,* 233–246.

Trueba, H., & Delgado-Gaitan, C. (Eds.). (1988). *School and society: Learning content through culture.* New York: Praeger.

U.S. Bureau of the Census. (1988). *School enrollment — Social and economic characteristics of students: October 1985 and 1984* (Current Population Report, Series P. 20, No. 462). Washington, DC: Government Printing Office.

U.S. Department of Education. (1990). *National goals for education.* Washington, DC: Author.

U.S. General Accounting Office. (1987). *School dropouts: Survey of local programs.* GAO/HRD-87-108. Washington, DC: U.S. Government Printing Office.

U.S. National Center for Education Statistics. (1991). *Digest of education statistics, 1990.* Washington, DC: U.S. Government Printing Office.

Wehlage, G. G., & Rutter, R. A. (1986). Dropping out: How much do schools contribute to the problem? *Teachers College Record, 87*(3), 374–392.

CHAPTER 8

Chart[er]ing Urban School Reform

MICHELLE FINE

This is the story of the first 3 years of high school reform; a story of reform in the midst. Our focus has been on the comprehensive high schools, those schools that sit at the bottom of a deeply stratified urban layering of secondary schools, where 80% of the city's students are assigned, disproportionately those who are low income, overage, African-American and Latino, and those who possess depressing academic biographies. While by most definitions these students would be called "at risk," our intent is to demonstrate that the notions of both *educational risk* and *educational resilience* reside more in the contexts of schooling than in the bodies of those students saddled with labels. Our strategy for reform has had two key elements: to fundamentally rethink and restructure the neighborhood high schools and to radically reform the central district.

This chapter will examine closely how the Philadelphia Schools Collaborative, a not-for-profit 501(c)(3), has worked at the interior of schools, with educators and parents, to transform existing schools in ways that have begun to produce increases in student outcomes and to reflect evidence of substantial teacher engagement and parental involvement. I will then review briefly the central district issues that are now percolating up from the schools as they pursue transformation. The radical transformation of urban central districts (and of state financing formulas) is, of course, a much larger topic than can be taken up in this chapter.

THE CONTEXT OF RESTRUCTURING

In 1988, a large urban school district began discussions with the Pew Charitable Trusts Foundation for what would ultimately be an $8.3 million grant to support the restructuring of the comprehensive high schools citywide. When the grant came to fruition, the Philadelphia Schools Collaborative was carved out as a 501(c)(3), located both inside and outside the district, working closely and collaboratively with the local teachers' union.

The task of the collaborative was to enable educators and parents to "restructure" the instructional approaches, systems, parent and community relations, assessment practices, and transitions into and out of the neighborhood high school. The collaborative became a forum, bringing together educators, parents, university and corporate representatives, the central district, and the labor union to discuss, imagine, and create educational communities for urban adolescents. With a small staff and substantial resources, the collaborative could provoke and respond to conversations about what is and what could be. Over the past 3 years, we have been engaged in this work, pressing issues at the district, union, school, and "charter" (i.e., school-within-a-school) levels. The question driving the work of the collaborative was not "how do we create alternative schools for urban youth" or "how do we stimulate shared decision making and school-based management for urban schools?" Surrounded by a statewide movement for vouchers for parent use in choosing public or private schools for their children, we pursued the big, systemic educational question—"How do we transform a system of deeply troubled high schools into many small, educationally and emotionally rich communities of learners with existing teachers, in existing schools, for existing students, and in existing communities, long abandoned by the federal, state, and local governments?" The task was ambitious.

In this city, the work of reform has been premised on the radical rethinking of "what is a school," the dramatic investment in critical, transformative conversations among teachers and parents, and the belief that reform is successful only if student outcomes are ultimately affected. While the improvement of labor conditions for teachers and the engagement of parents at school were central to our strategy, the task was to transform urban, public high schools for students at or near risk into educational and democratic communities engaged in ongoing public conversations about "what could be."

This restructuring work has developed within the high schools over the past 3 years with *charters* as the basic unit. Designed by and for teachers, students, and parents, these charters are small academic and emotional communities organized within high schools. Restructuring through charters is based on a framework with six critical elements.

1. *Governance: Communication and decision making.* Within these high schools, decision making is organized around principles of shared decision making/school-based management (SD/SBM). The first task of

shared governance is developing an educational plan for the school with provisions for charter development. The second task is developing a shared governance plan to support these charters. Charters are organized internally through shared decision making.

2. *School organization.* In high schools being restructured, the typical organization is dramatically transformed into educational communities called charters. The primary intellectual and student support work of secondary education occurs within these charters.

3. *Professional development: Curriculum and leadership development.* Teachers are granted time, space, and images to pursue charter-based professional development so that curricular and instructional strategies can engage students in active, multicultural, collaborative, and in some instances accelerated learning.

4. *Community: Student and family supports.* The relationship between school and community becomes enriched, both on a school-wide and charter-specific basis. Clear attention is focused on parental involvement, access to community-based services for adolescents in the school, relations with employers, and sites for community service implemented as part of the curriculum of charter schools.

5. *Assessment/Evaluation.* Student assessment strategies include some standardized testing but even more serious investment in portfolio, exhibition, and other performance-based assessment strategies. Each SD/SBM school is provided with a detailed, quantitative data base for tracking student progress within and across charter schools and with support for performance-based graduation projects.

6. *Partnerships: Focus on transitions.* Charters become the locus for school-based partnerships with universities, social service agencies, and employers. *All* partnerships with comprehensive high schools, to the extent possible, are connected to the needs of charters, and many are directed at facilitating transitions into ninth grade and transitions out of high school into college and/or employment.

The idea is that full schools be "charterized." Two to four hundred students constitute a charter, and they take classes together throughout their high school years. Sharing responsibility for this cohort of students are 10 to 12 core teachers who have a common preparation period each day and invent curriculum, pedagogies, and assessment strategies that reflect a commitment to a common intellectual project. Charters result in diplomas and prepare all students for college and/or employment; the student bodies of charters must, by definition, be heterogeneous.

Charters are not "programs" that meet once a week. They are not "transitional projects" for ninth graders or students in trouble. They are not pull-out remediation or advancement for students in special need or "with special gifts." No one charter should exist within a traditional high school (or it will be eaten—as we all know from experience). And charters should not be tracks. Instead, they work like intellectual and emotional communities of adults and students, teachers and parents, counselors and university faculty, who nurture together an engaging educational experience across 4 years and enjoy the richness of deep, sustained, and ongoing relationships, within and across generations, inside an urban, public high school. This is the vision.

Within this framework of restructuring, a fair amount has been accomplished over the past 3 years. In order to understand how the six elements of this framework permeate and transform daily classroom life, we need to telescope in on the development and characteristics of charters.

THE STORY OF CHARTERS: REJECTING "AT RISK" AND INVENTING "COMMUNITIES OF LEARNERS"

The work of the collaborative was begun in 1989. Through a series of conversations, urban high school teachers helped the staff of the Philadelphia Schools Collaborative imagine "what could be" the ideal educational experience in a comprehensive high school. In meeting rooms and in living rooms, after food and wine, we invented, together, images of small, intimate, and intellectually rich communities in which faculty would work closely and over time with each other and a stable group of students. These teachers cherished the idea of working within interdisciplinary teams and with an ongoing cohort of students. They bristled, however, at the idea of creating these communities in "your existing schools, with your present colleagues." They shuddered when we noted that charters would begin in the ninth grade. One teacher gasped, "Ninth graders! They're all hormones and feet!"

The point of restructuring was to engage *existing* comprehensive high schools in the task of full school transformation. That is, all teachers, staff, and students, as well as parents, it was felt, needed to feel attached to and be engaged with academic communities from ninth grade through twelfth. These communities would be their charters. And these charters would be what made the difference between "students at risk" and "educational communities of resilience." As one teacher explained, "More middle-class kids have the support and community and networks. These kids need it—and the charter delivers just that. A safe community in which they can learn, experiment, and be nurtured."

We have learned quickly the depths of "communitarian damage" in these schools, and the work it required to heal emotionally and engage intellectually. The damage of working in a deeply hierarchical bureaucracy shows in a diminished sense of possibility for community voiced by teachers. Nevertheless, at the core of restructuring lay both aims — to create relationally rich charters that care for the emotional and social needs and wants of students, and also to engage the intellects and passions of educators and students. The combination is essential. The point was not, simply (or naively) to "increase self-esteem" or to hug more, but to work with the long-neglected minds and meanings of these students. It meant taking teachers and students seriously as intellectuals. Most of our resources have been invested in "resuscitating" the sense of possibility held by teachers, strengthening their discipline-based work, and facilitating intellectually rich interdisciplinary work.

For some teachers, it was a chance of a lifetime. "This is why I entered education in the first place." For others, it was an assault on autonomy. "Create community with *my* colleagues, and *these* students? Have you met *my* colleagues, have you seen *these* students?" The work has been amazing.

Throughout the 22 public, comprehensive high schools in this city, 94 charters exist for grades 9–12. All 22 comprehensive high schools have developed, at minimum, two charters apiece; six of these schools are committed to fully charter their programs. In these schools, all students and all faculty belong to one of these within-school communities. A full one-half of the charters have been "home grown"; that is, they have been developed by interdisciplinary groups of teachers working in the schools. Charters are present-day versions of what we used to call "schools-within-schools," but they have quite specific criteria.

It is hard to recognize how radically different "life in the charters" is from typical "life in a comprehensive high school." So below I try to unravel the differences.

School Organization Before Charters

Before charters, most students in these high schools had six classes a year; were heavily tracked, with different students in most of their classes and different teachers every year; and they belonged, emotionally, to no *unit*. Anonymity prevailed, and only 45–55% of the typical ninth-grade class ever made it to tenth grade — much less graduation.

Teachers, likewise, were locked in an anonymous maze. They taught 165–180 students in a day, sharing them as a group with no one. Cut rates, discipline problems, and truancy were extreme. Discipline and counseling responsibilities were separated from teachers' work. Classroom educators enjoyed what some called autonomy, had (by all accounts) no power, and suffered what others called isolation. They rarely talked with colleagues at their school about their classroom work and typically were blamed for school failure. Most teachers knew little about the "personal" lives of students; counselors worked through the alphabet, dividing students from A through Z by the total counselors available; and parents were invited to school either because their child was in trouble or because there was a large, school-wide parents night, typically with terribly embarrassing attendance.

School Organization Within Charters

Within charters, students still have six classes a year, but they may be two at a time with deep concentration for 10 weeks for two credits over the period of time. Alternatively, they may have three classes a semester, or four "on site" at school and two "in the community" through employment and/or community service. They know the other students and the faculty with whom they share a charter, because they have an ongoing life (i.e., 4 years) together. In some charters, faculty have divided the students into "family groups" so that all students have one adult (maybe a teacher, counselor, aide, or janitor) with whom the personal connection is deep, sustained, and confidential over 4 years.

Teachers still have typically large urban loads, but they share their students with their charter colleagues. Common prep times are spent discussing curriculum, instruction, and assessment issues; worrying about and delighting over individual students; planning family nights for the "significant adults and children" in the lives of their students; strategizing on how to get Christina over the death of her father, Paul not to move down south with his grandmother, or Mr. Rodriguez not to deprive Cantada from the charter trip to visit a college.

Groups of charter teachers, with administrators and parents, are now involved in school-based policy making and in year-round ongoing seminars of their own design. Some are studying and inventing authentic assessments. Others are integrating vocational and academic work. Many are creating interdisciplinary curricula, developing multicultural classrooms, infusing technology into instruction, and sharing, with charter teachers from across the city, ideas on teaching and learning. Within charters, faculty are engaged in rich, critical conversations about the nature of learning and teaching in urban America.

Some teachers admit that their involvement in charters has provoked a sharp shift in their perspective on students. At a conference for charter educators, one of our teachers spoke passionately to a citywide group of faculty on just this topic.

> I have always thought of myself as a good teacher; but not always so creative. I have never enjoyed teaching as much as I do now. I am learning from my colleagues in the charter and, the most amazing thing, I never thought my students wanted to see themselves as students! We would all give the class away to the most disruptive students. Now the students tell Charlie to "shut up, and let us learn."

We can now appreciate how hierarchical, disempowering bureaucracies can keep teachers from seeing and hearing students' voices and from working with colleagues on "what could be" (Fine, 1990). Indeed, with these structural changes, teachers have become more radical in their demands over the past 3 years. Those most engaged in charter life now say, "Allow us to work over time, as an educational community, with this group of students and parents and with each other." For them that translates into:

> Don't bounce teachers out of the charter because the school has a momentary drop in enrollment, and don't appoint the next most senior person on the list to our charter. Teachers need individual and collective stability, we need time during the day to plan, reflect, and build curriculum, and we need to interview our peers to ensure that they know, and we know, how we can live together as a community. (composite comments, 1992)

These issues would be central to the making of any community, but they have been, until now, considered almost impossible to raise, much less resolve, in a bureaucratic urban school district. Working as a team of teachers on the issues of organizational change, curriculum development, and instructional strategies, many charter-based teachers now report feeling "reinvigorated." From charter faculty, we note that teachers who have taught together in more alienating arrangements for 20–30 years, are now providing each other with support and recognition for engagement, experimentation, and their contributions to improved student outcomes. Simply stated, charters have become a compelling vehicle through which a sense of connection among teachers, students, and parents has evolved.

Parents of high school students who have most recently been "folded" into restructuring work now comment that their relationships with schools have deepened because their involvement with charters allows them in, *not* for a discipline problem, truancy, or a special education referral, but as members of the charter community. One mother of a charter student reflected:

When he was first in the charter, I thought, "Something new again."
But then I saw him flourish, and the teachers took such an interest in
him. And in me. They called me, and we worked together. The
charter has given me something to connect to. Through it I became
interested in the school and, really, that was part of why I was willing
to serve on the governance council. I feel like it is my school, now,
too.

Based on preliminary evidence, parental involvement seems to be increasing in quantity and deepening in quality through the charter school experience.

CHARTERS AND STUDENT OUTCOMES

We now have good evidence (Foley & Crull, 1984; Meier, 1987,
1991a, 1991b; Oxley, 1990; Wolf & McMullan, 1988) that small educational communities, such as charters, can enhance academic and social
outcomes for students, including "holding power," attendance, achievement, promotion, sense of engagement, democratic participation, and
parental involvement (see also Wehlage, 1989). This is particularly true
for low-income, "low-achieving" students whose needs exceed most students', whose desire for relational attachment runs high, and for whom
dropping out bears disproportionate economic and social consequences.
Charters have become places where "risk" can transform into "resilience"
in a community.

Pertinent Research

The educational research that bears most directly on academic life
inside charters comes from Diana Oxley's 1990 study of "weak" versus
"well-designed" secondary school houses in New York City. Her in-depth
analysis of New York City house systems (which are similar to charters)
indicates the following features are critical to the success of house plans:

- Schools are organized into house units with no more than 500 students
  and a core teaching staff that instructs most, if not all, students' courses
  throughout their stay in school.
- Houses are divided into subunits containing an interdisciplinary teacher
  team and enough students to allow team members to instruct their
  required classloads within the subunit.
- Student support staff are attached to each house and work exclusively

with house students and collaboratively with each other and instructional teams.

- Extracurricular activities are organized within each house to give students more opportunities to participate in school life and to develop valuable skills not ordinarily pursued in the classroom.
- House classes, activities, and staff offices are physically located in adjacent rooms within the school building.
- Houses operate in semiautonomous fashion with the capacity to determine house policy, select staff, allocate resources, and discipline students.

Quantitative analyses compared small and large schools with what Oxley considered weak house designs with small and large schools with "strong" designs on both direct and indirect effects predicted on the basis of theory. Findings indicated that house systems or houses with stronger designs (more autonomy and identity for houses) had more positive effects on staff and students than did other houses. Well-designed houses, irrespective of school size, outperformed weak ones in large schools on most measures, including students' relationships with peers, teachers, and support staff; extracurricular participation; sense of community; academic performance; and teachers' knowledge of students' all around performance. In large schools, well-designed houses performed as well as weakly designed systems on most measures, and performed better with respect to sense of community and teachers' knowledge of student performance (Oxley, 1990).

Data from Charters

Charters are struggling to become learning communities that embody the very pieces of restructuring we would consider essential to full school transformation: democratic governance; creation of small intellectual communities with school-based, ongoing professional development; authentic assessment; deep parental involvement; and longer-term relationships between faculty and students resulting in college and/or work placements. Of the 94 charters in the school district, all are struggling to capture these layers of transformation. A few are exceptional. Most are mediocre. Many are struggling. None, however, is worse than the full, anonymous, bureaucratic school out of which it was designed.

There are still some schools in which charters look a lot like "tracks," and a few schools in which only two charters exist. Yet a growing number of charters are designed to be heterogeneously grouped, and as of September 1993, a number of SD/SBM schools were fully chartered. When we review our data, we can see first a dreary story of public high schooling in general. We could leave the analysis there and opt for vouchers, but instead we press on, noticing the moments of real possibility for change. But before we dive into charter data, a methodological and indeed substantive note is in order. There remains, still, an uneven distribution of special education and repeating ninth graders who are rostered outside of charters. Beliefs in tracking, the need for homogeneity, and categorical groupings are more deeply embedded in schools than we anticipated. And so these conversations among educators continue. Charter to noncharter comparisons must always keep this caveat in mind.

When we tell the quantitative stories of student outcomes and restructuring, we look closely at two broad questions — (1) Is this combination of restructuring strategies associated with discernible differences in the academic lives of students — that is, do charters make a difference in what students learn? (2) Is it fair to argue that the infusion of monies for the explicit purpose of school-based transformation — shared decision making/ school-based management — produces differences in student performance? To both questions we can now offer, with 2 years of data, a definite yes. (For a complete description of results from the formal evaluation of charters, see Center for Assessment and Policy Development, Final Report, 1992, and Richard Clark's evaluation memo, 1992.)

Academic improvements. Students in charters tend to outachieve their noncharter peers (although overrepresentation of repeaters among noncharters is a methodological confound). Further, we can see that selected comparisons of demographically comparable ninth graders within schools substantiate the positive impact of charters. For example, at one high school 77% of ninth-grade students in charters earned sufficient numbers of credits to move from ninth to tenth grade, whereas only 30% of noncharter ninth-grade students were promoted. At another school 59% of "charter" ninth graders were promoted, compared with 48% of noncharter, new ninth graders, and 41% of *all* (including repeaters) ninth graders not in charters.

Over time, the impact of 2 years of restructuring on students in grades 9–12, across comprehensive high schools, demonstrates steady incremental improvements in student outcomes. There have been substantial increases over time in the percentage of students passing major subjects (English, history, mathematics and science). For example, in one restructured high school, the percentages of ninth graders passing English classes were 78% for those in charters and 54% for those not in charters; history, 71% versus 41%; mathematics, 72% versus 47%; and science, 80% versus

50%. The rates for ninth and tenth graders are particularly noteworthy, since these are the grades that restructuring has most directly affected.

The impact of external investment and shared decision making/school-based management. Our data suggest that high investment for strategic restructuring can pay off; shared decision making can be associated with improved student outcomes; and, indeed, schools that started off in the worst academic shape ("low starting-point schools") seem to generate the most substantial initial increases in course passage and promotion rates. For example, between the 1988–89 and 1990–91 school years, the percentage of ninth graders passing major subjects at low starting-point schools increased 11% in English, 10% in social studies, 4% in mathematics, and 7% in science. The increases were similar at medium starting-point schools (6%, 11%, 7%, and 7%, respectively), but relatively small at high starting-point schools (2%, less than 1%, 4% and less than 1%). In looking at 12 schools that entered the shared decision making/school-based management process during the 1990–91 year, we again found that the increase in percentages passing major subjects favored students in charters: In English classes, the increase was 8% versus 3%; in social studies, 8% versus 7%; in mathematics, 8% versus 1%, and in science, 7% versus 3%.

Our primary work over the past 2 years has been facilitating a school-based capacity for radical transformation. Working primarily through the adults, we were surprised to find early, discernible improvements in student outcomes. We believe this to have occurred because *teams of adults* focus on school- and classroom-based changes. Most other reforms work with single teacher volunteers who are pulled out of their schools, "trained," and returned to what must feel like hostile environments. For this reason, we have insisted on working with teacher teams so as to accelerate the pace at which student outcomes can be affected.

As with the Oxley data, our initial evidence from those charters we would consider "well-designed" is very encouraging. Students, even those who began high school "at risk" (e.g., low-achieving and unmotivated), do improve, in the aggregate, in terms of "survival" — as measured by attendance, grades, and level of credit accumulation — relative to their noncharter peers. Charter students' attendance seems to be up, as are their course passage and promotion rates. We expect, with early encouragement, that graduation and college-going rates will also be enhanced after 4 years of charter life. And, as with the students, teachers' sense of themselves as intellectuals and professionals within charters has been enhanced. We hear delight from many educators, and some are requesting help to try new approaches. From these requests, for example, we began to employ social work interns in classrooms as support staff to teachers in charters.

THE POLITICS OF REFORM—ENGAGING EDUCATORS IN COLLECTIVE CHANGE

When we first entered the work of restructuring, a fair number of teachers in the school district had already been engaged with professional development networks within and beyond the city, including the rich experiences with PATHS/PRISM (see Lieberman & McLaughlin, 1992). The challenge, then, was to translate what had been rich, individual, faculty development projects into sustained, collective, school-based transformations toward improved student outcomes. This proved not to be such an easy shift. While some teachers remarked that they had felt alone within their schools, they were nevertheless energized by local and national professional networks and quite weary of trying to create school-based change. They were well socialized to a centralized, hierarchical system; they were used to little freedom and no authority.

Early on, I naively thought that if only educators could be free to dream, individually and collectively, to imagine and ask for the conditions of labor and schooling they sought, then they would produce rich, educationally progressive notions of "what could be." But, the shrinking pool of students citywide meant that the last time a secondary English teacher or social studies teacher was hired was 1972. Teachers in the school district had lived through the installation of state-mandated graduation credits, generation of centralized "initiatives," and piloted school-based projects; they had worked with the same colleagues for more than 20 years under disempowering structures. Union–district relations had been deeply adversarial, although they had improved recently. Budget cuts from the state and city were imminent, and the principals had voted to join the Teamsters union during this administration.

So, at those early meetings, when asked to imagine "what could be," teachers sought more freedom from district prescriptions, and they envisioned "fewer overage students" (the school district had a promotion policy that resulted in 20% to 25% of ninth graders being substantially overage), "more tracking," and "more special education placements." It was not that these teachers were ill-informed about best practices or harsh in their judgments about students. They had the categories of experience that they had, and from these they generated images of what could be—"more teachers and counselors."

So the work of reform was clear. Neither top–down nor naively bottom–up, the collaborative worked with educators and parents through *ongoing critical conversations* about practice, which came to be known as guided school-based change. What we failed to anticipate, however, was the depth of "communitarian damage" that had infiltrated, divided, and defined the culture of their schools. Even those principals and faculty who were still energized and enthusiastic could barely imagine working *with* their weary colleagues to create rich educational communities. Few could imagine that the district would allow them the room for radical change, and fewer could imagine a sufficiently collective effort among colleagues to produce improvements in student outcomes. The damage ran deep and wide. It took about 2 years to begin to melt it (Sarason, 1992). In many instances, we are still slogging through power struggles. I consider it progress that at least people are fighting aloud.

We were committed to transform *with*, not *despite* and not *around*, existing public schools. Radical vision meant slow, incremental changes in practice. With teachers and parents, this work has been terrific. Each has a vested interest, ultimately, in understanding the needs, strengths, and passions of students. Most, when supported, are willing to stretch to get there. But it took a while to move out of "despair" and into a sense of possibility.

DILEMMAS OF REFORM

Across 3 years, the development and impact of charters has been much more encouraging than we anticipated over such a short period of time. Charters are up in numbers, transforming how teachers, students, and parents feel about the work of schooling; as pointed out earlier, the charters are already resulting in what seem to be modest increments in students' persistence in school, attendance, course passage, and promotion rates. But we are entering the next generation of dilemmas, struggles, fights, and, indeed, battles over how to invent a district committed to serious, effective, caring, and intellectually rich education within the inner city.

Some of our dilemmas derive almost "naturally" from the commitment to transforming "what has been" into "what could be," rather than peeling off motivated students and parents into voucher schemes, new or alternative schools, or magnets. Many are fundamental dilemmas of organizational transformation in the public sphere. Dilemmas of bureaucracy emerge because educators and parents are interrupting a dehumanizing discourse of rationality and efficiency with a percolating vision of educational democracies and a press for improved student outcomes.

Quite a few are the dilemmas of working in the urban public sector in the 1990s, inheriting and combating a Reagan/Bush legacy that nationally has constrained the lives and dreams of low-income African-American and Latino youngsters and their families. Below I review these dilemmas within charters, schools, and the central district.

Dilemma One: Doing "What Is" as We Envision What "Could Be"

In the midst of restructuring we live inside a moment of institutional schizophrenia. A micro-example of a macro-problem, teachers are caught between a radically new world and the relatively untransformed bureaucracies that stand around them and in their heads, rigid and controlling.

The work of (charter) restructuring within existing (school) contexts is markedly different from creating new schools, alternative schools, or privatization with eager, "willing" volunteers. Each is differently exhausting and invigorating. However, in creating rich educational settings within existing bureaucracies, educators and parents must juggle contradictions and invent educational possibilities in the midst of enormous educational constraints and hierarchical resistance. Trying to grow a series of educational communities from amidst the crusty, fragmented organizations we have called urban high schools requires that parents and educators who are front-runners do double duty—create "what could be" and transform "what has been" in our schools and in the central district. In the process, they offend almost every vested interest at some point. The political reverberations may be enormous.

Dilemma Two: Autonomy Versus Community

When we undertook restructuring, we were naive about the realities of life inside secondary urban schools. We didn't realize that one of the only perks left in the "comps" was autonomy—getting to shut one's door. We also didn't realize that few reforms in the past asked educators to transform their individual and collective practices, as well as systemic policies and practices, in ways that would improve student outcomes. So we didn't know that among educators left in the comprehensive high schools, few would initially believe that full-blown institutional, collective change would be possible. Now, an ongoing struggle for faculty and students is how to create charters as rich communities that respect both collective work and autonomy. At present, much of charter work actually begins to address what seemed to be contradictory needs of educators— for autonomy and community. We have come to see that these needs are necessarily co-existent. That struggle persists.

Dilemma Three: We Can Only Educate—We Can't
Deal with Their Personal Needs Too!

Early on, this line was common among the educators with whom we worked. That is no longer so. Working within charters has opened up the "personal" lives of students and faculty. And there is no going back. It took time for us all to realize that there are good reasons that faculty get "burned out" or "callous" to students' lives. Educators today are picking up the pieces of a society ravaged by class and race stratification, and they are being held accountable for turning students who carry the weight of the bottom of the social hierarchy into compliant, loyal, educated, and optimistic citizens. In particular, high school educators inherit histories of academic defeat that they need to reverse. In this process, many educators, although certainly not all, have opted *not* to know the pains and struggles experienced by their students. "If I knew," said one very committed teacher, "what would I do?" And yet, charter-based education takes us deeply into the lives, strengths, and survival strategies of urban adolescents.

The emotional, social, and psychological challenges of young adolescents are played out in our schools, masked as attendance problems, acting out, discipline, or even learning problems. We now know, in charters, that the problems of "at-risk youth" can often be unraveled to reflect homelessness, family or community violence, learning difficulties, or cultural differences—the kinds of issues public education has ostensibly stayed away from. But we now know that young people import these issues into our schools. The dilemmas for those of us committed to reform is to figure out how to support educators who are willing, but understandably reluctant and sometimes ill-equipped, to "take on" the lives of these youngsters. This dilemma asks how we can create, in charters, safe places to discuss and to educate through the social issues that present themselves like embarrassing "personal problems," so that students don't have to feel alone with the difficulties of living that so many have survived so well.

Dilemma Four: Bottom–Up Images, Multicultural Curriculum,
and Heteroge.ieous Groupings

At the collaborative, we were committed to restructuring being a bottom–up design (that is, working for ideas and strategies generated primarily by educators and parents). We were also committed, however, to what was known to be the "best of practice." So we pressed for multicultural education, mainstreaming of students labeled in need of special education, heterogeneous groupings of students, and teachers/parents' substantial roles in decision making. We didn't realize that these two commitments are not necessarily compatible within institutions of urban public education today. For instance, given the research on educational problems that derive from deep and rigid segregation and tracking, we knew that charters should be "mixed ability." Yet, we heard early on from many educators and parents raised and practiced in the comforts of tracking that this would be impossible or educationally irresponsible. Indeed, most schools exempted ninth-grade "repeaters" from their first year of restructuring, and many, initially, worked "around" special education.

So we continue to struggle with how to get more educators and parents to imagine the virtues of heterogeneity, when it looks like, feels like, and may indeed mean more work for them and less attention for their children. This is particularly tricky for principals of some schools that have become "last resorts" and who want an elite track to attract "good" students, for educators who have accrued enough seniority to be placed out of lower-track teaching, for educators working within special education, or for parents of "advanced-track" students. Further, we wrestle with how to get federal and state regulations sufficiently pried open (e.g., Chapter 1, special education, Perkins monies, dropout prevention grants) so as to enable, and not constrain, the mixed-ability groupings of students. We have begun to move toward school-wide use of Chapter 1 monies, integration of special education students and faculty, and school-basing of Perkins. But these shifts are slow, hard, and often place us in politically treacherous territory. Finally, we debate how to get each of us to shift consciousness so as to recognize that students are not born into a track, but indeed develop over time into their own forms of intelligence. Being educated is a process, not a given. This is only slowly sinking in as an insight for us all.

Dilemma Five: Efficiency and Efficacy

This dilemma is, perhaps, the most powerful. Today, in the 1990s, it is no longer a mystery how to educate, and even educate well, low-achieving, low-income urban students, those smothered in the perverse box called "at risk." Collectively, we have the knowledge, methods, and assessment strategies to transform our classrooms into engaging, critical, and creative sites of intellectual growth and personal development. What is a mystery in the 1990s is whether we have the political will to enable urban public schools serving low-income students of color to flourish.

If we are serious about creating intellectually engaging and personally supportive communities of adults and students, we must work to ensure that intellectual depth, continuity, care, community, and trust are nourished inside those public high schools that have been deprived of such a history. It is important to realize, from our experience, that restructured schools are not more expensive than traditional, failing schools, although resources need to be deployed in radically different ways; the central district bureaucracy needs to be trimmed enormously; fragmentation of "innovation" must come to a halt; and state monies for larger graduating classes (instead of dropouts) must be forthcoming. However, we also realize that it does take substantial investment to get from "here" to "there."

The question that we are now facing asks, is *institutionalization* of reform an oxymoron? Can the radical transformation of schools into autonomous communities survive within the public sphere? Can we collectively and seriously reinvent the public sphere of public education to be a contested site of what Ann Swidler (1990) would call the Good Society, in which the "vested" but also shared interests of educators, students, and parents can engage together in a sense of community?

LOOKING BACK/MOVING FORWARD

Eight million dollars and 3 years later, five major policy conclusions can be drawn from the evaluation of the first phase of the Philadelphia Schools Collaborative.

1. We can make a difference in existing, urban comprehensive high schools, with existing faculties, "at-risk" students, and their families. School-based restructuring, as a relentlessly supported strategic agenda focusing on transformed governance, instruction, structure, assessment, and student supports, appears to be associated with improved student outcomes even in one of the most poverty-ridden school districts in the state.
2. External investment can enhance student outcomes — especially monies targeted to instigate systemic change. Schools that enjoyed "high external investment" from the collaborative, earmarked to enhance schools' institutional capacities to educate, did report substantially greater increases in student outcomes than "low-investment" schools. It takes investment — in the near term — to instigate the change process, to enhance institutional capacity, and to sustain ongoing organizational self-reflection toward improved student outcomes.
3. Participatory and strategically guided decision making can promote contexts for improved student outcomes. Shared decision-making schools pursuing full-school restructuring have advanced further, in terms of

improved student outcomes, than have schools that have deferred shared decision making. We presume that a school's engaging in shared decision making/school-based management reflects a school-wide commitment to invest in educational restructuring. Thus, it would make sense that student outcomes would improve in those contexts in which investment is most comprehensive.

4. Those schools most "at risk" are, indeed, most susceptible to early improvements. Schools that reported the most troubling student data in 1988–89 appear to have progressed more rapidly than "high-start" schools. Such improvement was especially apparent when there was evidence of high external and deep school-based investment.

5. Learning communities that are educationally rich and intimate will enhance student learning, teacher collaboration, and parental involvement. Placing students and teachers within learning communities, or charters, appears to yield increases in attendance, course passage, promotion, and, we believe, "holding power," particularly for those students considered most "at risk." Risk is a contextually created—and removable—feature of academic life.

These conclusions have informed the strategies of restructuring pursued over the past 3 years, and they will shape our work in the future.

If this round of reform fails, the New Right press for privatization will prevail. A deepened underclass will be abandoned. Many of us will know that public-sector bureaucracies may have publicly resisted but implicitly buoyed the privatization agenda in their refusal to change radically to meet the needs of children. It is neither too expensive nor too late to transform the educational outcomes of urban adolescents—even those we have collectively placed "at risk."

REFERENCES

Center for Assessment and Policy Development. (1992). *Final report.* Philadelphia: Author.

Clark, R. (1992). Evaluation memo to Pew Charitable Trusts. Philadelphia, PA.

Fine, M. (1990). *Framing dropouts: Notes on the politics of an urban high school.* Albany: State University of New York Press.

Foley, E., & Crull, P. (1984). *Educating the at-risk adolescents.* New York: Public Education Association.

Lieberman, A., & McLaughlin, M. (1992, May). Networks for educational change: Powerful and problematic. *Phi Delta Kappan, 73*(9), 673–677.

Meier, D. (1987, Fall). Central Park East School—Success in East Harlem—How one group of teachers built a school that works. *American Educator.*

Meier, D. (1991a, March 4). Choice can save public education. *The Nation*, *252*(8), 253–258.

Meier, D. (1991b, September 23). The little schools that could. *The Nation*, *253*(9), 321–325.

Oxley, D. (1990, June). *An analysis of house systems in New York City neighborhood high schools*. New York: Bank Street College.

Sarason, S. B. (1992). *The predictable failure of school reform*. San Francisco: Jossey-Bass.

Swidler, A. (1990). *The good society*. Berkeley: University of California Press.

Wehlage, G. G. (1989). Dropping out: Can schools be expected to prevent it? In L. Weis, E. Farrar, & H. G. Petrie (Eds.), *Dropouts from school: Issues, dilemmas, and solutions*. Albany: State University of New York Press.

Wolf, W., & McMullan, B. (1988). *Reclaiming the future*. Philadelphia: Wolf & Associates, Center for Assessment and Policy Development.

CHAPTER 9

The Dropout Prevention Initiative in New York City

Educational Reforms for At-Risk Students

JOSEPH C. GRANNIS

New York City may be the ultimate test of whether a large city school system is simply condemned to bureaucracy or can respond humanely and effectively to students with diverse strengths and extraordinary needs. This chapter will analyze the New York City Dropout Prevention Initiative to discover the obstacles, incentives, and inventions that figure in efforts to reduce risk in schools. The analysis encompasses the programs that originated in the mid-1980s, their evaluation, and their restructuring in the early 1990s. The basic finding of the evaluation was that the original initiative focused too narrowly on students identified as at risk, rather than on schools as risk-enhancing institutions. At the same time, the early programs did pilot certain strategies that, now implemented on a broader scale, are beginning to get more positive results. Fundamental to the evolving approach are systemic school change and collaboration with community-based organizations. The analysis emphasizes the importance of student-oriented goals that are both feasible and challenging, and of information that is collected and fed back to the schools for making progress toward the accomplishment of these goals.

CONTEXT OF THE PROBLEM

School System

Throughout the period between 1984–85 and 1990–91, the New York City school system included 632 elementary, 179 middle, and 119 comprehensive, vocational-technical, or alternative high schools. Between the beginning and the end of this brief span of years, the number of students enrolled increased from about 930,000 to about 970,000. The proportions of students who were Hispanic or Asian-American increased, while the proportion of white students decreased. In 1990–91, 38% of the students were African-American, 35% were Hispanic, 19% were white, 7.9% were Asian or Pacific Islander, and 0.1% were American Indian.

Since 1970, the hiring and supervision of elementary and middle school staffs has been carried out by 32 community school districts covering the five boroughs of the city: the Bronx, Brooklyn, Manhattan, Queens, and Staten Island.[1] By contrast, the central Board of Education exercises direct control over budgets and the appointment of principals for the high schools. This is essential background for understanding the dropout problem in the city. Whatever the difficulties of articulation between junior and senior high schools might be in the nation's schools generally, they are exacerbated in a system where these levels are as differently governed as they have been in New York City.

The "Board of Education" signifies for many the quintessence of bureaucracy. Still, in its very size and differentiation into myriad separate departments and offices, it has historically fostered innovation on at least a limited or compartmentalized basis. Dale Mann (faculty colloquium, Teachers College, Columbia University, Spring 1991) has referred to New York as the "I've got one!" system, because whenever someone suggests a new program for the schools, the system turns out to have it already installed in one location or another. However, recent chancellor Joseph Fernandez took a decidedly more comprehensive approach to reform than any previous chancellor.

Dropout Information

Newspapers and advocacy groups in New York City pointed to high dropout rates in the city schools with increasing stridency during the early 1980s. In 1983, Aspira of New York claimed that as many as 68% of students entering ninth grade in New York City public schools never graduated from high school (Aspira, 1983). The cross-sectional technique used by the Board of Education at that time estimated a citywide high school dropout rate of 38.4% for 1982–83 and again for 1983–84. This percentage began to decline in 1984–85, reaching an estimated 26.2% in 1986–87, but then turned up again in 1987–88 to 26.8% and in 1988–89 to 28.7%[2] (Office of Research, Evaluation, and Assessment [OREA], 1990). The preceding decline was at least partly a function of the board's and the schools' learning how to discharge fewer students as dropouts, by tracing them to new schools when they left the city, transferring them to alterna-

tive schools and General Equivalency Diploma (GED) programs, and keeping truant or failing students on roster for a longer time. Since 1987, the
board has analyzed discharge status by racial-ethnic category and has
consistently found, parallel to national findings, that Hispanic students
drop out at the highest rate, followed by African-Americans, with Asian/
Pacific Islander and white students dropping out at the lowest rates.

The most "at risk" students in the city are concentrated in the zoned
high schools and alternative schools, and the elementary and middle schools
that, directly or indirectly, are their feeders. A triage structure is widely
recognized to involve five levels of high schools in the city: the special
public science and art schools, secular independent schools and parochial
schools, magnet theme and vocational public schools and programs within
schools, the comprehensive zoned high schools, and alternative schools[3]
(see, for example, Hess, 1986; Hill, Foster, & Gendler, 1990).

THE DROPOUT PREVENTION INITIATIVE

The bulk of the explicitly designated "dropout prevention" effort in
the city school system between 1984–85 and 1989–90 was conducted
through the New York State funded Attendance Improvement/Dropout
Prevention (AIDP) program. A program of supplementary student "services" in six areas (see below), the AIDP was implemented in 26 high
schools and 69 feeder middle schools. In 1985–86, a Dropout Prevention
Program (DPP) was funded by the city to extend the effort into a new set
of 10 high schools and 29 feeder middle schools, but to go beyond the
AIDP in stimulating systemic interventions in these high schools and in
experimenting more broadly with the use of community-based organizations (CBOs) at both the middle school and high school levels. Teachers
College, Columbia University, was retained for 3 years, beginning in April
1986, to evaluate the effort in the 39 DPP schools and, for purposes of
comparison, three of the 26 AIDP high schools. The programs in these 42
schools constituted the Dropout Prevention Initiative (DPI) that is analyzed in this chapter.

The Teachers College evaluation was intensively qualitative as well
as quantitative. A research assistant was assigned to each DPI high school
and its feeder middle schools to observe, interview, and administer surveys. The Board of Education supplied a mass of data on the characteristics of students, services recorded, prior-year and program-year attendance, courses passed, credits earned, test scores, and school or discharge
status. The evaluation was monitored by a Steering Committee consisting
of representatives of the Board of Education, the Mayor's Office of Youth
Services, and the Office of Management and Budget. Eight interim and

final reports were produced between 1986 and 1990.[4] At the insistence of the Steering Committee, the reports were not distributed directly to the CBOs or the schools. As it became apparent that the actual reports never did filter down to the schools and CBOs during the span of the evaluation, Teachers College took the liberty of sending abstracts and site-specific findings to the local programs.

The original Request for Proposals for the High School Dropout Prevention Program, issued in early 1985 by the Board of Education, summarized succinctly the thrust of both the middle school and the high school programs at that time: "The purpose of this initiative is to identify those high school students most at risk of dropping out of school, to offer them services and to help them maintain a successful academic career" (New York City Board of Education, 1985, p. 11).

DPI Students, Staff, and Budget

Each year between 1985–86 and 1987–88, an average of 150 students were enrolled in the DPI in each of the 29 middle schools; an average of 425 students a year were enrolled in each of the 13 DPI high schools. These students met one or more criteria for program eligibility, beginning with poor attendance or a low rate of passing academic courses. They typically were overage for grade. *The number of students targeted for the DPI in the schools was substantially smaller than the number who met the program's eligibility criteria, especially in the high schools.* Some of the non-DPI students may have received services from other programs, particularly bilingual education programs. But many others were not targeted by any special program, although it was hoped that the DPI would have a positive "trickle-down" effect on them.

Each of the schools in the DPI had various staff especially designated for the program. In the middle schools, some of the program teams consisted entirely of staff hired by the school system, while in other schools the teams included staff employed by one or another CBO. The school-only staffs generally included a facilitator (coordinator), an attendance secretary, two family assistants, a guidance counselor or substance abuse worker, and teachers retained for extended-day (before- or after-school) activities. Where a CBO was contracted to work with the school, most of the DPI staff were provided by the CBO — as case workers, for example — but the program facilitator and an attendance secretary were still school-system personnel. Larger and much more varied combinations of these kinds of staff were employed in the high schools, all of which involved at least one CBO, and many of which had more extensive alternative education components than did the middle schools.

In the middle schools, the total budget for the program was set at \$150,000 a school per year for each of the 3 years of the DPI: In a school collaborating with a CBO, \$100,000 was allocated to the CBO, while \$50,000 was provided to the school; in a school where no CBO had been retained, the entire \$150,000 was controlled by school staff. In the high schools, the total budgets varied between about \$400,000 and about \$800,000 a school per year. Approximately half of the high school funding went directly to the CBOs and the other half to the schools, the proportion in each school depending on how heavily it used a CBO to provide services to the targeted students. The total cost of the DPI alone was over \$40 million during the 3 years monitored by Teachers College, while an even larger sum was spent in the parallel AIDP program funded entirely by the state. Nearly all of this cost was in addition to the regular tax levy funding that the schools qualified for on the basis of their enrollment.

Services to Students

The DPI was meant to combine six components of service to students: attendance outreach, guidance and counseling, middle school/high school linkage, health services, alternative educational programs, and increased school security in most of the high schools. To capture the intent as well as the difficulties associated with each, these components must be discussed separately. The specific issues and tactics differed between the middle school and high school levels, while more fundamental problems emerged at the two levels in common.

Administration of the program was carried out by a facilitator in a middle school and by a coordinator in a high school. Although it involved extensive budgetary responsibilities, this position was usually filled by a teacher. Facilitators and coordinators found their jobs were more manageable if they had full-time appointments. But even if they were full time, the effectiveness of facilitators and of the dropout prevention team generally depended not only on their own skills but on DPI staff's being empowered by an actively supportive principal.

MIDDLE SCHOOL PROGRAM AND OUTCOMES

Program Components

Attendance outreach. Attendance outreach consisted of letters, phone calls, and home visits to absent students. School and CBO staff, including teachers, repeatedly testified that home visits were valuable. In the middle schools, they were often characterized as the most important parts of the program. Records showed that home visits frequently cast light on reasons for students' behavior in school, and sometimes elicited increased attendance support from a parent or guardian. Home visits were usually made, or attempted (often no one was at home), by two family assistants traveling together. The Office of Student Progress (OSP), the school system central office that monitored the implementation of the DPP and the AIDP program in the middle schools, expected teams to make at least 15 home visits a week and required each participating school to complete a monthly form detailing how many home visits and other services each student received.

Guidance and counseling. OSP also expected guidance counselors to hold at least 15 individual and 10 group guidance counseling sessions a week. OSP personnel were quite explicit with the evaluators about the necessity of challenging the "culture" of guidance in the middle schools, where at least some counselors felt that only much lower numbers of guidance sessions were possible, given the paperwork they had to do, not just for the program but for high school admissions and various reports. Another key aspect was the intensity of help that some students required. Analysis of the service records showed that some students were the focus of a large number of services, while at the other extreme a substantial fraction received few or no services. Group counseling is one solution to the problem of reaching a large number of students, but most guidance counselors or social workers had not been trained for group counseling.

Middle school/high school linkage. School linkage activities were intended to smooth middle school students' transition to high schools. Of various activities, the most valued was a middle school student's shadowing a high school student for part of a day. Access to information about high schools was, and continues to be, a major problem for the typical middle school student. Linkage activities of any kind, however, were recorded less than once a year for the average DPI middle school student.

Health. Illness was far the most common explanation students surveyed by the evaluation cited for their absence from school. Yet, health services also were recorded less than once a year for the average DPI middle school student. DPI staff surveyed said that health services were quite inadequate for students' needs. Like the gap in middle school/high school linkage, the shortfall of health services stemmed partly from the difficulty of coordinating two administratively separate systems, in this case the Board of Education and the Board of Health.

Alternative education. Alternative education began as a combination of pull-out, "enterprise" career education sessions and, for a relatively few students, before- and after-school tutoring, homework help, and recreational activities. Successive attempts were made to implement, first, more academic career education and, later, a regularly scheduled class for basic skills remediation or enrichment. Very mixed results were obtained from each of these. Overall, alternative education was never more than a supplement to the regular academic program of the middle schools, rather than a true alternative to conventional curriculum and teaching.

Middle School Service Intensity and Outcomes

In each year of the DPI, tens of thousands of services to targeted students were recorded. At the same time, one had to be skeptical of the impact the program would have on the long-term success of the students in school. In addition to the health and linkage problems, the services did not seem to be enough to counterbalance the boredom and failure students experienced in their academic classes. Program staff in some of the schools and CBOs particularly questioned how effective they could be with students if regular academic staff were not equally involved.

For each year of the DPI, the evaluation compared targeted middle school students' attendance rates and rates of passing courses with the same students' rates in the previous year, when most of them were not yet enrolled in the program. No progress in arresting middle school students' attendance declines was demonstrated between the first and the third years of the DPI (see Table 9.1). In all 3 program years, the targeted students in the middle schools did improve slightly in the average proportion of courses passed over the previous year (see Table 9.1). The largest gain was found for the second year of the program, when targeted students passed 70% of their courses, compared with a pass rate of 65% for the same students during the prior year. It appears that the program arrested a decline in the number of courses passed that might otherwise have been expected. Still, the resultant rate of passing courses in each program year was substantially below what would be required to predict that these middle school students would have a good chance of succeeding in high school.

An Exceptional Middle School

Of course, there were variations among the middle schools in how they implemented the DPI and in student outcomes. In each of the four most successful schools, something special transformed the program into more than the sum of its components. One middle school, in which program students gained in attendance in all 3 years of the DPI and where there were substantial gains in courses passed by targeted students, com-

TABLE 9.1 Attendance and courses passed by students targeted for services in dropout prevention initiative middle schools

	1985–86	1986–87	1987–88
Average Attendance		$(n = 2,756)^b$	$(n = 4,372)^b$
Prior Year		78%	77%
Program Year		77%	74%
Change	−4%	−2%	−4%
Courses Passed		$(n = 3,269)^b$	$(n = 3,574)^b$
Prior Year		65%	66%
Program Year		70%	73%
Change[a]	2%	4%	2%

[a]Change does not necessarily equal the difference between the prior year and the program year, because the published averages in each row were obtained for all the students for whom data were available in that row, i.e., there were different *n*'s for prior year, program year, and change.
[b]In both sections of the table, *n* is the number of evaluation sample students for whom data were available both from the prior year and the program year, i.e., the students represented in the change row. Only the percentages of change were published in the 1985–86 report; the evaluation sample for this year was all of the 4,726 1985–86 targeted middle school students. In both 1986–87 and 1987–88, the evaluation sample was again all targeted middle school students, and in these years the *n* was reported.

bined extensive monitoring of services to individual students with substantive and structural changes for staff, students, and their parents. DPI students in this school were block-programmed for part of the day. Program staff kept very close track of students' attendance throughout the school day. Teachers and program guidance and outreach staff ate lunch together every day — a very unusual situation in the professional and social life of school staff generally. The program involved large numbers of parents in dinners, health workshops, and career fairs, again in distinct contrast to nearly all of the other schools. Career enterprise activities in the school included a chocolates factory, a greenhouse, and a school supplies store. The principal's "creative rule bending" helped make these activities possible.

HIGH SCHOOL PROGRAM AND OUTCOMES

The DPI in the high schools was much more varied than in the middle schools, not just because of individual school variation, but because of planned variation in the schools' mode of delivering services to students. Some schools relied more heavily on CBOs and used a case-management approach, while others invested more in strengthening sectors of the school that included targeted students.

Program Components

Attendance outreach. Attendance monitoring and outreach tended to be treated as a school central office function that was carried out for DPI and non-DPI students alike, even where DPI funds paid for additional staff. For a variety of reasons, the school-wide monitoring of attendance sometimes duplicated, but was rarely coordinated with, monitoring by a counselor, social worker, teacher, or other staff involved with the dropout prevention program. The sheer size of the problem (i.e., the number of students who might be absent on a given school day, perhaps 500 in a school of 2,500), a lack of up-to-date information on students' addresses and phone numbers, and a shortage of resources, especially telephones, were the main factors that typically had to be dealt with by attendance outreach. A great deal of time was devoted in the fall to resolving questions about which students should even be expected to attend, and "long-term absentee" (LTA) cases soaked up time throughout the year. Many inventive ways to deal with these problems were discovered. This resourcefulness notwithstanding, however, in most of the DPI high school programs the lists of targeted students were not used to provide more intensive attendance outreach to these students than to students who were not targeted. Limited communication between the CBOs and the schools contributed to this problem in many of the DPI schools.

Guidance and counseling. In most of the high schools in the DPI, more staff were hired for guidance and counseling, or casework, than for any other component of the dropout prevention program. Despite this heavy investment, counselors were generally perceived both by themselves and by other high school staff as very overloaded. Substantial fractions of the counselors' time were devoted to trying to reach students. A typical comment from an evaluation survey of staff was, "Caseloads for CBO workers are very high, approximately 110 students per CBO counselor, the crises in our students' lives are often unremitting and debilitating."

Orientation. The dimensions of the problem the high schools faced are illustrated as well by orientation, the high school counterpart to the middle school linkage component. At one high school a very well-planned program for the week before school began — late August–early September — had a daily schedule of breakfast, assembly, activities, lunch, and sports. Upper-class students served as mentors in the program. At the time of planning for the orientation, about 500 students had been identified from notices sent from the middle schools and were mailed announcements; of these 500 letters, about 150 were returned as having the wrong address. Orientation staff members reported that the actual attendance totaled about 80; this represented a small fraction of the 600 students new to high school who eventually registered at the school. Interviews of randomly selected samples of ninth-grade students from four of the high schools found that very few reported having gone on tours of their high school either the spring before, during orientation, or during the first few weeks of school. Indeed, surprisingly few of the students targeted for DPI services in their first year in high school had even been in a DPI program in middle school.

Health. Extensive health services were available on site to students in two of the 13 high schools. These two schools had a comprehensive health program funded by the Robert Wood Johnson Foundation. One of these schools also had a program that supported young mothers in school, including day care for their infants. At the other extreme, one school did not even have a city-mandated health coordinator. Other schools had greater or lesser availability of a nurse or a health coordinator, had pregnancy prevention advice, a drug counseling program, or other special services, but nothing that began to approach a comprehensive health program.

Alternative education. Between the first and the third years of the DPI, there was an increasing emphasis on the alternative education component of the high school program. In the third year, over half of the students were involved in one or another of a variety of activities, including peer and adult tutoring, enrichment courses, mini-schools or blocked academic programs, career education and job training, and a part-time jobs program. However, these were rarely complementary activities. That is, some students got tutoring, others got a special program or flexible scheduling, and still others received part-time jobs, but few students had a combination of these supports. Two program inventions that showed particular promise were a "PM School" attended voluntarily by students in the late afternoon, to make up courses or gain credits toward early graduation, and an on-site GED program in which career education and counseling staff of a CBO worked closely with school academic staff.

Security. In the 10 DPP high schools, program funding was used to beef up security personnel and equipment. An automated building entry/attendance system was installed in each of the schools under this component.

Testimony and incident reports indicated, at best, mixed returns from these investments. Consistently positive results were found, however, for another intervention, a peer mediation and conflict resolution program implemented in five of the DPP high schools by Victims Service Agency, a CBO. In all five of these schools, the incidence of suspensions for aggression against other students dropped dramatically in the year following the startup of the program.

High School Service Intensity and Outcomes

DPI staff exerted themselves tremendously. They cared about the students, were continually involved in crisis management of one kind or another, and contributed to a variety of program innovations. Nonetheless, the picture that emerged from reviewing the services overall was one in which the average student did not receive anything like the full complement of services that the program rationale called for. As in the middle schools, the DPI for most of the students was an add-on rather than a transformation of their school experience. Even where a mini-school attempted to create an island of security for students, the surrounding school environment continued to be an overwhelmingly negative factor in students' lives.

Targeted high school students had substantial attendance losses in all 3 years of the DPI (see Table 9.2). Likewise, in each program year the targeted students passed fewer courses than they had the year before (see Table 9.2). Students entering a high school from another school, usually a middle school, suffered particularly disastrous results. Course failure led to retention, students piled up in the ninth and tenth grades, and the highest rates of dropout discharges were incurred by these students.

A longitudinal study examined outcomes for targeted students from each of the three cohorts of the DPI — Year One (1985–86), Year Two (1986–87), and Year Three (1987–88) — cumulatively from 1984–85 through the end of the 1987–88 school year. Both middle school and high school targeted students lost as much attendance in the year following a given program year as they had during the program year itself. By the end of 1987–88, 15% of the First Cohort of targeted high school students had graduated from high school or received a GED and another 12% were still in school or were enrolled in a GED program. At the same time, 51% had been discharged as dropouts. (Another 10% were discharged not as dropouts and data were missing for 12%). The dropout discharges began in the program year at the rate of 16%, proceeded at a higher rate (21%) in the following year, and then occurred at close to the initial rate in the third year (i.e., 14%). A similar pattern was seen to be developing for the

TABLE 9.2 Attendance and courses passed by students targeted for services in dropout prevention initiative high schools

	1985–86	1986–87	1987–88
Average Attendance		$(n = 1188)^b$	$(n = 1640)^b$
Prior Year	72%	71%	69%
Program Year	63%	62%	64%
Change[a]	−9%	−10%	−6%
Courses Passed		$(n = 1180)^b$	$(n = 1460)^b$
Prior Year	44%	45%	44%
Program Year	35%	40%	42%
Change[a]	−9%	−7%	−4%

[a]Change does not necessarily equal the difference between the prior year and the program year, because the published averages in each row were obtained for all the students for whom data were available in that row, i.e., there were different *n*'s for prior year, program year, and change.

[b]In both sections of the table, *n* is the number of evaluation sample students for whom data were available both from the prior year and the program year, i.e., the students represented in the change row. Number of students was not published in the 1985–86 report; the high school evaluation sample for this year was all of the 6,068 1985–86 targeted high school students for whom both 1984–85 and 1985–86 attendance was reported. In both 1986–87 and 1987–88, the high school evaluation sample was a randomly selected subsample of the total population of students targeted in the high schools.

Second and Third Cohorts, so that the school completion rate anticipated for all three of the high school cohorts was very low.

OVERALL APPRAISAL OF THE DPI IN RELATION TO ITS GOALS

One goal of the program was that at least 50% of those targeted students who had failed a course in the previous year improve their course pass rate in the program year. When *all* targeted middle school students in 1987–88 were considered, however, only 37% passed more courses during the program year than they had the previous year, 32% passed fewer, and 31% stayed the same. Similarly, when *all* targeted high school students were considered in 1987–88, 36% had gains in courses passed, 15% stayed the same, and 49% had losses in percent of courses passed.

One reaction program administrators had to these findings is that the students had such great needs that it would be unreasonable to expect the school to be able to ameliorate their situation. But focusing so centrally on students' needs seems to have diverted attention from the schools' role in the problem. An analysis of the records kept by Pupil Personnel Committees (PPCs) in the middle schools showed that the principal concerns for male students were home problems and discipline, and for females, home problems and health issues.[5] Even more significant than the gender stereotyping that this reflected was the finding that staff *never* attributed students' absences or their inadequate academic performance to difficulties arising from teachers, curriculum, or some other feature of the school itself. *The targeted students attended school for the greatest percentage of days in September and then for decreasing percentages through most of the subsequent months,* suggesting that more than problems at home accounted for the attendance patterns. Indeed, this particular finding, as much as any other, seized the attention of the incoming Chancellor Fernandez's staff reading the final report in 1990, and galvanized the argument for a more thoroughgoing, school-wide approach to dropout prevention.

What the Teachers College evaluation increasingly called for was a comprehensive restructuring of students' experiences in school. For example, although there was some evidence that when students increased their attendance by more than about 10% their course performance also improved, attendance changes of this magnitude occurred for very few students. In addition, to improve the rate of courses passed, the evaluation concluded that instructional issues had to be addressed; current problems could not be addressed just through remedial instruction, but also required reform of the core academic program.

Most of the intermediate and junior high schools of New York City bore little resemblance, in organization, curriculum, or social climate, to what the term "middle schools" has come to stand for in educational discussions today. This observation translated into recommendations that classes combine direct instruction with hands-on or experimental activity, that teachers seek opportunities for positive communications with students and their families, and that greater communication be promoted within schools and with CBOs, the high schools, and the Board of Health. Central and district Board of Education personnel needed to share expertise and decision-making power with local school personnel.

In the high schools as well, dropout prevention needed to become a school-wide concern, rather than the special responsibility of add-on staff. The evaluation recommended that instead of funding simply on the basis of the number of students identified as at risk in a school, three levels of funding be used for successively more comprehensive and systemic approaches in a school. The schools were urged to combine flexibly scheduled, experience-based courses, courses preparing students for GED programs and examinations, and part-time employment and appropriate academic and social supports, for all students who wished to pursue these options. Houses or subschools of fewer than 500 students, combined with advisory or mentoring programs, were recommended to promote bonding and facilitate communication and problem solving among staff and with students.[6] Major increases in the schools' resources needed to be obtained through alliances with employers in both the private and public sectors. CBOs, especially those with closer ties to local communities, needed to be integrated more centrally into the work of the schools.

A central recommendation was that student outcomes, not just levels of service, be examined regularly in order to make successive approximations to program objectives. "Keep your eye on the ball" was argued to be a commonsense way of saying what studies of individual and organizational behavior confirm — that goals are essential for regulating complex programs and actions. Schools were urged to set long- and short-range goals that were both challenging and attainable, and to be accountable for these goals. For the most part, top administrators and DPI staff had dismissed the negative findings of the first 2 years regarding attendance rates and courses passed, holding that it would take 3 or more years for the interventions to produce substantial results. This stance ensured greater continuity than had been possible in earlier programs with shorter timelines. On the other hand, it also led to underestimating the importance of the evaluation findings. The results were taken seriously only when two new chancellors — first Richard Green in 1988 and then Joseph Fernandez in 1990 — each came from outside to head the school system, and each used the evaluation reports to get a picture of the system that he was inheriting.

SCHOOL SYSTEM RESPONSE

Project Achieve

In May 1990, the Board of Education announced Project Achieve, a new dropout prevention program designed by the Division of High Schools. Thirty-two high schools were selected to participate, and committees in the participating schools were to first engage in a comprehensive self-assessment to determine site-based needs. Their findings were to be prepared for presentation to external visiting teams, each comprising a borough superintendent, a representative of the Division of High Schools, a principal or assistant principal, teacher and parent representatives, and a university and/or corporate representative. A plan jointly developed by the internal and the external teams would be submitted to the Division of High Schools for approval and funding. At critical junctures during the school year, the school teams would be asked to meet again with external review teams to review progress, develop joint strategies to improve student outcomes, and revise the program as appropriate. Schools were urged to "utilize all available resources — both internal and external, public and private, tax levy and reimbursable — to address compelling problems creatively" (Division of High Schools, 1990, p. 2) and were given full latitude to pursue school-based solutions. Critical elements to be included in the plans were accountability for student performance outcomes, school-based management/shared decision making (SBM/SDM), systemic changes to redesign the delivery and integration of instructional and support services, use of CBOs in this process, focus on the needs of incoming students, continuous monitoring of students' performance outcomes, effective parental involvement programs, and "commitment on the part of schools, superintendencies, and the High School Division to *collaborate* and to take *collective responsibility* for the *success* of this program" (p. 3, emphasis in original). Goals were specified for dropout rates, attendance, credit accumulation, and Regents Competency Tests in reading, writing, and mathematics. Schools could apply for one of three levels of possible funding — $150,000, $250,000 or $350,000 — for successively more systemic plans. But at all three levels of possible funding, goals and objectives had to be projected in three areas: restructuring/houses, improving the instructional program, and school-based planning and management.

In a bold move to add resources to the dropout prevention effort — not least, a heavy ally to hold CBOs accountable for their work with the schools — the United Way of New York City was engaged to serve as an umbrella organization for the identification of community groups to provide needed services and for management and monitoring of CBO participation in Project Achieve and in the elementary and middle schools. For this purpose a Community Achievement Project in the Schools (CAPS) was funded at $12 million for 1990–91 (and has since been renewed at this level).

Middle and Elementary School AIDP Program

Shortly after Project Achieve was announced, the Board of Education issued a special circular revising the middle school dropout prevention program. As it had begun to do in the late 1980s, the board allowed districts to include elementary schools in the program. Significantly, the elementary/middle school effort in New York City continued to be identified as the AIDP program, while the high school effort reached for a new identity as Project Achieve. Both the 1990–91 and the 1991–92 circulars mandated just three components of the AIDP program in elementary and middle schools: attendance outreach, counseling/case-management services, and parental involvement. *Health services, extended school day programs, school linkage programs, alternative instructional programs, and school restructuring initiatives were presented as optional components.* As was also the case for Project Achieve, the circulars gave a broadened range of risk criteria for identifying students who qualified for the AIDP program, and they mandated integration of students in temporary housing and pregnant and parenting students into existing or newly installed programs. Both a school-based model and a school–CBO collaborative model were described, giving districts and schools a choice over whether to engage CBOs. The 1990–91 circular announced essentially the same attendance and course pass performance objectives for students as had pertained to the DPI. The 1991–92 circular referred to improved academic achievement at various points, but concentrated solely on attendance in specifying goals for targeted students of 40%, 45%, and 50% improvement over their prior-year performance, for 1991–92, 1992–93, and 1993–94, respectively.

It is apparent that the board's plans for dropout prevention were much more ambitious in the high schools than in the elementary or middle schools. This reflects both the stronger leadership in the Division of High Schools at that time and, more fundamentally, the greater control the board has over high schools than over elementary and middle schools.

APPRAISING THE NEW PROGRAMS

There has not yet been a study of the new programs on the scale of the evaluation of the DPI. My appraisal of the progress of the programs is based on interviews of various officials at the Board of Education and in CBOs, examination of recent reports, visits to a few schools, and extensive involvement with a dropout prevention program at one school. Since the high schools selected for the visits were identified by the Board of Education, and the middle and elementary schools by a district recommended by the board, these schools have to be taken as examples of what the board is striving for, rather than as representatives of how things are proceeding in all the schools. Thus, what is reported may describe more of the desired process than currently can be observed in the system.

High School Progress

One senses at the Division of High Schools and in visits to selected Project Achieve sites a thoroughgoing, data-driven effort to establish dropout prevention as a central agenda of the host schools. Project Achieve funds are being used to leverage systemic changes within the schools as a whole. At the same time, large areas of the program and culture of the schools are very difficult to change, or are even moving in a direction counter to the development of a thoroughly supportive and productive high school environment.

One high school visited, a vocational school, has been restructured into three houses, each occupying a different floor of the building. The integration of academic and student support functions is manifest in a commons that each house has, a large room in which a counselor and a house coordinator have their desks in the open, and where students can come to relax, study, play games, or purchase snacks from vending machines that pay for student activities. Each house also has an "academic leader," a teacher who meets weekly with the heads of the academic departments (English, mathematics, science, social studies) to exchange information about students and their achievement. Several years ago, the average rate of passing courses was below 55%; now the rate is 65%, and the school's goal is to reach 75%. A long list of "decentralized house functions and responsibilities" includes outreach, orientation, social events, tutoring, makeup work, newsletters, theme clubs, assemblies, awards/incentives, and parental involvement, among others.

A second high school visited is a zoned school that has integrated CBOs extensively into its work with students. This school had been a principal site for observations during the DPI evaluation, when an incipient house system did not include the DPI-targeted students because they supposedly had their own program. Today, all ninth-grade students are in one of five houses, and tenth-grade students who were in the houses last year have been continued in them. Eventually, students at all grade levels will be in houses. Whereas previously a few hundred students had been targeted for dropout prevention, now every student in the school is considered eligible for Project Achieve programs. At the same time, different specific populations of students have been assigned to different programs, especially those offered by CBOs. For example, one CBO works with ninth-grade students who have been truant or LTAs. These students start their day in school with a breakfast club that combines food and guidance. The CBO not only calls homes to locate students who have not come to school, but also has a van that may go to the home to bring the student to school. A tutoring program is run by New York University for students with various needs, ranging from basic skills remediation to preparation for regents examinations. A nearby medical center operates a health clinic in the school, staffed by a regular nurse full time and a medical doctor twice a week. The center is also equipped and staffed to provide dental services to students in the school. A variety of organizations are involved in community outreach, to strengthen relationships with families and the image of the school in the community. Again, a variety of corporations are involved with the school, particularly to sponsor part-time job programs that are now available to about a quarter of the students. The school's overall attendance climbed from about 79 % in 1987–88 to 84 % in 1990–91.

A third high school visited is another zoned school that I had visited during the DPI. Here, as in the vocational school described earlier, the entire school is organized into houses. Unlike in the first and second schools, however, the houses here have been detracked, following a hotly contested discussion of the issue in the SBM/SDM committee. A College-Bound House is being phased out, while houses called Science-Tech, Humanities, Business, International (bilingual), and Sigma (Special Education) all include students with college aspirations. Project Achieve's most salient success in the school right now is a Discovery Mini-School for all ninth-grade students not in International House or Sigma. Discovery is itself divided into three clusters, each having a coordinator, a counselor, a family assistant, and a CBO social worker. An Academic Olympics recently involved the students in intense competition, and the closeness of the final totals for the three clusters demonstrated that they were fairly evenly matched. Attendance increased and the number of LTAs decreased for ninth-grade students in the first 5 months of 1991–92, compared with the same period in 1990–91. These results were almost reversed for tenth graders in the school, however, and only slight attendance gains were found for the school as a whole. Likewise, the percentage of courses passed increased only for Discovery ninth-grade students. A Project Achieve committee meeting I attended examined these findings and identified the strengthening of tenth-grade as a principal problem to be focused on in an upcoming SBM/SDM retreat.

In all three of these schools, the principals work with their staffs and CBOs in a combination top–down, bottom–up style that, on balance, promotes both initiative and accountability. A multiplicity of programs and functions appear to be well-coordinated, and the schools are striving to incorporate still more. Data collected and analyzed by the Division of High Schools are regularly fed back to the schools for problem solving.

A report released by the Board of Education in May 1992 shows that the dropout rate for the city high schools overall fell from 28.7 % in 1988–89 to 24.0 % in 1989–90 and 20.1 % in 1990–91 — using the old, noncohort method of projection. Using the cohort method, the dropout rates for the classes of 1989, 1990, and 1991 at the end of the fourth year were 20.9 %, 19.2 %, and 17.2 %, respectively (OREA, 1991). The last two years coincide with the implementation of the evaluation recommendations, and the chancellor and the press have credited the evaluation and Project Achieve with these results. For the first time in years, the city's dropout prevention effort has received positive publicity, including claims that the city dropout rate is below that of the several next largest cities in the nation (Berger, 1992).

Whether the cup is half full or half empty is a question posed by the more sobering finding that ninth graders in Project Achieve high schools overall still are passing just a bare majority of their courses. The rate of graduation for the classes of 1989, 1990, and 1991 at the end of the 4 years hovered around 38% (OREA, 1991). Unfortunately, at the very time when the need to improve classroom instruction is most transparent, funds are being shifted heavily into security budgets. Two of the three high schools visited are now participating in a very expensive weapons scanning program. On the day I visited one of the schools, I was scanned from shoulder to toe and had a sense of what students are experiencing every day as they enter the school. One well-placed observer has suggested that there is an increasing resemblance between the classroom and the street, as force is brought in to counter force. More and more teachers say they cannot deal with it, and this may be a factor in the high teacher absentee rate in many schools. Still, in the three high schools I visited, teachers and administrators manifestly cared for and held high expectations for their students.

The AIDP Program in Elementary and Middle Schools

It is acknowledged at the Board of Education that there is great variation in how effectively the AIDP program is carried out in the elementary and middle schools through the different community school districts. Of course, there is also substantial variation among the high schools. However, the board has not only less political control over the elementary and middle schools, but also less information. In particular, the board does not have the capacity to give elementary and middle schools the swift feedback on attendance and course pass rates that has become central to the high school strategy. The board office that directs the AIDP program citywide still relies on tallies of student services to monitor the program in the schools.

To see the AIDP program at its best, I was referred by the board office to the AIDP coordinator in the same district in which I have been working in a middle school. The AIDP program in this district has been renamed the AIMS program, for Attendance Improvement Means Success. This responds to a feeling that many DPI staff in the schools have expressed, that the program should have a more positive emphasis than "dropout prevention." Still, district AIMS staff stressed the enormity of the problems that the DPI staff face. A heavy influx of immigrants to the district has crowded the schools to 130% capacity, with many elementary as well as middle schools having enrollments well over a thousand. The children themselves are heavily affected not only by factors such as hunger, illness, abuse, drugs, and separation and divorce, but also by homelessness, abandonment, guns, and incarceration or death of a close relative. Staff saw it as a miracle that the children were able to function in school at all.

A middle school I visited enrolls 636 children in fifth grade, sixth grade, and special education classes. The school is divided into five houses, named Mango Street, Strivers Row, and the like. Four of the houses have both fifth and sixth grades. A student entering the fifth grade remains in the same homeroom (usually called the "official class" in the New York system, but not in this school) through the sixth grade. Furthermore, while the teachers specialize in different subject areas, they come to the homerooms to instruct, rather than the classes traveling to the teachers. During the mornings, double periods are scheduled to allow more integration of subjects. With the exception of those who attend extended-day activities, the AIMS students are not grouped together at any time of the day. The coordinator, who in this school functions as both facilitator and guidance counselor, has placed a premium on communicating directly with the teachers, knowing the students in their classroom situations, and mediating between teachers and families. This school has a parents' room and has had a variety of parent involvement activities throughout the year. Since the current principal's arrival here 5 years ago, attendance and test scores have risen dramatically in the school. The principal started with a demoralized staff, but in time some left, others joined, and the faculty as a whole cohered. AIMS appears to be thoroughly integrated into the life of this school.

I also visited a K–4 elementary school with over a thousand students, along with a nearby shelter for 49 homeless families. The typical family in the shelter is a mother with three children. A Schools and Families for Education (SAFE) program, which is coordinated with the AIDP program throughout the city, assists the families with many facets of their daily living and helps them seek acceptable permanent housing. A guidance counselor is employed full time to work with the families and the school. Every morning she accompanies the children from the shelter on a bus that makes the rounds of the several schools in which the children are enrolled. Staff were deservedly proud that the shelter children had an average attendance of 94% in their schools through February of the 1991–92 year. There is an AIMS corner in the shelter office, as there is a SAFE corner in the AIMS room at the school. Both in the shelter and at the school, a prominent cabinet includes dictionaries, educational games, school supplies, and other incentives given to the children for attendance and successful school performance. As also holds in the middle school observed, every AIMS child's attendance and a record of attendance outreach are posted daily on bold wall charts. The principal told how the school had "tried everything" to try to improve attendance, but in recent years could not bring it up beyond 86%. The first year that the AIMS program was in this school, attendance was over 90% in 10 classrooms and 88% for the school overall. Recognizing the ability of the teacher who was appointed the AIMS facilitator, the principal would like to have designated the SBM/SDM coordinator for the school as a whole. However, the district is not yet willing to support this larger responsibility for the facilitator.

During 1990–91 and 1991–92, I directed a New York State funded Stay in School Partnership Program (SSPP) in a 6–7–8 intermediate school in the same district in which two of the schools I visited are located. The partnership with Teachers College emphasized a systemic collaboration with school staff to strengthen the core program of the host school. Working with two of the eight clusters of students in this school of more than 1,400 students, the SSPP made substantial progress in developing a bilingual career education program in one cluster and a life environments enrichment program in another. The SSPP was de-funded statewide for 1992–93, and the (now volunteer) partnership has concentrated on completing the life environments curriculum as a vehicle for a more engaging approach to teaching in the cluster as a whole. A fundamental limitation from the start was the very low press for achievement in this school. Recently, however, a state-initiated School Under Registration Review (SURR) investigation concluded that major priority has to be given to "instruction and the effective delivery of curriculum." This was entirely consistent with the SSPP approach, which the SURR report cited as a positive factor in the school. One of the eight clusters in the school—not one that the SSPP worked with—was made up of students targeted for the district AIMS (AIDP) program. The program facilitator was dedicated to students. However, the SURR report observed that "the AIDP program, which should give potential dropouts a particularly rich and attractive school program, was found to be unappealing and under-developed compared [even] to the other programs [in the school]" (New York State Education Department, 1992, p. 9). This report has resulted in the dissolution of the AIDP cluster and the dispersion of its students into other clusters in the school. Still, the fact that this situation could have persisted even in a district with strong AIDP leadership suggests the limits of the program in the middle schools more generally.

PROSPECTS FOR FUTURE IMPROVEMENT

The kind of progress observed in all three of the high schools and the elementary and middle school that were visited is one basis for believing that the system's response to students at risk is being improved. The United Way's orchestration of CBOs appears to be bringing a rich array of new resources to the schools, although funding needs to be greatly expanded. Project Achieve is working very deliberately to foster the integration of academic and personal-social supports for students. The strategy combines resources for comprehensive programs with accountability for results. Central board personnel are currently considering ways to undertake a more systemic approach in the elementary and middle schools, perhaps through the strategy of different levels of funding that seems to be effective in the high schools. School change has to be brought about in contexts that are highly resistant to change (Sarason, 1982) and in concert with the indigenous forces and resources of schools (McLaughlin, 1990). The fact that only for untenured administrators and teachers in the New York City schools are professional development activities mandated outside of designated school hours means that professionalism and accountability have to be fused in new frameworks to result in more positive outcomes for students.

"Involvement in schooling" has emerged as the bottom line in dropout prevention (Finn, 1989), and this calls for a commensurate involvement of educators with students. The recently completed evaluation of the Annie E. Casey Foundation's New Futures Initiative for restructuring urban schools found that little progress had been made at this level in the project schools (Wehlage, Smith, & Lipman, 1992). On the other hand, the characterization of that project applies more to the DPI as the Teachers College evaluation found it in New York City in the 1980s than to the restructuring that has developed since that time.

A still unresolved issue is what balance there should be between a systemic approach to school reform and the targeting of individual students at risk. The evaluation made clear that targeting alone did not substantially improve outcomes for students, as long as the larger school environment was not dealt with. But the opposite may equally apply. It is possible that, as was true before, programs that demonstrably benefit some students still do not affect the students most in need. However, this may be less likely to be the case in the high schools now because the examination of results for specific groups of students has become a more central part of the dropout prevention process overall.

Virtually all of the problems that were identified in the DPI evaluation could still be problems in individual schools. At the same time, the central

administration's serious effort to learn from its experience and to anticipate these problems in the schools is unparalleled in the system's recent
history. Of course, changes in education have to be accompanied by and
are interdependent with improvements in health, housing, and employment. Efforts in the schools to link students with resources in these areas
need to be multiplied many times over. Still, the schools have to act as if
the future were now. We cannot just begin in grade 1 and build gradually.
Schools at every level need to support and empower students so that they
may become part of the solution. The New York City school system has
taken important strides in this direction, especially in its high school dropout prevention initiative, Project Achieve, and the Community Achievement Project in the Schools.

NOTES

1. For the origins of the community school board system, see Ravitch, 1974.
2. These percentages are derived from projecting over 4 years the survival
rate of students in a given year. The Board of Education adopted a more accurate
cohort tracking system beginning with the class of 1986 and has since reported
both the cross-sectional projections, to conform with New York State requirements, and its cohort findings. The dropout rate calculated by the cohort method
for the class of 1987 as of the end of the 1986–87 school year (the class' fourth
year) was 22.4%. For the class of 1988, the fourth-year dropout rate was 20.8%,
and for the class of 1989 it was 20.9%. The dropout rates for each of these cohorts
rose by the end of their seventh and final calculated year to 29.4%, 27.5%, and
27.7%, respectively.
3. The special public science and art high schools include Bronx Science,
Brooklyn Technical, Stuyvesant, and LaGuardia Art and Music and Performing
Arts, all of which require a written or performance examination for admission.
Secular independent and parochial schools range from highly selective and expensive schools to those admitting virtually all students whose families can afford a
relatively modest tuition. Magnet theme and vocational public schools and programs include whole schools emphasizing business, graphic communication arts,
automotive trades, and so forth, and special option programs within the comprehensive high schools. A great expansion of these programs throughout the 1980s,
and the recent introduction of a system that admits 50% of the students to each
magnet by lottery stratified by achievement test levels, resulted in 62% of the
system's high school students being in magnets of one kind or another in 1990–91
(Crain, Heebner, & Si, 1992). The comprehensive high schools include a variety
of special option programs, but are also required to accept students from their
attendance zone who do not gain acceptance to an option school or program.
Programs for students admitted in this way tend to be dominated by entry-level
and remedial academic courses. Finally, the alternative schools have tended to be
much smaller and less conventionally structured than the comprehensive high
schools and to admit high proportions of students who have not been successful in
other high schools.

4. All of these reports are accessible through ERIC. The evaluation was carried out by the Institute for Urban and Minority Education at Teachers College. In addition to this writer, the authors of the reports included Carolyn Riehl, Thomas Bailey, Selina Bendock, Luisa Contreras, Robert Crain, Kiveli Filmeridis, Robert Futterman, Carole Gayle, Joseph Gerics, Judith Goldwater, Kenneth Jewell, Bruce A. Jones, Young-sil Kang, Nava Lerer, Yvonne Martinez, Aaron Pallas, Sanna Randolph, Michele Reich, David Rindskopf, Carolyn Springer, Diana Stewart, Susan Sullivan, Maria Torres-Guzman, Miriam Westheimer, and Denise Willis. I am deeply indebted to all of these individuals for their contributions.

5. A variety of studies suggest that individuals conform more to gender stereotypes when they are under stress or as a way of coping with stress. See, for example, Freedman, 1975; Grannis, 1992. The evaluation linked this phenomenon to the repeated finding that, in both the middle schools and the high schools, males got substantially lower grades than females despite the fact that male students' attendance was not significantly different from female students' attendance, and even though these samples of males and females did not have significantly different reading or mathematics achievement test scores.

6. The development of houses in New York City high schools had already begun in 1986–87. For a well informed study of the house system in New York City high schools during the start-up years, see Oxley and McCabe, 1990.

REFERENCES

Aspira of New York, Inc. (1983). *Racial and ethnic high school dropout rates in New York City: A summary report*. New York: Author.

Berger, Joseph (1992, May 20). Dropout rate down sharply for New York schools. *The New York Times*, pp. A1, B2.

Crain, R. L., Heebner, A. L., & Si, Y. P. (1992). *The effectiveness of New York City's career magnet schools: An evaluation of ninth grade performance using an experimental design*. Berkeley: National Center for Research in Vocational Education, University of California at Berkeley.

Division of High Schools. (1990). High school memorandum no. 128: PROJECT ACHIEVE! A school improvement program for at-risk students. NY: New York City Board of Education.

Finn, J. D. (1989). Withdrawing from school. *Review of Educational Research, 59*, 117–142.

Freedman, J. L. (1975). *Crowding and behavior*. San Francisco: Freeman.

Grannis, J. C. (1992). Students' stress, distress, and achievement in an urban intermediate school. *Journal of Early Adolescence, 12*, 4–27.

Hess, G. A., Jr. (1986, Fall). Educational triage in an urban school setting. *Metropolitan Education, 2*, 39–52.

Hill, P. T., Foster, G., & Gendler, T. (1990). *High schools with character: Alternatives to bureaucracy*. Santa Monica, CA: Rand.

McLaughlin, M. W. (1990). The Rand Change Agent Study revisited: Macro perspectives and micro realities. *Educational Researcher, 19*(9), 11–16.

Mann, D. (1991, Spring). Faculty colloquium, Teachers College, Columbia University, New York City.

New York City Board of Education. (1985). *Request-for-proposals: New York City*

   Board of Education High School Dropout Prevention Program. New York:
      Author.
New York State Education Department. (1992, March 16). *Registration review
      report.* Albany, NY: Author.
Office of Research, Evaluation, and Assessment. (1990). *The cohort report: Four-
      year results for the class of 1990 and follow-ups of the classes of 1987, 1988,
      and 1989, and the 1989–90 annual dropout rate.* New York: New York City
      Public Schools.
Office of Research, Evaluation, and Assessment. (1991). *The cohort report: Four-
      year results for the class of 1991 and follow-ups of the classes of 1988, 1989,
      and 1990, and the 1990–91 annual dropout rate.* New York: New York City
      Public Schools.
Oxley, D., & McCabe, J. G. (1990). *Restructuring neighborhood high schools:
      The house plan solution.* New York: Public Education Association.
Ravitch, D. (1974). *The great school wars. New York City, 1805–1973: A history
      of the public schools as battlefield of social change.* New York: Basic Books.
Sarason, S. B. (1982). *The culture of the school and the problem of change.*
      Boston: Allyn & Bacon.
Wehlage, G., Smith, G., & Lipman, P. (1992). Restructuring urban schools: The
      New Futures experience. *American Educational Research Journal, 29,*
      51–93.

CHAPTER 10

Chicago School Reform

A Response to Unmet Needs of Students At Risk

G. ALFRED HESS, JR.

All too frequently, discussions of students at risk proceed from the assumption that these students exist at the margins of the regular student enrollment. This is particularly the case, I have noticed, with scholars working from national data sets such as High School and Beyond. So, for example, Hammond and Howard (1986) suggest that African-American and Hispanic students (with survey-reported dropout rates at unbelievably low 17% and 19% levels, respectively) "display some rather interesting anomalies in their statistical behavior" (p. 55). They suggest that dropping out can best be understood as behavior at one end of the performance spectrum.

> At the other extreme are students whose performance suggests that they have essentially dropped out (or have been dropped out) of the academic process though they have remained in the school building. Still further to this side are students for whom school attendance is not only minimally productive, but even painful. For them dropping out is a rational response to an intolerable situation. (Hammond & Howard, 1986, p. 55)

Such an analysis leads the authors into an individualized and psychologized definition of the problems of at-risk students and to remedies that call for all teachers to have high expectations for black students.

Similarly, Wehlage and Rutter (1986) describe dropouts as marginalized students who "do not expect to get as much schooling as their peers" and who experience "conflict with and estrangement from institutional norms and rules" (p. 381). The authors propose a solution that is based on the presupposition that at-risk students are primarily marginal students on the edges of normal student bodies. They propose alternative schools within regular schools that can be more attentive to the special needs of at-risk students. These alternative schools would have a few teachers who worked intensively with those who were at risk in small and mutually supportive groupings of students. But how applicable are such approaches to the urban schools that many at-risk students attend?

At Chicago's Austin High School, where the longitudinal dropout rate for the class of 1982 was 62.1%, only 18.4% of the entering ninth graders could read within a range that might be considered "normal" (above the twenty-seventh percentile nationally, or no more than 2 years below grade level; Hess & Lauber, 1985). For the class of 1985, the dropout rate increased to over 80%. In segregated urban schools like Austin, where 54.2% of the students are from low-income families, or nearby Crane, where 73.2% are low-income students, at-risk students are not on the margins of the student body. They *are* the student body. And it may be argued that these students are rejecting, in massive numbers, the structures and performance of contemporary urban schools as being inadequate to meet their needs.

It is for this reason that reform activists in Chicago abandoned the effort to add specialized programs in individual schools to meet the needs of at-risk students and began to focus on the problem of changing at-risk schools. With the recent emphasis on accountability and vouchers, these schools may be more at-risk than reformers understood during the movement to bring reform to the Chicago Public Schools. The Chicago reform activists were convinced that it was inappropriate to "blame the victims" and therefore sought to provide opportunities for schools to change to become more effective with low-income students. It was out of this conviction that they persuaded the Illinois General Assembly to pass the Chicago School Reform Act of 1988 (P.A. 85–1418).

PREVALENCE AND NONSUCCESS OF AT-RISK STUDENTS IN THE CHICAGO PUBLIC SCHOOLS

As Chicago reformers were mounting a legislative effort to foster extensive change, the data they were presenting showed a school system that was made up predominantly of at-risk students who were not being successfully educated. During the 1987–88 school year, 80.2% of all elementary school students qualified for a free or reduced-price lunch. There were 96 elementary schools in which every student qualified, and another

112 in which more than 90% of students did. Two-thirds of the system's primary and intermediate students attended schools in which at least 80% of the students were from low-income homes. Only 32 of Chicago's 440 regular elementary schools had fewer than 30% of their students from low-income backgrounds, and these schools were attended by fewer than 5% of the city's public elementary school students (Hess, 1992). These statistics have not changed appreciably in the intervening years.

During the 1989–90 school year, the first under the reform act, 165,842 elementary students (42% of the elementary-aged children) qualified, using a much more restrictive definition of poverty [combining Aid to Families with Dependent Children (AFDC), census, and free-lunch data], for federal Chapter 1 support for disadvantaged students, but the funds were so limited that they were concentrated into only 288 of the city's 491 public elementary schools and served only 50,733 students, almost exclusively in pull-out programs. Despite the relaxation of federal regulations, only five Chicago elementary schools were permitted by the system's bureaucrats to use funds for school-wide programs. Thus, most low-income students in Chicago schools were not served by these federal funds at all, and the majority who were served had to experience the labeling effect of participating in a pull-out program, which probably negated whatever benefit the program itself provided.

For years, special education programs in the Chicago Public Schools had been in chaos. This catastrophically mismanaged program was highlighted in the 1982 report of Designs for Change entitled *Caught in the Web* (Moore & Radford-Hill, 1982). The authors charged that Chicago steered black students into Educationally Mentally Handicapped (EMH) classes at rates triple those of other major cities. They claimed that as many as 7,000 of the 12,000 EMH students were misclassified. More recent data indicate that as many as 4,000 Chicago students (1% of the total enrollment) are tuitioned out to specialized schools or residential placement centers at a cost of more than $50 million a year.

As reform was beginning in Chicago, the system was a predominantly minority school system. Only 12.3% of the students were white; 59.6% were black; 25% were Hispanic; and 3.1% were Asian or American Indian (Chicago Panel, 1990). Just over 9% were limited in their English proficiency. The Chicago Public Schools had had a long history of de facto segregation. Although the system had been legally desegregated in 1874, residential segregation, reinforced by Chicago Real Estate Board policy and restrictive covenants incorporated into property titles until as late as 1969, combined with the system's emphasis on neighborhood schools, led activists in the 1950s to claim that 91% of Chicago schools were attended by 90% or more of one race. However, it was not until 1980, when white enrollment had dropped to 18%, that the system entered into a consent decree with the U.S. Department of Justice to desegregate. At that time, nine of the city's high schools had more than 70% white students, enrolling 45% of all white high school students in the city. Only a quarter of white high school students attended schools where more than half of the enrollment was minority. By contrast, 85% of the black high school students attended schools with fewer than 15% white students. At the elementary school level, there were 74 schools with more than 70% white enrollments, and 347 schools with fewer than 15% white students; these segregated elementary schools enrolled 93.1% of all black students and 58.2% of all Hispanic students (Hess & Warden, 1987).

Thus, students who might be considered at risk because they belonged to a racial or ethnic minority were generally isolated in schools primarily attended by other similar students. At the elementary school level, students in these racially isolated schools achieved at lower levels than did students attending schools with more white students. On the eighth-grade Iowa Test of Basic Skills in 1985–86, the median grade-equivalent score for students in schools with at least 30% white students was 8.5, 3 months below the national norm; the median for students in schools with less than 15% white students was 6.8, 2 full years below the normal grade level.

The implementation of the 1980 agreement eliminated the few remaining predominantly white schools in the system, but left the vast majority of minority students attending the more than 300 schools that were 100% minority in enrollment. The Chicago Panel's assessment of the effect of the desegregation program was that only 4% more minority students were attending schools in desegregated settings at the end of the decade than had been doing so before the desegregation agreement was signed (Hess & Warden, 1988). One of the primary mechanisms utilized in the desegregation plan was the dramatic expansion of magnet schools. The study showed that these schools were disproportionately funded and provided disproportionate benefits to white, middle-class students. Thus, despite an increase in desegregation funding from $9.8 million in 1980–81 to $77.3 million in 1985–86, for the most part minority students continued to attend schools in which at-risk students were aggregated and were performing less successfully than were students attending the system's relatively few integrated schools. But, due to the small number of remaining white students, desegregation, as a school improvement strategy, had done about as much as it could do (Easton & Hess, 1990).

Economically disadvantaged and minority students in Chicago were not being successfully educated. In addition to the intolerably high dropout rates already mentioned, Chicago students were scoring badly on every form of standardized measure being reported. But, as noted in the

Panel's initial dropout study, the most disadvantaged students were shunted into one set of schools, while the most successful were "drawn" into another set of schools in a system of "educational triage" (Hess, 1986). Students with the best elementary school preparation were enrolled in one set of high schools, while those with the worst scores were shunted to neighborhood schools, predominantly in low-income, inner-city neighborhoods. Overage students were funneled into the worst schools and prevented from attending the more selective high schools. The best schools were more than a third white in enrollment, while the worst enrolled only 6% white students, and most of these students were in 4 of the 21 schools. The percentage of low-income pupils was twice as high in the worst schools as in the best.

This means that half of all low-income high school students, half of all students entering high school overage for their grades (which usually means they were retained in grade at least once in elementary school), 45% of all black students, and 49% of all Hispanic students were shunted into neglected schools that then lost more than half of their students before graduation. The aggregate dropout rate for these schools was 55.8%, and none of them graduated as many students as dropped out. On the other hand, half of all white students were enrolled in selective high schools or those that enrolled few minorities or low-income students. These selective or exclusive schools, in the aggregate, had dropout rates below the national average and less than half of the neighborhood "dumping ground" schools. The triage assignment of students created great disparities in school success at the high school level.

Although one Chicago high school was at the seventy-eighth percentile on scores from the American College Testing Program (ACT), 31 were in the first (i.e., the lowest) percentile. Only six of 58 Chicago high schools ranked at the tenth percentile or higher (Chicago Panel, 1990). The story was similar on other measures and nearly as dismal in the elementary schools as in the high schools.

When we studied elementary schools (Hess & Greer, 1987), we discovered that 20% of these schools enrolled nearly two-thirds (63.1%) of all white eighth graders; in those schools, only 11.4% of the students were from low-income families. In the aggregate, only 18% of these elementary school graduates started high school reading at below normal rates, and only 19% eventually dropped out. These schools tended to be smaller than most schools in the system, and they had more experienced faculties. By and large, they sent their students to the system's selective and exclusive high schools. Students in the other 80% of Chicago elementary schools included few (13.5%) white students, and generally one-third to one-half of their students were from low-income backgrounds. When we tracked the sending patterns from elementary schools to high schools, we found these schools dividing their graduates — that is, sending the more successful to the selective and exclusive high schools and the less successful to high schools in their own neighborhoods. Dropout rates for students sent to the selective and exclusive schools were generally 20 percentage points lower than for students sent to inner-city neighborhood high schools.

The school system was failing its students, most of whom were at risk when they entered the system. It tended to aggregate the most at-risk students in at-risk elementary schools, sorting out the most successful to enroll in more selective or exclusive high schools. It left the rest to attend more neglected inner-city neighborhood high schools. To compound this problem, it focused its resources on schools with fewer at-risk students in attendance.

Federal compensatory funds were concentrated in schools that were attended overwhelmingly by low-income students, but their effects were undercut by lower levels of basic resources provided to those schools. State compensatory funds were blatantly diverted to provide bureaucratic overhead. The Chicago Panel's research showed that basic funding to elementary schools with 90% to 99% low-income students was nearly $1,995 per pupil, $344 less per pupil than that provided to schools with 100% low-income students ($2,339) and, more surprising, $355 less per pupil than was being provided to schools with *fewer* than 30% low-income students. This situation existed even though nearly one-third of the system's students attended these 90% to 99% low-income schools. Base-level funding at these schools, exclusive of the compensatory state Chapter 1 funds, was $630 per pupil lower than at the more affluent schools (Hess, 1992). This lower spending at the schools with more low-income students reflected, in part, the fact that these schools also were staffed with the most inexperienced teachers (Hess & Greer, 1987).

If one begins to define at risk as referring to students who come from economically disadvantaged families and adds to that being from minority families that are racially isolated, and then includes poor academic preparation, it is clear that such students are disproportionately enrolled in inner-city and rural school systems. Within urban systems, such students frequently are further isolated in inner-city neighborhood elementary schools; they are underrepresented in selective schools and in schools in more exclusive neighborhoods. Such is the case in Chicago.

What emerged to Chicago activists was the picture of a school system that was at risk. It was a school system in which most of the students started school at a disadvantage and remained in that condition throughout their school years. The system's resources, however, were husbanded for those students who showed the most promise. These students were steered into a few well-performing schools that were provided with the most experienced teachers and, frequently, were provided extra resources. Those individual students who had overcome the risks, who had battled against the odds to maintain good attendance and achieve good grades, were steered into the system's better high schools. Meanwhile, most at-risk kids were concentrated in "holding pens" until they reached an age when they could officially drop out. Many had unofficially dropped out years before. If the facts were available, I suspect many other large urban systems could be similarly assessed.

Following the Panel's publication of several of its dropout studies, it convened a symposium of university scholars and leaders from the city's nonprofit, school support agencies to examine solutions to the dropout problem. This symposium quickly dismissed the ad hoc proposals that treated potential dropouts as marginalized students. It adopted a sociological, rather than a psychological, perspective to address student failure. The members built a matrix of student needs and potential solutions that covered all years from infancy to age 18 and included hours both in school and out of school. It was agreed that a comprehensive approach would be needed. Otherwise, students could be expected to continue making what were apparently "rational" decisions to drop out of school: If one was unprepared for high school level work when one graduated from eighth grade and had been unable to accumulate any course credits during the first 2 years in high school, dropping out would seem more rational than investing another 4 years in the current school system. At the same time, however, these dropouts were being blamed for future life failures because *they* did not make it through a system that was stacked against them.

Chicago reformers decided it was the system that had neglected and stacked the odds against at-risk kids. Primarily, it was the system that was failing the kids, rather than the kids who were failing in the system. Such a conclusion was incomprehensible to school system administrators, who were more comfortable with psychological explanations of the failures of individual students. When the Panel described the ways in which Chicago high schools regularly shortchanged their students through 20% shorter subject periods, chaotic classrooms, and phantom study halls (Hess, Wells, Prindle, Kaplan, & Liffman, 1986), the school superintendent's only response was that the Panel was trying to "trash" the school system. When asked by the news media why the system could not do better by its students, he could only respond by citing the high number of low-income students in the system ("Byrd Defends," 1987). Refusing to only blame the victims, Chicagoans set out to reform the school system.

FIX THE SYSTEM INSTEAD OF FIXING THE KIDS

Aided by a 19-day school strike that mobilized massive political pressure, reform activists were able to persuade Illinois legislators to enact a thoroughgoing reform bill (P.A. 85–1418, adopted December 2, 1988). (See Hess, 1991, for a fuller description of the effort that led to the passage of the Chicago School Reform Act and for additional details on its components and early implementation.) The Chicago School Reform Act had three major components. The first was a set of 10 goals that can be summarized as requiring the Chicago Public Schools to lift the achievement levels of their students to match the national norms. While many of the reform activists recognized the near impossibility of achieving these goals within the initial 5-year timeframe of the legislation, they were committed to putting such high expectations before schools in the hopes that school faculties would develop and hold similarly high expectations of their students. These goals were expressive of the educational philosophy that was held by the more thoughtful reform advocates and was rooted in the research literature on effective schools. Based on this literature (e.g., Brookover & Lezotte, 1979; Edmonds, 1979; Purkey & Smith, 1983), provisions in the legislation were designed to provide the opportunity and to foster efforts of schools to change so as to embody these more success-oriented characteristics.

The second component in the legislation is frequently overlooked in accounts of the Chicago reform act but is seen, in Chicago, as the engine that has driven much of the improvement effort. The act requires that the resources of the school system be reallocated to be focused on the students with the greatest needs. This reallocation was accomplished by two mechanisms. First, a cap was placed on the proportion of noninstructional expenses within the school system, limiting that proportion to the average proportion of such expenses in all other school systems in the state. This provision alone forced a reallocation of about $40 million in the first year of reform, resulting in the elimination of about 500 positions in the bureaucracy's central and district administrative units and the granting of an average of $90,000 in new discretionary funds to individual elementary schools. The second mechanism was the requirement that all schools receive equitable base-level funding, with categorical grants and state compensatory funding added as the basis of the number of qualifying students. The reallocation of the state Chapter 1 compensatory funds, for example, which amounted to about $250 million in the initial year of reform implementation, was eventually to be phased in over 4 years, and these funds would become progressively discretionary at the decision of local school leaders over that time.

The third component of the reform act is the best known — the establishment of school-based management in the form of elected Local School Councils (LSCs) at each school site. These councils were given three basic responsibilities: to create a school improvement plan (SIP); to adopt a school spending plan; and to select the principal to lead the school under terms of a 4-year performance contract. The school improvement plan was to be drafted by the principal with significant input from an advisory teacher committee (the Professional Personnel Advisory Committee, or PPAC), from the council itself, and from the community. The improvement plan was to be built on the basis of a needs assessment of the school's students, its facilities, and its educational program. Through the school improvement plan, local schools were being given the opportunity to shape their curriculum in diverse ways to meet the particular needs of their enrolled students. The school budget was then to be shaped to support the components of the improvement plan. LSCs were given the opportunity to add or delete positions, shift the focus of program resources, or add programs as required by the improvement plan, subject to existing laws and union contracts. While these limitations were very significant, the legislation provided LSCs with the means to gain waivers of contract provisions or board regulations. This mechanism was mirrored in the next contract signed between the Chicago Board of Education and the Chicago Teachers Union, and union leaders have claimed they granted every legitimate request for waivers that was received.

Local School Councils were also given the right to select the principals to provide educational leadership for their schools. Since about 1970, Chicago schools had been able to recommend their choice of a new principal to the General Superintendent when a vacancy occurred. In most cases, their choice was appointed to the school. Once chosen, the principal had lifetime tenure, usually in the same school, if he or she desired. The reform act eliminated principal tenure, substituting a 4-year performance contract for the principal. All existing principals were deemed to be completing such contracts and half the councils would be able to select a new principal, if they so desired, during the first year of implementation, with the second half choosing in the second year. The significant new power granted LSCs was the ability to terminate a principal a LSC thought was no longer being effective.

There were several other important provisions of the reform act. Principals were given the right to select educational staff for newly open positions (either through a vacancy in an existing position or for newly created positions) on the basis of merit. Teachers would no longer be assigned to schools on the basis of seniority, with the consequent "bumping" of teachers that the prior seniority assignment system had fostered. Accompanying this new assignment pattern, the teacher remediation and termination procedures for teachers evaluated as "unsatisfactory" were shortened from the year-long remediation period adopted in statewide reforms in 1985 to a 50-day remediation period (cf., Hess, 1991, p. 90; Nelson, Yong, & Hess, 1985). Again, these provisions were ratified in the ensuing contract with the teachers union.

Finally, a procedure was established for the identification of schools in which SIPs were not adopted or in which the plans were not being adequately implemented. Frequently referred to as the "bankruptcy" provision for nonperforming schools, this provision allowed a subdistrict superintendent (with the agreement of a district council made up of one representative from each school council) to place a nonperforming school in remediation for a year and to provide it with direct assistance and guidance. If the school still did not improve in its efforts, the subdistrict superintendent, again with the agreement of the district council, could recommend more drastic steps to the Board of Education, ranging from new Local School Council elections to removal of the principal, replacing the entire faculty, or closure of the school. This bankruptcy provision was applicable only after schools had had 3 years in which to improve themselves.

A MIDWAY REPORT ON CHICAGO SCHOOL REFORM

At the end of February 1992, the Chicago Panel issued *A Midway Report* on the implementation of the Chicago School Reform Act (Hess, 1992). The act had envisioned an initial implementation period of 5 years, beginning with the initial LSC elections in October 1989. The report presented an assessment of progress after two-and-one-half years.

The report noted that it was still much too early to assess student achievement changes. The reform effort had been in operation for two-and-one-half years. The first year was a planning year in which Local School Councils were elected and carried out their initial needs assessments, built their first SIPs, and adopted their first budgets. Half of the schools evaluated their incumbent principals and selected their leadership for the ensuing 4 years. During the second year of implementation, LSCs first began to put their newly adopted improvement plans into operation, and the second set of principals was selected that spring. The most recent student achievement tests were taken in April of that second year, during the eighth month of the initial SIP. Even in the schools where radical changes were planned, 8 months would be far too short a period to expect significant impact on achievement scores.

In one recent study, for example, the Chicago Panel demonstrated that graduation and dropout rates could be predicted with nearly 90 % accuracy on the basis of second-, third-, and fourth-grade teacher-assigned academic grades and attendance records (Hess, Lyons, Corsino, & Wells, 1989). Since early experiences with schools evidently have powerful influences on students' later school performance, it would be naive to think that a few months of even radical innovation, at the high school level, for example, would be able to change basic student achievement patterns. Generally speaking, it is the consensus in Chicago that it will take sustained efforts at the school level to bring about significant, positive changes in student achievement. At the halfway point in the reform process, most schools in the city were still at a very early stage of operation.

The data collected on student performance during the first 3 years of reform in Chicago reflect this early stage of implementation. Test scores from the second year of reform implementation showed no significant pattern of change from the previous year. On the Illinois Goals Assessment Program tests for 1990–91, 77 % of all elementary schools fell below state averages; for eleventh-grade reading and math, 92 % of students were below the state average. Dropout rates, largely responsive to earlier student experiences of neglect in the city's schools, continued to be discouraging; during most of the 1980s, these rates hovered between 40 % and 45 %, jumping to 48 % in 1989 and then declining slightly to 46 % for the class of 1990 but rising to 51.5 % for the class of 1991. Attendance data for the system's elementary schools showed very little change; at the high school level, the data showed a continuing pattern of decline over the past 6 years, due in part to more stringent record-keeping procedures enforced by the state as a result of the Panel's 1986 dropout study (Hess et al., 1986). Although some individual schools have shown improvement in this area, little citywide progress on reducing absences has been made to date.

The Chicago Panel will continue to monitor student achievement and behavior on a series of measures throughout the reform effort. The Panel will examine individual student achievement gains from year to year and compare those gains with previous achievement gains for these students to see if there are increases or decreases in the yearly gains for each student in the system. This work has been complicated to an extent by the Chicago Board of Education's decision to use different forms of standardized tests to increase test integrity during the reform implementation years. In order to compare scores, the Panel has been forced to mount annual equating studies, with the cooperation of the board's evaluation staff and a number of volunteer schools. The pattern of individual student increases and decreases will eventually be aggregated to the school level and correlated with data on each school's improvement efforts: program changes, staffing changes, changes in resource allocation, and school responses on surveys of teachers and principals. In future reports, the Panel will seek to provide some assessment of which improvement efforts are associated with improved student achievements.

Organizational Change

On the basis of system-wide data and an intensive study in 14 representative schools, the Panel's *Midway Report* reached two major conclusions: first, organizationally speaking, the major elements of reform had all been put into place and are functioning relatively adequately; second, the number of schools that have entered into school-wide efforts to change the nature of classroom instruction is still quite low. The amount of organizational change that has taken place in this $2.5 billion operation is quite astounding. In particular, the report listed four dimensions of organizational change that were and are noteworthy.

Establishment of local school councils. In every school Local School Councils have been established, and for the most part they function adequately. LSCs were first elected in October 1989 and then re-elected in October 1991, with about 45 % of first-term members re-elected for a second term on the same LSC. Since the children of some parent members had graduated from those schools, disqualifying their parents from further LSC membership, this continuation rate seems appropriate. Despite initial chaos about where LSCs would meet and what immediate duties they were to perform, most LSCs successfully completed their major responsibilities: adopting a school improvement plan and enacting a school budget for the ensuing year. All councils, during their first 2-year terms, evaluated their principals and selected a person to serve in that position for the next 4 years. At 38 % of the schools, a different person was installed as principal than had been providing leadership when the reform act was signed in December 1988.

LSC attendance varied from school to school, but overall it averaged about 70 %, with principals attending most frequently. LSC chairs and teacher representatives had meeting attendance rates over 80 %, while rates for community representatives and parent members other than the chairs were nearer to 60 %. Although LSCs spent nearly a third of their time on organizational matters, they also devoted a third of their time to topics related to the school program. Building, finance, and personnel (primarily principal selection) items dominated the remainder of their discussions.

Leadership of principals. Principals have adopted new roles and are providing new leadership. As already noted, by the third year of reform implementation, 38% of Chicago schools were led by a principal who had not been in that position when reform began. A similar percentage of schools in the Panel's intensive study were being served by new principals. The selection process went smoothly in some schools, but others had a more difficult time in keeping their incumbent evaluation process objective and separate from the launching of a search for a new candidate. In some schools, the principal selection process so dominated council agendas that they could not adequately conduct other business, such as revising their improvement plans or adopting a school budget. The *Midway Report* described the selection process in three schools that represent the range of experiences schools encountered.

During the initial years of reform, principals found that time demands were excessive. They found themselves playing new roles, not all of which seemed appropriate to them. One participating principal complained that she now had to be a public relations figure, a referee between factions in her school, and a glorified clerk compiling lots of reports. The extra work occasioned by interacting with the LSC had "opportunity costs" for principals, resulting in less time for staff supervision and other areas of program leadership. But some principals also saw the reform effort as providing more opportunities, particularly relative to staff selection and to the additional support they receive from more involved LSC members, parents, and teachers.

At the end of the third year of reform implementation, a survey of principals was conducted by the Consortium on Chicago School Research (1992). About 83% of the system's 550 principals responded to the survey. Generally, principals then serving in the system were optimistic about the prospects for school reform. One set of questions focused on their relationships with the central administration. While the central administration no longer exercised direct line supervision over most matters affecting local schools, it was expected to provide significant support for schools. In 13 separate areas, ranging from school budgeting and curriculum and instruction issues to capital improvements, principal dissatisfaction was relatively low. Generally, central office assistance was deemed to be not helpful or not timely by between 10% and 20% of the principals. In the areas of school maintenance and capital improvement, dissatisfaction was expressed by about 50% of the principals. More information about principal perceptions of reform is available in *Charting Reform: The Principals' Perspective* (Bennett et al., 1992).

Involvement of teachers. Teachers have become increasingly involved and positive about reform. Based on two surveys and interviews with a series of key school-level teacher leaders, it appears that teachers may now be quite active in reform efforts at most schools. A small survey conducted before the first LSC elections (Chicago Panel, 1989) showed that teachers did not then see themselves becoming extensively involved in reform. They thought increased parental involvement would be the primary strength of the reform effort, but worried that such involvement might lead to greater classroom interference. A much more comprehensive survey of 13,000 elementary school teachers, carried out in the spring of 1991 (Easton et al., 1991), showed that a majority of teachers had positive opinions about school reform. In 62 schools, teachers were very positive about reform, while in another 241 they were moderately positive. In 89 schools, teachers were somewhat negative, while in 9 schools, they were very negative. Most teachers felt they were fairly represented by LSCs, they had increased their involvement in policy making, and they were involved meaningfully in implementing their school improvement plans. Interviews in the 14 study schools indicated that teachers had major roles in determining their schools' improvement plans, which were generally accepted as proposed by the LSC. Although the survey indicated teachers were mildly optimistic that their schools would improve, fewer than half indicated their own instructional practices had changed or would change in the future.

Reallocation of resources. Resources have been increasingly focused on the schools, with the greatest increases in schools enrolling the highest proportions of disadvantaged students. Between 1988–89, when the reform law was being enacted, and 1991–92, the Chicago Public Schools increased revenues by $403 million, mostly from increased property tax receipts (state aid increased by only $25 million). Most of these new revenues were reallocated to schools (primarily through changes in the distribution of state Chapter 1 compensatory funds). At the same time, some 840 administrative unit positions were eliminated (to meet the cap on noninstructional expenses and the pressures of budget balancing), and the numbers of school staff were increased by 3,365. One-half of these positions were classroom aides hired by schools to assist teachers; schools also added just over 1,000 teachers and other professional staff.

Funds are now much more equitably allocated to schools. As pointed out earlier, in the year before school reform began, elementary schools with 90% to 99% low-income students averaged nearly $400 less per pupil in expenditures than did schools with fewer than 30% low-income students. In 1991–92, the schools with the heaviest concentrations of low-income students had nearly $1,000 more per pupil than did those with the fewest disadvantaged pupils. The average elementary school had $340,000 in supplemental discretionary funds. Supplemental funds in the average high school amounted to $478,000. Disadvantaged students in Chicago have far better access to (additional) educational resources under the reform initiative than they did previously.

Instructional Change

The amount of institutional change that has occurred in the Chicago Public Schools in just two-and-one-half years is quite amazing. Few other $2.5 billion organizations have ever undergone such rapid and far-ranging changes. But the point of the Chicago School Reform Act was not just to change the system. It was to help low-achieving students, particularly low-income disadvantaged students, to become more active and successful learners. For this to happen, significant instructional change must also occur. Two major findings in this area relate to the increase in reform assistance from outside Chicago and to the nature of school improvement efforts being undertaken with the Chicago Public Schools.

Reform assistance for Chicago's schools. In one of the more exciting by-products of the Chicago reform effort, the Panel found that national school improvement efforts have "marched on Chicago" to assist many schools. Whereas in 1988 few national school improvement efforts were working in any Chicago schools, by 1992 a wide variety of reformers from across the nation had formed links to assist more than 170 Chicago schools. The Chicago Panel has been chronicling the activities of a number of these efforts in its monthly newsletter, entitled *Reform Report.* Some of these projects have a distinctly Chicago flavor (e.g., Mortimer Adler's Paideia program, the Illinois Writing Project, and the federally supported desegregation program — Project CANAL — which has provided school improvement planning training to about 70 racially isolated schools in the city). Other projects are products of major school reformers, such as Ted Sizer (Coalition of Essential Schools), Henry Levin (Accelerated Schools Network), and James Comer (Comer School Development Program). More than 60 elementary schools have been trained in the principles of the New Zealand Reading Recovery program. These national and international efforts are providing valuable resources to schools and school staffs as they work to improve Chicago's schools. Many are supported by grants from Chicago's major foundations and corporations, which continue to support the reform effort. These outside reform resources were largely unavailable to the city's schools prior to the school reform initiative begun in 1988.

School improvement efforts. For all of this outside encouragement, only a minority of Chicago schools have yet brought radical change to their instructional programs. School improvement plans in the city's schools have focused more on "add-ons" than on altering the regular instructional programs of schools. In the first year of school improvement planning, most schools focused on solving practical problems like overcrowding, discipline in the school, controlling gangs, and increasing attendance. About a quarter of the observed schools planned quite significant changes in their instructional programs, while another quarter approved very rudimentary plans. An analysis of the revised plans adopted in the second year showed curricular changes were most prevalent, and pedagogical improvements next most frequent, with organizational and other changes following. About a quarter of the studied schools were attempting changes that would affect regular classroom instruction throughout the school, while another quarter were planning changes in some classrooms. More frequently, schools were favoring "add-on" programs such as additional classes (art, music, science or computer labs) and additional instruction (after school, preschool, full-day kindergarten, or summer school). Most add-ons can be implemented easily if money and new staff are available.

Initiatives that may affect the regular classroom experiences of students require significant commitments and time on the part of teachers. One school is emblematic of efforts to change regular classroom instruction. It is implementing a literature-based reading program, extensive use of hands-on learning in mathematics, an experimental approach to science, an innovative school-wide writing program, and Socratic seminars in an attempt to improve the content and intellectual level of classroom discussion.

As we tried to track significant changes in the instructional programs of schools we were studying (Flinspach & Ryan, 1992), we discovered that the extent of implementation frequently reflected the type of planning that had been undertaken. While teachers had been engaged in school planning from the beginning of the reform effort, school-level leaders indicated that the involvement of teachers was becoming more extensive as their confidence grew that their suggestions would be heard, would have the support of their principals, and would receive adequate funding in local school budgets. But not all schools were equally effective in their planning.

As we assessed the evaluation of the school improvement plans operative during 1991–92, it became obvious that in a third of our schools, the formally adopted SIP had little effect on the regular, daily life of the school. In these schools, the SIP was rarely discussed by anyone; teachers were unaware of its contents; principals could not find a copy of the plan. In most cases, these plans were not realistically related to the life of the school. In another third of the schools, the plan was occasionally discussed, but was not a regular part of the life of the school. In a third of the schools, the SIP played a much more vital role; it was regularly discussed in Professional Personnel Advisory Committee meetings, and teachers were actively engaged in revising the plan for 1992–93 implementation. We labeled the unrealistic plans the result of "symbolic planning," planning that was characterized by vague or generalized descriptions of existing practice, initiatives that sounded good but were unlikely to be implemented, or goal statements without accompanying descriptions of implementing activities or programs. By contrast, where plans were having important effects, they were much more pragmatic. Frequently, in schools with pragmatic plans, the persons expected to implement plan components had had a major hand in the planning process and were willing to be accountable for the plan's implementation.

Case Studies

We have been studying three schools more intensively because their plans were more focused on instructional change than were the plans of other schools in our sample. In these schools, we found the planning to be characterized by pragmatic approaches. A brief description of the planning process of two of these schools may make the distinction between symbolic and pragmatic planning clearer.

Montgomery Elementary. At a school we are calling Montgomery Elementary, the incumbent principal, obeying the mandate though not the spirit of the reform law, drew up the first school improvement plan by himself. The plan included vague initiatives and perfunctory descriptions of routine operations, such as "monitor instruction and pupil progress" and "organize school for instruction next year." He also included items that "sounded good" but were not meant to be implemented, such as "utilize computers and calculators in the instructional program" (though none were made available to teachers) and "evaluate pupil progress in all subject areas and adjust instruction to meet individual pupil needs as is necessary." His real attitude toward reform, however, was revealed in this passage from the plan.

> School reform is a paper-intensive, meeting-oriented, time-consuming effort that diminished the energy and creative talents of the staff and parents who are sincerely attempting to meet the demands placed upon them. If legislative mandates are all that is needed to correct social conditions and shortcomings, there would be no problems with drugs, crime, poverty or the myriad other problems facing society. (Flinspach & Ryan, 1992, p. 13)

Thus, this principal was rejecting the notion that mandated changes in school organization and governance could provide a better answer for at-risk kids. He observed the newly mandated actions required of him, but communicated his disdain for the approach. Needless to say, little changed as a result of the plan he proposed to the LSC.

During the following year (1990–91), the Montgomery LSC was charged to evaluate the principal and decide on his retention or replacement. It was decided to not retain the incumbent. Two days before the second-year SIP had to be adopted, a new principal began her tenure. The outgoing principal had prepared the second-year SIP in the same way he had the first. Too late to completely change the process, the new principal added three of her own initiatives, in response to concerns expressed by staff and parents: hiring another teacher to extend the kindergarten classes to a full-day program; devising an after-school program; and hiring a security guard. These three very practical initiatives, characterized above as "add-on" planning, were instituted at the beginning of the 1991–92 school year; the rest of the SIP was ignored as irrelevant.

During the third year of reform, these new initiatives were seen to be significant improvements in the life of Montgomery School. The full-day kindergarten was seen to be beneficial, as was the after-school program. The new security guard relieved feelings of danger that had pervaded the school previously. More important, the man hired, a moonlighting Chicago policeman, saw his job not only as providing a sense of security in the school, but also as an advisor to students; he was actively engaged in the effort to improve Montgomery, interacted regularly with the principal, and was very responsive to requests for assistance from individual teachers. These add-on initiatives had created a climate under which more fundamental change could be undertaken.

Not surprisingly, when the new principal began the planning process for the SIP to be adopted in the spring of 1992, teachers were much more willing to participate. The principal chaired the 10-week process of developing the plan. She reviewed the record of student achievement in the school and the system-wide goals and objectives of reform adopted by the Board of Education. She gave a list of suggestions, but solicited input from the faculty members. The final plan presented to the Local School Council was prioritized to reflect the new funds available in the next year's school budget and was focused on the five subject areas included in the system's guidebook to improvement planning. It was full of very practical plans, each building on existing programs and capacities. We have called this type of planning *pragmatic incremental planning*. In our opinion, it represents the first level of realistic planning for school improvement.

Winkle Elementary. Further along in the improvement planning process is a school we are calling Winkle Elementary. During the first 3 years of school reform, Winkle had introduced many new initiatives, implementing Socratic seminars to improve the intellectual content of classroom discussion, shifting to a literature-based reading program, beginning extensive use of hands-on learning in mathematics, focusing on experiments in science, and utilizing the Illinois Writing Project to implement a school-wide writing emphasis. Teacher involvement in the planning process had been high in 1991–92; Teachers accepted the idea that they were accountable for plan implementation; they had undertaken numerous incremental improvements and had moved on to more *thematic improvements* (see Louis & Miles, 1990), with shifts in the means of instruction for writing, math, and science. Winkle was doing the kind of instructional improvement planning we hoped other schools would emulate.

During the 1991–92 school year, with teachers struggling to incorporate the many changes they were already undertaking, the principal decided it was time to shift the focus of improvement planning from staff development to student development. This was part of her vision of a renewed partnership among staff, students, and parents at Winkle Elementary that had guided the integrated SIP adopted in the spring of 1991. In an effort to make upper-grade students "responsible for what they produce in school," the principal proposed establishing stiff, minimum eighth-grade graduation requirements, combined with a revamping of the seventh and eighth grade ("junior high") into an ungraded, project-oriented, portfolio-assessed school within the larger school (Flinspach & Ryan, 1992, p. 33). While the teachers claim they have accepted the vision put forward by the principal, they watered down the radical changes incorporated in the principal's original proposal, retaining the grade structure and reducing the project structure to activities already included in the year's planning. By utilizing incremental planning, rather than *directed planning* that would seek to put a more radical implementation of the professedly agreed-upon vision of student responsibility into place, the teachers slowed the amount of instructional change to a pace with which they were more comfortable. The principal, recognizing the importance of staff conseı.sus in the planning process to engender staff accountability, agreed to the compromise on the implementation plan for the 1992–93 school year.

Analysis of School Improvement Plans

Based on the experiences of these schools, which we have been studying intensely, Panel staff have devised a model of school improvement planning, drawing significantly upon the work of Louis and Miles (1990). On one side is the *symbolic planning* that is largely disconnected from reality, whether due to generalized statements, abstract goals without implementing plans, or "sound good" initiatives disconnected from the school improvement plans. On the other side are plans characterized by pragmatic planning. These plans frequently were begun with *incremental changes* building on currently existing school efforts. They progressed to *thematic changes*, which integrated some incremental plans. The fullest development of this pragmatic planning is an integrated SIP that is built upon a shared vision derived from previous improvement planning efforts of the school community. We refer to planning that is instituted and designed to carry out this vision as *directed planning*. To date, only four of the 14 schools we are studying are seriously engaged in pragmatic planning about the instructional program of the school. Only one of these four has reached the point of having a shared vision, and it is the only one that has yet attempted directed planning. However, if school reform is to be effective in Chicago, more of the system's 540 schools must be about the job of directed planning to improve the instructional program for all of the city's students, and particularly for its students who are at risk.

CHICAGO: A SYSTEMIC ATTEMPT TO ADDRESS AT-RISK STUDENT NEEDS

In far too many settings across the United States, at-risk students attend schools that are themselves at risk of failing their enrolled students. While these at-risk students may not come to school with all of the advantages of their more affluent peers, at least in terms of the behavior characteristics that schools currently value and reward, they bring other strengths and maturities that frequently are ignored or devalued by school staffs trying to emulate their more "successful" neighbors located in more affluent communities. Instead of emphasizing the strengths their students bring to school and adapting their programs to successfully guide these students in the learning enterprise, these at-risk schools too frequently try to force their students to abandon the characteristics that make them successful on the streets of their own communities and to adopt those other behaviors schools have traditionally rewarded. Without examining their own assumptions about what will make young people successful, these at-risk schools continue to emphasize the behaviors characteristic of a manufacturing century in an economy increasingly focused on information and service. In this context, it is at least reasonable to raise the question as to whether it is the students or the schools that are most at risk of failure. The assumption, at least among reformers in Chicago, is that *it is our schools that are seriously failing our city's students.* If our schools are unwilling to build on the strengths their students bring with them, or are unable to restructure themselves to better meet their students' needs, then it is the schools, even more than the kids, that must be changed.

The Chicago School Reform movement is an effort to address more adequately the previously unmet needs of at-risk students by creating a systemic opportunity for schools to restructure. Halfway through the initial reform period, the degree of organizational change is quite encouraging. Despite the chaos created by fiscal and administrative mismanagement on the part of officials who were unwilling to accept their responsibility to change a failing system, the major elements of the Chicago School Reform Act have been successfully established. Local School Councils are functioning in almost every Chicago school. Nearly 12,000 people are present during local discussions of school concerns each month of the school year. In some schools, important efforts are underway to change the way in which instruction is carried on in regular classrooms. In other schools, important practical problems have been addressed, and new programs have been added to meet the special needs of some students. In some schools, little of significance has occurred. If student achievement is to improve measurably, more schools must turn their attention to changing the ways in which students and teachers interact in the majority of the city's classrooms.

The Chicago School Reform Act embodies a very different philosophy of meeting the needs of at-risk students. It is a grand experiment in attempting to force schools to change to meet the needs of their students. It is still too early to tell whether this experiment will be successful. At the midway point, it is encouraging that so much organizational change has occurred. But much must be done to embody a similar amount of change in the instructional programs of the city's schools.

REFERENCES

Bennett, A. L., Bryk, A. S., Easton, J. Q., Kerbow, D., Luppescu, S., & Sebring, P. A. (1992). *Charting reform: The principals' perspective.* Chicago: Consortium on Chicago School Research.

Brookover, W. B., & Lezotte, L. W. (1979). *Changes in school characteristics coincident with changes in student achievement.* East Lansing: Michigan State University.

Byrd defends school anti-dropout role. (1987, January 18). *Chicago Tribune,* Sec. 4, p. 2

Chicago Panel on Public School Policy and Finance. (1989). *Teacher attitudes toward school reform.* Chicago: Author.

Chicago Panel on Public School Policy and Finance. (1990). *Chicago public schools databook: School year 1988–1989.* Chicago: Author.

Consortium on Chicago School Research. (1992). *Data brief: Assistance provided by central and district offices to principals of Chicago public schools.* Unpublished paper released to the press and circulated by the Consortium.

Easton, J. Q., Bryk, A. S., Driscoll, M. E., Kotsakis, J. G., Sebring, P. A., & van der Ploeg, A. J. (1991). *Charting reform: The teachers' turn.* Chicago: Consortium on Chicago School Research. [Reprinted in *Catalyst*, 1991, September, *III*(1), 1–16.]

Easton, J. Q., & Hess, G. A., Jr. (1990). *The changing racial enrollment patterns in Chicago's schools.* Chicago: Chicago Panel on Public School Policy and Finance.

Edmonds, R. (1979). Effective schools for the urban poor. *Educational Leadership, 37*, 15–18.

Flinspach, S. L., & Ryan, S. P. (1992). *Vision and accountability in school improvement planning.* Chicago: Chicago Panel on Public School Policy and Finance.

Hammond, R., & Howard, J. P. (1986, Fall). Doing what's expected of you: The roots and the rise of the dropout culture. *METROPOLITAN Education, (2),* 53–71.

Hess, G. A., Jr. (1986). Educational triage in an urban school setting. *METROPOLITAN Education, (2),* 39–52.

Hess, G. A., Jr. (1991). *School restructuring, Chicago style.* Newbury Park, CA: Corwin Press.

Hess, G. A., Jr. (1992). *School restructuring, Chicago style: A midway report.* Chicago: Chicago Panel on Public School Policy and Finance.

Hess, G. A., Jr., & Greer, J. L. (1987). *Bending the twig: The elementary years and dropout rates in the Chicago public schools.* Chicago: Chicago Panel on Public School Policy and Finance.

Hess, G. A., Jr., & Lauber, D. (1985). *Dropouts from the Chicago public schools.* Chicago: Chicago Panel on Public School Finances.

Hess, G. A., Jr., Lyons, A., Corsino, L., & Wells, E. (1989). *Against the odds: The early identification of dropouts.* Chicago: Chicago Panel on Public School Policy and Finance.

Hess, G. A., Jr., & Warden, C. A. (1987). *Who benefits from desegregation now?* Chicago: Chicago Panel on Public School Policy and Finance.

Hess, G. A., Jr., & Warden, C. A. (1988, Fall). Who benefits from desegregation now? *Journal of Negro Education, 57*, 536–551.

Hess, G. A., Jr., Wells, E., Prindle, C., Kaplan, B., & Liffman, P. (1986). *"Where's room 185?" How schools can reduce their dropout problem.* Chicago: Chicago Panel on Public School Policy and Finance.

Louis, K. S., & Miles, M. (1990). *Improving the urban high school: What works and why.* New York: Teachers College Press.

Moore, D. R., & Radford-Hill, S. (1982). *Caught in the web: Misplaced children in Chicago's classes for the mentally retarded.* Chicago: Designs for Change.

Nelson, F. H., Yong, R., & Hess, G. A., Jr. (1985). *Implementing educational reform in Illinois.* Chicago: Chicago Panel on Public School Policy and Finance.

Purkey, S. C., & Smith, M. S. (1983). Effective schools: A review. *The Elementary School Journal, 81*(1), 426–452.

Wehlage, G. G., & Rutter, R. A. (1986). Dropping out: How much do schools contribute to the problem? *Teachers College Record, 87*(3), 374–392.

CHAPTER 11

Children At Risk in America's Rural Schools

Economic and Cultural Dimensions

ALAN J. DEYOUNG

During America's early twentieth-century Country Life Movement, many citizens began to have serious second thoughts about the abandonment of rural America that had accompanied our industrial development (e.g., Grantham, 1983). Since then, a vision of the countryside as some sort of a paradise lost appears related to episodic flights of many urban Americans away from perceived problems of the city, even registering briefly on the demographers' scale as a "reverse migration trend" in the 1970s. Yet, the data on rural life in America do not support many of the benign assumptions about the quality of life available to those who work and live there now. The cruel irony is that while many Americans express interest in rural or small town life, those living in the countryside now are often belittled and stereotyped in a variety of negative ways.

IMAGES AND REALITIES OF RURAL AMERICA TODAY

Demographic information about rural America suggests an incomplete but complicated picture. According to the U.S. Census, metropolitan areas comprise counties with a central city of at least 50,000, together with their surrounding suburbs; everything else constitutes "non-metro." Under such a nomenclature, approximately 25% of the U.S. population lives in non-metro (by default, rural) areas. However, among non-metro counties, those with the largest growth rates this century typically have been in counties adjacent to metropolitan ones, suggesting the growth of employment and cultural ties between many non-metro communities and metropolitan America.

One fact that demographic information accurately suggests is that rural America is no longer primarily agricultural, nor has it been for decades. Actually, there are eight primary types of economic activities to be found within America's 2,443 non-metro counties: farming, mining, manufacturing, retirement, government services, federal lands, persistent poverty, and "unclassified." Of these counties, only 702, or 29%, are farm "dependent." There are also 242 non-metro counties categorized as persistent poverty counties; 200 counties whose economies rely on mining; and 515 counties whose economies are based on retirement income (Bender et al., 1985).

This suggests that non-metropolitan America is very diverse, that much of it is nonagricultural, that much of it is poor, and that many of the contexts and subcultures of rural America are heavily influenced by the age, income, and extractive nature of occupations of those who live and work within them. Even where agriculture is the dominant industry, most modern farming is really "agribusiness," meaning that fewer and fewer people are actually engaged in farming even as crop yields rise. Successful farmers today more typically consider themselves to be high-technology businesspeople engaged in agriculture. And, there are entire rural states that do not generate enough farm income to be considered agricultural by the U.S. government, due to modern agricultural production and distribution factors. Accordingly, fewer and fewer American rural children live on farms in stereotypical farm households. Rather, only about one-twelfth of all rural children live on farms, and only one of 11 rural jobs is a farm-related job (Children's Defense Fund [CDF], 1992).

Poverty in Rural America

Most chronically poor counties in the nation continue to be located in non-metro areas, particularly in Appalachia and the South. In 1986, the non-metro poverty rate was 50% higher than the metro rate (O'Hare, 1988). In fact, general poverty rates for all non-metro counties nearly equaled the poverty rate for our central cities in the late 1980s (CDF, 1992; Porter, 1989). Rural poverty in the 1980s also stayed higher, rose more rapidly, and fell more slowly in the "recovery" period (O'Hare, 1988). Displaced rural workers were unemployed more than 50% longer than urban workers and, when they did return to work, were more likely than urban workers to take pay cuts and lose insurance benefits (Podgursky, 1988). Among the 242 persistent poverty counties in 1985, average per capita income has been in the lowest U.S. income quintile over at least the past 4 decades.

For that matter, average per capita income declined substantially during the 1980s even in counties with high outputs from manufacturing and extraction. Jobs created in rural America are typically positions paying either minimum wage or close to it (Reid, 1990). Manufacturing plants that locate in the countryside tend to be of the low-wage and routine production type, resulting in lower wages compared with those earned in metro America (Lyson, 1989). In addition, workers in rural service occupations — where the bulk of new rural employment is projected to occur — are also having economic difficulty. Even full-time workers in service industries have extremely high poverty rates. Controlling for inflation, annual pay per job *fell* 7% from 1979 to 1988 for rural off-farm workers, even as more and more rural families moved closer to metropolitan areas in order to seek employment.

Although some communities attracted manufacturing plants in the 1960s and 1970s, many of these left rural America during the 1980s to go "off-shore." The net loss of manufacturing jobs even between 1979 and 1986 in rural America was 12% (McGranahan, 1987). As mining operations continue to be mechanized, coal tonnage continues to rise, as do rates of unemployment among miners. At the same time, compensatory government assistance programs have changed and had negative consequences for many rural children and families. In 1979, federal government benefits reduced poverty levels for approximately 20% of rural families. In 1987, only 10% of rural families so benefited. Aid to Families with Dependent Children (AFDC) benefits in rural states are typically much lower than similar benefits in more metropolitan states (CDF, 1992).

Racial and ethnic inequality is also well-represented in rural America, for 29% of the rural poor are minorities, and they suffer more severely from poverty than either rural whites or urban minorities. For example, 44% of rural African-Americans were poor in 1987, compared with 33% of their urban counterparts. The poverty rate of rural African-Americans exceeds the poverty rate of rural whites by 200%, and similar contrasts characterize the relationships of poverty rates among rural Hispanics, American Indians, and Alaska Natives.

Great Society writings on the status of poor rural children typically suggested that rural places and their inhabitants could be positively affected once rural citizens had access to the knowledge and social programs emerging in metropolitan America (e.g., Harrington, 1962). Later assessments in general have been more critical, suggesting that many local communities and their children remain trapped in declining local economies with few real avenues of upward social mobility, save for the "escape" to the city where they become city problems rather than country problems. In any event, rural poverty has not disappeared with further maturation of our national economy.

An important misconception about rural families living in poverty is that their living costs must be lower as housing costs and agricultural products both must be significantly cheaper in the country. While dwelling costs generally *are* lower in rural America, related costs such as garbage collection, sewage, and water are rarely included in urban versus rural comparisons. When separate costs for water lines, gas lines, septic services, and garbage disposal are factored in, rural costs of living more closely approximate those of cities. In addition, few rural families produce more than a fraction of their foodstuffs today. And transportation costs in rural America are significantly higher than in metropolitan areas (CDF, 1992).

Schooling Issues Related to Rural At-Risk Children

Twenty-two percent of America's schools are non-metro, and 12% of our children attend them. Beyond that, we have only recently begun to investigate the status of rural education as it pertains to children at risk. The National Rural Development Institute (NRDI, 1990) completed a large national survey of rural, urban, and suburban school districts specifically related to perceptions held by school administrators regarding the nature and severity of at-risk conditions in rural schools. While return rates for this survey were arguably too low for the sorts of statistical analyses policy makers might desire, the tentative findings were consistent with images created by the previous review of income and family conditions in rural America.

Among the at-risk categories proposed by the NRDI were substance abuser, depression/low self-esteem, child abuse victim, sexually active, disabled, illiterate, and poor. The NRDI also included several student disability categories and school levels to co-vary with their at-risk categories. Respondents were asked to describe the percentage of their students (both handicapped and nonhandicapped) who fell into the various categories provided. In comparisons of rural versus nonrural children across all student types and at-risk categories, 39 of the variables analyzed yielded significant differences between rural and nonrural students using multiple analysis of variance protocols. Of the 39, reported incidences of at-risk situations/conditions were *higher* for rural students than nonrural students in 34 comparisons. That is, in only 5 of 39 comparisons did nonrural (typically urban) school administrators report higher incidences of at-risk situations in their schools than did rural school administrators. In the nonhandicapped category, 19.3% of rural students were reported to be from dysfunctional families; 18.8% from poverty households; 13.7% as being depressed or having low self-esteem; and 11.4% as being victims of child abuse.

In a report to the National Rural Small Schools Task Force, by the Council for Educational Development and Research (CEDaR, 1987), 2,445 rural school teachers, superintendents, and school board members were queried regarding their perceptions of priorities for rural schools across the nation. Among their responses were many that reflected national concerns as well as rural ones: For example, 60% believed that the thinking and reasoning skills of their students were inadequate and required attention, and 36% believed that the quality of staff inservice programs needed to be improved. In addition, 60% of survey respondents were particularly concerned with the academic performance of their (rural) students from low-income families, 48% were concerned with their inability to reward or recognize outstanding teachers, and 41% feared for the levels of self-esteem and aspirations of their students. Regional differences were also clearly recognizable in the CEDaR survey: School administrators in Appalachia and the South reported far worse schooling situations than in any of the other regions.

The Children's Defense Fund summarized a variety of data-based studies related to children at risk, and argued that rural schools and their students suffer a number of important weaknesses compared with schools in much of metropolitan America. The CDF notes, for example, that providing equal educational opportunities in rural places is more costly than in metropolitan places, given economies of scale considerations. In sparsely populated school districts, costs of offering services and/or courses similar to those in larger schools is typically higher when calculated on a per-student basis. Yet, since many rural states have no or minimal cost equalization formulas based on population density, local taxes must be relied on heavily to equalize expenditures. Naturally, poor school systems have difficulty in generating such extra taxes, leading to significant inequities. These inequities become translated into fewer mathematics and advanced placement courses in rural high schools, fewer programs for either gifted and talented children or alternative school programs and programs for pregnant teenagers, or in some cases even the failure to provide transportation to and from school (CDF, 1992).

The CDF study also reported on a number of other metro/non-metro comparisons of schools based on national studies like the High School and Beyond survey and the National Assessment of Educational Progress. Among the findings are: Rural teachers are less experienced, less well-trained, and have faster turnover rates than metropolitan teachers; achieve-

ment scores for rural students are slightly below those of students in metropolitan areas; high school dropout rates are higher in rural America than
in metropolitan America; rural school dropouts are less likely to return to
school than are those in cities; out-migration of young people who have
completed high school is high, leaving more poorly educated citizens behind; and the rural college-going and college-completing rate is lower for
rural high school graduates than for graduates of metro schools.

SCHOOLING, INSTRUMENTALISM, AND
RURAL EDUCATION REFORM

Accounts of rural poverty and rural schooling difficulties typically
cite the sorts of economic and sociological data just presented, prior to
making programmatic suggestions. Unfortunately, most policy briefs on
such concerns pay little attention to local school and community *histories*
and *cultures* as they pertain to school improvement issues. In rural regions
contiguous to metropolitan areas and/or where economic development
trends have culturally transformed a host of local institutions and employment possibilities, such a focus may be comparatively unimportant. On
the other hand, in depressed and isolated schools and school districts —
where arguably the majority of at-risk students live and go to school —
such factors are probably quite central to anyone interested in positively
intervening in rural public education.

Extensive formal schooling in the United States has by now become
an economic ultimatum rather than an opportunity. Although there remains a strong (and perhaps valid) academic criticism of educational "cre-
dentialism" in American culture, it remains the case that most of the
children who are not equipped with at least a high school diploma are
and will remain economically and socially at risk throughout their lives.
Yet, such a conviction was *not* the basis on which rural schools in the
United States were historically based, and equivocal feelings about such
usefulness of education in many (often depressed and isolated) rural communities remain even today.

Educational traditions in much of rural America predate the advent
of common schooling and secondary education, both of which were more
specifically instituted toward instrumental outcomes of schooling in a mul-
tiethnic and rapidly urbanizing America. Expenditures for public education and expectations for student success today remain underlying themes
of contemporary schooling dedicated to the view that educational investments are investments in the national economy, improving worker productivity, and promoting national citizenship (Schultz, 1981). Such reform

efforts are similar to those internationally, yet with our decentralized system of school governance, school improvements must be filtered through literally thousands of state and local education agencies.

Boli and Ramirez (1986) suggest that contemporary educational policies and practice internationally rely on various world views and institutional structures that directly conflict with the underlying beliefs and economic experiences of many rural families and communities. For example, market-driven national economies depend on individuals (not families or communities) becoming primary social units, and children (rather than adults) are the main focus of public schooling. Schools thus increasingly become sites for the creation of individual actors oriented toward occupations and careers potentially far removed from local communities.

Pedagogical orientations of modern schooling, according to Boli and Ramirez, involve curricular and organizational teachings that undercut the importance of place and kinship bonds, which are still of significance in many rural American communities. In their place, children are taught to believe that individual success in contemporary America occurs primarily as a function of state economic development policy and national/international trade success. Further, as the key to economic participation is ideologically linked to educational attainment, citizens are encouraged to accept the centrality of school certificates and credentials in their lives — one of the assumptions on which this work is also partly based. School documents and credentials thus legitimate the individual's entrance into the national workplace, a workplace at least partly controlled by the state.

Creating "One Best System" in the United States

The public school revolution that occurred in this nation during the late nineteenth and early twentieth centuries was primarily an *urban* and *industrial* inspired revolution, although at the time it was announced as a unilateral victory for the forces of moral uplift and social progress (Tyack, 1974). Exploding city growth during this period was fueled by rural inmigration and foreign immigration. Such demographic changes were also accompanied by labor unrest and middle-class perceptions that newly arriving city dwellers were driving down their previous quality of life. As a consequence, school building and school reform movements quickly gathered momentum.

In searching for institutional models upon which to organize city schools, city leaders and professional educators quickly judged rural educational models as too archaic and unprofessional for their purposes. Schooling was increasingly championed by reformers as an activity best guided by specialized knowledge as supervised by administrators well-versed in both the science of child development and scientific (i.e., efficient) management. Professionalizing public education statewide meant that teachers and principals required better certification and that enhanced accountability measures were needed. In the main, late nineteenth and early twentieth century school reformers had little but pity and/or contempt for rural schools and rural communities (Cubberley, 1914).

The urban "critique" of rural school governance and finance was probably correct by contemporary standards. Many of the rural organizational characteristics were viewed as archaic by metropolitan-based school reformers. Untrained school board members and trustees made many school decisions; attendance rates were generally lower than in the city; dropout rates were high; building maintenance was usually performed on a volunteer basis by parents; rural teachers frequently were less well-prepared than city teachers; classes were typically mixed-grade; supervision of one- and two-room schools was administratively almost impossible, and so on (Tyack, 1974).

Reformers interested in "improving" rural schools generally believed improvement could happen in only one of two ways: Either rural schools would disappear, as continued out-migration removed children from rural places, or rural schools could be made to look and operate more like urban ones. An alternative interpretation is that various rural school characteristics represented cultural values quite different from the ones that helped found the common school movement. And then as now, many religious, locally based, and nonindustrial rural cultures were frequently at odds with the emerging conventional wisdom of schooling (DeYoung & Theobald, 1991).

Rural Views of Schooling

With important exceptions, many rural parents challenged the alleged superiority of mental over manual labor inherent in late nineteenth-century calls for secondary education, which appeared to many as preparatory for college enrollments in towns and cities and not as an education that would return native sons and daughters to the land (Perkinson, 1991). In the current era, high school completion rates remain lower where graduation appears to bear little local utility due to large-scale unemployment and/or where low-skilled extractive and/or service industries provide the major source of employment (DeYoung, 1985).

Other bases of rural school support also came under attack by metropolitan school reformers later in the twentieth century. For example, Christian moral instruction was an important curricular orientation of most American schools before the progressive era; yet, the secular and professional interests of many school reformers directly challenged these moral underpinnings and led to significant resistance in much of rural America. Even today in rural states like Kentucky, Arkansas, Tennessee, and West Virginia, there are ongoing challenges to proscriptions against displaying the Ten Commandments, challenges to the teaching of evolution, and/or battles over "offensive" textbooks (Page & Clelland, 1978).

Rural School Consolidation

Historically, rural communities placed high value on traditional family (and extended-family) relationships, sense of community, and the importance of "place." Rural school reform throughout the twentieth century, however, devalued and undercut such traditional interests via school consolidation efforts dedicated to professionalism, curricular diversity, and efficiency. As late as 1930, there were 128,000 school districts and over 238,000 schools in America. By 1980, however, the number of school districts had dropped to 16,000 and schools to 61,000 (Stephens & Perry, 1991).

Even today, at a time when many urban school systems have begun to decentralize schools for various pedagogic reasons, some primarily rural states continue massive rural school closure policies under economies of scale arguments (Sher, 1986). The students and communities most inconvenienced — in terms of bus-ride times for students and inaccessibility to parents — are those most isolated and impoverished.

AN ILLUSTRATIVE CASE STUDY

The problems of rural U.S. students at risk of school failure and/or incompletion are in many ways similar to problems of low-income children and young people in metropolitan America. Yet, many chronically depressed and isolated rural communities still involved in extractive economies or dependent on single labor-intensive and unskilled industries often are characterized by schools without the funds to remediate many schooling deficiencies associated with rural poverty; family and community values inconsistent with modern career orientations and instrumental schooling; and parents who believe that college is financially unavailable.

The West Virginia county school system that is the subject of this research provides a good illustration (unfortunately) of many of the topics discussed so far, as well as of a number of school-based strategies for addressing the needs of rural at-risk children.[1] This system actually contains two administratively distinct populations: a K–4 elementary school and a small 5–8 middle school that share one building. Total enrollment of all grades plus kindergarten and prekindergarten is approximately 295. The school in question was constructed between 1916 and 1925 and designed as a "town" school for grades 1–12. Over the years, however, the town's once prosperous economy collapsed, and the school is considered rural. Its attendance area has also changed so that "the rural kids" in the countryside, who used to sometimes continue their schooling in town after elementary grades, are now all bused into the former town school daily. All of the former one- and two-room schools that flourished earlier in this century in outlying areas of the county have been closed during the past 3 decades.

Burnsville, the town in question, was a bustling American community until the 1930s. Today, there is virtually no local economy, and most families remaining in and around the town are economically disadvantaged in multiple ways. The majority of county households either depend on some form of government income assistance and/or have absent household heads working in far-removed construction or timbering industries. Frequently, children of Burnsville School dwell in trailers or small-frame housing located strategically along rural roads, and often they live in multiple generational units. Life in and around Burnsville today would undoubtedly disappoint city dwellers looking to escape to rural America.

Braxton County: A Brief History

Burnsville is located in Braxton County, West Virginia, the central-most of West Virginia's 55 counties. Its history is critically tied to America's industrial revolution, but its ties to this revolution, many claim, have been to its detriment (e.g., Eller, 1982). The county has depended on the extractive industries of timbering, coal mining, and gas and oil drilling during the past hundred years. Unfortunately, many of these industries usually have been owned by outside corporations who pay little tax on the wealth they control underground. In addition, with a nationwide recession in manufacturing, reducing the need for natural resources, even the extractive jobs remaining in Braxton County typically require little formal schooling.

Agricultural opportunities in central West Virginia have been quite limited in size and scope during this century. Most of the small-scale farming in the "hollows" of thousands of rivers and streams in West Virginia led to a more marginal/subsistence life-style than was available in better located agricultural settings to the east and the west. The isolation of communities in central West Virginia led to primarily local economic, social, and kinship systems whose social organization of production and reproduction differed from that in other regions of the United States.

Yet Braxton County was geographically and economically fortunate in the nineteenth and early twentieth centuries compared with other Appalachian regions. Two navigable rivers linked the county with the outside world and enabled a number of successful commercial activities to develop there. Transportation made possible by the Elk and Little Kanawha Rivers also enabled the construction of several small towns in Braxton County, including Burnsville, Sutton, and Gassaway. Each of these towns had newspapers, banks, hotels, department stores, various mainline church denominations, and public schools—in other words, all the accoutrements associated with a strong and growing middle class.

The schools, in particular, showed signs of "progress" during the period, as the old subscription schools and later one-room schools increasingly became eclipsed in the larger population centers by larger and graded schools—much like the earlier pattern in northeastern states (Cremin, 1961). Reading central West Virginia teacher oral histories of the early twentieth century makes schooling there sound very similar to schooling to be found in most American communities prior to the Great Depression.

By the 1920s, Braxton County contained approximately 140 rural schools and four high schools. Some children graduated from outlying one- and two-room schools and came into the high schools. Most probably did not. Until the past several decades, employment in extractive industries usually did not require a high school education. And when there was work in the mines, in gas exploration, and in timbering—typically the major sources of work in Braxton County—there was invariably little incentive to develop the sorts of advanced professional skills that might have led to jobs in some distant place whose industries fed off Braxton County's extractive economy.

Burnsville's economy was at first based on extractive industries and local manufacturing, both made commercially possible by the Little Kanawha River. This river passes through oil and gas country and into the Ohio at Parkersburg. Timber extraction, oil and gas drilling, several veneer factories, a (wooden) wheel factory supplying Ford and other companies, and a wagon factory put Burnsville "on the map" in the late nineteenth and early twentieth centuries. Yet, as the boom periods of coal, timber, oil, and gas subsided, and as the railroads and local manufacturing firms were undercut by the "hard roads" that went around central West Virginia more than through it, regional economic decline also became personal and institutional disasters. By the 1950s, Braxton County had joined the ranks of most economically depressed regions of the country, where unemployment was high, wages were low, and dramatic outmigration of many of its citizens had been occurring for at least 2 decades.

Decline occurred in almost every positive economic area. In 1930, agricultural workers in the county constituted over 60% of the workforce. By 1980, they accounted for less than 3%. While paved roads were built in the county, interstate commerce made possible by major highways mostly bypassed it, at the same time undercutting rail transportation. With the demise of the railroad, hundreds of employees throughout the county lost their jobs, visitors no longer traveled by rail into and through the county, and markets for the few agricultural and manufactured goods still being produced in the region became even harder to reach.

Economic Decline and School Consolidation

Educational decline began to set in around the time of the larger national depression of the 1930s. During this period, many large tracts of land held by outside interests were forfeited to the state for nonpayment of taxes — taxes that supported public education. Without jobs and incomes, many remaining residents faced loss of property if previous tax rates continued, and a statewide constitutional amendment was passed in 1932 that placed a cap on property assessments. This had a further predictable impact on revenues available for local school funding. Due to lack of funds, many teachers remained unpaid, and school terms were either shortened or the schools closed altogether. In 1933, the state's 398 school districts were consolidated into 55 districts to coincide with county units. In so doing, the state of West Virginia took on significant responsibility for the financing of schools in the 55 county districts, making more than state-required funding minimums dependent on special local elections.

Many metropolitan counties in West Virginia have been able to raise extra taxes for schooling (i.e., excess levies), while the poorer rural counties, like Braxton, have not. Since growing transportation costs and teacher salaries use the bulk of county funding in places like Braxton County, building maintenance and construction typically have suffered. Coupled with out-migration, the net effect was dramatic school consolidation.

Educational Instability

Burnsville schools and their children have inherited a great number of legacies from the boom-and-bust county history. When the county's high schools were consolidated for financial reasons in 1969, Burnsville's former ninth to twelfth graders were all bused to the new (but unfinished) county high school. Shortly thereafter, Burnsville's remaining movie theater, bowling alley, and several restaurants, which depended on the high school crowd for business, all went out of operation.

All of these developments were made possible by the completion of I–79, which runs virtually overhead of Burnsville School. The interstate has in some ways dealt a deathblow to Burnsville: Half of the town was torn down to build it, and the people who are still left and own a car now use the interstate to drive either north or south to shop. The county high school was also made possible by the interstate, for it sits at the Flatwoods exit some 12 miles south of Burnsville.

Burnsville's middle school is being consolidated with the county's two other middle schools in order to (again) save money for the district. Like the former high school consolidation project, middle school consolidation is supposed to provide an attractive new facility with a larger and more varied curriculum. Not surprisingly, many if not most Burnsville residents remain opposed to the school consolidation. They fear further deterioration of their small town and are dubious about the claimed quality of the county middle school. They have good reason to be suspicious.

Instabilities associated with the proposed new facility continue to affect school climate throughout the county. On the one hand, construction appears behind schedule, and not even the contractor is certain if the new building will be completed on time. In addition, changing state policies on seniority versus staff quality in the hiring of teachers, bus drivers, and custodial staff for consolidating school districts have colored many personnel issues for almost 2 years. The county administration had hoped that building and staffing a completely new school facility would allow for hirings independent of traditional seniority-based protocols. However, after staff had been chosen and partially trained for the new school based on applicant qualifications, the state overruled such attempts in another county school system, and Braxton County decided to comply with seniority guidelines in their final staffing decisions.

Many teachers throughout the system thus had their 1992 career expectations significantly altered in the spring of 1991, and a number who were previously chosen to teach at the new middle school were cut completely from the county teaching roles based on seniority considerations. All eight of Burnsville Middle School's regular classroom teachers were at first chosen to teach at the county middle school based on their teaching evaluations, but seniority protocols reduced this number to six, and the two "losers" were RIFfed (reduced in force) and had no job in the school system for 1992–93.

How the county statistics on economic decline, population outmigration, and school consolidation are experienced in Burnsville is a general concern of this research. A central theme that has emerged involves the numbers and types of people who "are not around" anymore in Burnsville. These are probably the sorts of people who used to provide a major source of financial and emotional support for Burnsville School. In an age in which community support of learner outcomes increasingly has been championed as an important strategy for improving all schools, the absence of the most accomplished white-collar graduates of Burnsville High may be significant.

For quite some time, Burnsville has been a place where the only time highly educated and professional people — other than schoolteachers — can be seen on the street is during the spring and summer when large groups have their reunions. One of the biggest annual gatherings in Burnsville is that of the Kanawha Alumni Association, which meets on Memorial Day weekend every year. This association of approximately 500 members all are graduates of Burnsville High (or graduates of the county high school who would have graduated from Burnsville) and is the largest high school alumni association in the state — even though Burnsville hasn't been a high school for more than 20 years. Unfortunately, there is almost no interaction anymore between Kanawha alumni and current students at Burnsville schools. Most alumni live hundreds of miles away, and, as the current president phrased it recently, "there really hasn't been much enthusiasm for the school (programs) once the high school was taken away."

Children above the age of 10 and adults who used to be found in Burnsville but have migrated out won't "be around" any longer, but the school *building* will remain. The Braxton County Board of Education would like to build a new elementary school facility on Kanawha Street, but they haven't got enough money. So, 150 or so young children will remain in portions of the old facility for at least a few more years. This appears somewhat ironic to local residents, who were told that one reason older children were being removed was because of the asbestos hazards of the old building that were too expensive to remove.

At-Risk Students in Braxton County Schools

Assuming poverty as a primary indicator, more than half of all Braxton County's students are officially at risk. The county's economy has been depressed for over a decade, and the official unemployment rate in mid-1992 was approximately 20%. Of course, the unofficial rate was probably much higher. Current economic development patterns there are of four different types, but each is unlikely to transform the economic future of the county. Coal operations are scheduled to begin again in several years in the southern end of the county, but the jobs they may provide will just about offset those lost at another site. Several years ago the operator of the county landfill applied for a permit to enable his facility to begin bringing in large quantities of out-of-state garbage. At the current time, this "economic development" scheme remains on hold.

A rapidly growing service industry based on interstate travel *has* emerged in the past 5 years. The Flatwoods exit on I–79 now has a host of fast food, truck stop, and motel franchises. All of these places provide many minimum-wage jobs for local citizens, but few require advanced education or inspire career orientations at the county high school located just a stone's throw from most of these businesses.

Another development near the high school and the fast food restaurants is the soon to be completed regional jail. The regional jail is eagerly awaited by many, since dozens of county residents will get a chance to work there as cooks, janitors, and guards. The county already has lots of people who may be able to cook and clean at the prison: These are the sorts of jobs also fought for at the county schools. And since the county's largest employer (i.e., the school system) is laying off workers due to consolidation and state funding cutbacks, competition for these jobs is likely to be intense.

Meanwhile, more than 50% of the children enrolled in the system's nine elementary and middle schools (99% of whom are white) were below the poverty line in 1991. In one elementary school, 77% of the children received free or reduced-price lunches; in the least poverty-affected school, 53% fell into this category. At the combined Burnsville elementary and middle schools, 63% of the students received free or reduced-price lunches and/or breakfasts. According to Mr. McCoy, the principal, however, the actual figure would be much higher if all those eligible applied. Many parents, he suggests, remain poor but proud.

To signify how the national economy affects Braxton County schools, enrollment levels in the county's prekindergarten programs have risen significantly during the past 3 years. Central office staff believe that many families now coming into Braxton County are back living with parents and siblings in the wake of job losses in metropolitan America. Many of these families allegedly are waiting for (typically minimum-wage) jobs to be restored. Meanwhile, the number of prekindergarten poor children qualifying in 1992 for Head Start money increased by almost 20% (to 74%) over 1990 levels.

Statistical information on Burnsville students and their families suggests the socioeconomic status of those who attend and teach at the elementary and middle schools. Sixteen percent of the student bodies are from "professional" households — many are the children of teachers. Twenty-eight percent are from blue-collar homes; frequently children from these homes live in households where one parent is absent on a weekly basis, engaged in work in another county or state. Thirty percent of the schools' 297 students come from homes where parents work in unskilled trades or service industries; 18% from families with just enough income to not qualify for welfare; and 7% from families on AFDC.

Of the 31 students who started seventh grade in September, 28 finished the school year. Of these, 14 lived in households with both parents working, four had at least one working parent absent on a weekly basis, two lived in multigenerational homes, and 12 lived either in homes without both natural parents or in single-parent families. Mr. McCoy classified 8 of these 28 students as at risk because of either their attitudes toward school, the attitudes of their parents toward school, or the attitudes of the parents toward their children. Unlike many principals in metropolitan areas, Mr. McCoy claimed his knowledge of each student's situation was based on 22 years of experience with each of the families of these children and from working with most of them for 7 or 8 years.

District Philosophy for At-Risk Students

Almost all county instructional programs are based on what the district superintendent argues is an at-risk educational philosophy. In his judgment, Braxton County schools can be successful only if they provide local children with the types of programs and instruction that will make them successful in life and that will win the larger support of the entire community. He suggests this has not always been the case in Braxton County.

District philosophy is built around the notion that basic literacy and numeracy are a must. Therefore, academic instruction, constant monitoring of pupil performance, strong building leadership, high expectations, and a positive learning climate are emphasized at all schools. In effect, then, guidelines of the Effective Schools movement underlie many of the day-to-day operations of Braxton County schools, and almost half of the county's principals and a significant percentage of the district's teachers have been sponsored to attend state-level workshops on Effective School organizational strategies. Apparently the system-wide emphasis on academic skills has paid off in Braxton County, for its schools have been among the state's highest grade-level scorers (at the earlier grades) since the mid-1980s.

In addition, district education policy subsidizes a number of out-of-school educational endeavors as support services to the school system. The superintendent and school board believe that building public trust in the schools and providing positive learning experiences for children require recreational and literary support systems in the larger community as well as the schools. Thus, even in the face of district budget shortfalls, the school system has helped fund the three town libraries and helped raise funds for the county recreational park, located not far from the high school. The system also is quite aggressive with regard to its GED and active parenting programs, seeking out state and federal grants for supplemental programs consistent with district educational philosophy.

At-Risk Programs in the Burnsville Schools

The Burnsville schools historically have had significant community support, although instructional programs currently involving parents are relatively low. Many poorer families live out of town and aren't able to drive to the school easily. Other families have two wage earners, which makes volunteering to help difficult. There are adult education and active parenting programs available in Burnsville, but these are both small and run out of the board office and the library rather than the schools themselves. And, unlike metropolitan schools that may be able to bolster community support via school–business partnerships, such partnerships are less feasible in Burnsville, for it has very few businesses to speak of.

Nevertheless, there remains a belief in town that Burnsville schools provide a sound education and moral instruction, and that the teachers there usually do a good job. Most teachers and noncertified workers have been in the school for a number of years. Many who work in the school graduated from it when it was a high school. Thus almost all school people are well-known locally, and they appear very trusted by the public at large.

Mr. McCoy has also been at Burnsville for 22 years and is involved with many if not most civic groups in town. He is an elder in the Methodist Church; he teaches hunter safety to most of the middle school children; he is a county scout leader; he is treasurer of his bowling league; and he is a member of the Masonic Lodge. He also symbolizes a bridge to a more cosmopolitan world, for his father used to be an engineer when trains ran routinely through the region; and his teaching area is science.

Even in the face of constant budget shortfalls and school closings, an air of staff stability exists at Burnsville School. Budget cutbacks have cost the school teachers and staff over the years, but almost never do teachers in Braxton County resign and move away. Both the elementary and middle schools retain an emphasis on instruction and academics, and several teachers have won statewide awards for innovation in instruction. Community support, both historically and currently, is high, and like other rural schools, support of athletic events (which draw the most parents to school now) is a major indicator of how the community identifies with the Burnsville middle school. Faculty morale was high at both schools in 1991 and 1992, and the fact that almost every teacher who had children enrolled them in the school is a testimonial to the respect teachers have for the school and its programs.

Paradoxically perhaps, Mr. McCoy reports few formal programs for at-risk children in the school. While arguing that most Burnsville children are developmentally or socially at risk, he continues to emphasize the caring environment directed toward school success that is focused on enhancing positive self-concepts among all children. Such school-wide programs as Assertive Discipline and School-Based Assistance Teams have been proposed and instituted in the Burnsville schools, but special pull-out programs where children are identified as needing extra help are not part of the schools' philosophy. There is a part-time gifted education teacher, a part-time speech and hearing teacher, and a full-time special education teacher; however, because these individuals typically have multiple certifications, have worked "both sides of the street" with exceptional learners, and frequently share instructional spaces and materials, younger children would probably find it difficult to comprehend how they had been grouped for particular attention in these schools.

One of the specific efforts undertaken at most Braxton County schools appears to be routine school-wide award ceremonies that publicize student success. Good grades, positive citizenship, and other special achievements are widely proclaimed throughout the school during the year, and most of these ceremonies are covered in both county newspapers, even though many parents cannot or do not attend such events.

Concerns at Braxton County High School

While reorganizing elementary and middle school programs toward a general "at-risk" philosophy appears to have been successful, the major battle in Braxton County during the past decade has been at the high school level. Arguments over vocationalism versus academics and school-wide emphasis on meeting student needs versus subject-matter specialization have been pronounced. By 1992, a school-wide climate of caring and open communication appeared to have been achieved, but as recently as 2 years earlier, the school system that produces among the highest elementary reading scores statewide had longitudinal dropout rates of approximately 30%, among the state's highest.

Since Braxton County is a place where few jobs requiring a high school diploma are available, where poverty and dysfunctional families are prevalent, and where higher education opportunities historically have been absent, "explaining" the dropout rate as a function of extra-school factors has a long history. Under the rationale of improving the school climate to improve the likelihood of school success among the at-risk student population, however, the high school was in effect told to take "ownership" of the dropout problem rather than to attribute dropout rates to contextual factors or to "problem" students (DeYoung, 1991).

In 1987, monies from the Job Training Partnership Act and Appalachian Regional Commission were used for an innovative dropout prevention program based loosely on cooperative learning strategies. According to the program, dropping out of school is the final event in a student's career, an event that can be negated if/when teachers and other school-based staff undertake the task of analyzing and remediating the causes for student decisions to leave school. Accordingly, "student advocacy teams" composed of teachers, staff, and students were formed to intercede in the school careers of identified at-risk students. Great pressure was put on the school to utilize such tactics over and above the wishes of the building principal, who was alleged to be less committed to this agenda than the central office was.

By 1992, the longitudinal dropout rate had declined to approximately 12%, and the 4-year college-going rate for 1991 graduates soared to almost 50%, up from 25% only several years earlier. Three school improvement thrusts were reported to have been responsible for the turnaround. The primary thrust involved a change in school climate. A new principal was hired after the former principal's death in 1990 and announced his intention to have *all* students succeed in Braxton County High School, not just those academically inclined. At the same time, he instituted a number of rewards for perfect attendance, including early school dismissal for some students and free entry into a number of school functions. According to the school guidance counselor, his philosophy (much changed from that of his predecessor) was that the role of high school "is not to punish students but to help them." He is credited by the guidance counselor with treating all BCHS students with "dignity."

It seems highly unlikely that one person — that is, the new principal — could transform BCHS as dramatically as the statistics indicate in just 2 years. More plausibly, his appointment to the school also served as a catalyst for school improvement already present but underdeveloped in the years just prior to his hiring. While developing and maintaining a "climate of success" appears to have become a major preoccupation of school staff, specific skills and programs for at-risk students were also developed.

In addition to remedial and tutorial help, programs to heighten the expectations of students for post-high school opportunities have been installed in BCHS during the past 2 years. For example, a student "shadowing program" was put into place, whereby students go into the few local businesses and workplaces to observe the world of work. More recently, BCHS obtained external funding to underwrite its Aim High program, which enables all interested students to visit various higher education institutions in the state and helps them understand the requirements and protocols for admission.

Tensions between vocational and academic programs and interests abound in rural high schools like BCHS. In order to expand the curriculum to accommodate both academic and vocational interests, the school system has pushed some of the college-prep courses down into the eighth grade, while striving to continue most of the vocational programs (like keyboarding) of potential relevance to both academic and vocational students.

In effect, then, Braxton County schools, with their new middle school reorganization, are hoping to better prepare young adolescents for eventual college enrollments. At the same time, efforts to make BCHS less impersonal continue, and, in addition to a more student-centered school climate and high expectations and support services for at-risk students, BCHS also is working with outside community agencies and programs targeted at adolescents. In a number of ways, then, BCHS seems to have altered a more traditional model of high school as a site for academic instruction to one of advocacy, referral, and instruction.

CONCLUSION

The educational stories I am interested in telling about Braxton County, West Virginia, and its schools reflect but one set of iterations of rural life and rural education in the United States. There are virtually no majority–minority conflicts in this county, and there are no open political feuds that frequently affect community life and schooling dynamics in many rural places. People here trust the schools and revere the good teachers who have labored for so long for comparatively little reward. Nevertheless, there are significant educational issues and problems here that approximate many of those mentioned early in this chapter as specifically related to the futures of students at risk.

Braxton County schools, like most schools in economically depressed and isolated places, face a number of problems in dealing with their at-risk student populations. Because local tax dollars still are a primary funding mechanism for schools, places with few resources have difficulty in funding special programs for at-risk students. Thus, *inherited* economic disadvantage in rural places usually has consequences *for the present and for the future.* Redefining the economic base on which depressed rural schools can build their programs has to be near the top of the list of any systematic effort to improve the life chances of at-risk rural students.

Redefining the *purpose* of schools must also be a primary concern of schools with significant numbers of children at risk of not completing school. In places where desired role models are absent and the local structure of opportunities is limited, schools must attempt to demonstrate and inculcate the incentives necessary for students to complete school. Such incentives may more often be taken for granted in suburban schools, but they cannot be in places like Braxton County. School people there recognize that they are enmeshed in an economic, historic, and cultural battle, not just an instructional one.

Braxton County schools probably do more with what they have than many school systems do. They provide sound academic instruction, comprehensive services, and an attitude of caring. They intervene forcibly in the cultural politics of the United States, for they instill values and teach skills required for a national culture and an international economy in a region arguably socially and economically scarred by national success in such areas.

Effective rural schools typically "export" their best "products," leaving behind families and communities that often are or ought to be anxious or ambivalent about school success and school completion. In places like Braxton County, schools are arguably a more central institution to the individual success of at-risk students than they are in metropolitan America; yet, they have an even more difficult time in providing the sorts of education and cultural services necessary to facilitate student persistence and school completion. National efforts to improve the life chances of rural at-risk children ought to better recognize and better support rural schools like those of Braxton County. They are not the cause of economic decline in rural places. Rather, they are the institutions that have to live and work with the consequences of such decline.

ACKNOWLEDGMENTS

The brief case study presented in this chapter was partially funded by the Spencer Foundation of Chicago, IL, and the Claude Benedum Foundation of Pittsburgh, PA. I would also like to thank the Appalachia Educational Lab of Charleston, WV, and West Virginia University for their particular contributions to my research and the composition of this manuscript.

REFERENCES

Bender, L., Green, B., Hady, T., Kuehn, J., Nelson, M., Perkinson, L., & Ross, P. (1985). *The diverse social and economic structure of nonmetropolitan America* (Rural Development Research Report Number 49, United States Department of Agriculture, Economic Research Service). Washington, DC: U.S. Government Printing Office.

Boli, J., & Ramirez, F. (1986). World culture and the institutional development of mass education. In J. Richardson (Ed.), *Handbook of theory and research for the sociology of education* (pp. 65–90). New York: Greenwood Press.

Children's Defense Fund. (1992). *Falling by the wayside: Children in rural America*. Washington, DC: Author.

Council for Educational Development and Research. (1987). *Building on excellence: Regional priorities for the improvement of rural, small schools*. Washington, DC: Author.

Cremin, L. (1961). *The transformation of the school*. New York: Vintage Books.

Cubberley, E. (1914). *Rural life and education: A study of the rural school problem as a phase of the rural life problem*. New York: Houghton Mifflin.

DeYoung, A. J. (1985). Economic development and educational status in Appalachian Kentucky. *Comparative Educational Review, 29*(1), 47–67.

DeYoung, A. J. (1991). *Struggling with their histories: Economic decline and educational improvement in four rural southeastern school districts*. Norwood, NJ: Ablex.

DeYoung, A. J., & Theobald, P. (1991). Community schools in the national context: The social and cultural impact of educational reform movements on American rural schools. *Journal of Research in Rural Education, 7*(3), 3–14.

Eller, R. (1982). *Miners, millhands and mountaineers*. Knoxville: University of Tennessee Press.

Grantham, D. (1983). *Southern progressivism: The reconciliation of progress and tradition*. Knoxville: University of Tennessee Press.

Harrington, M. (1962). *The other America: Poverty in the United States*. Baltimore, MD: Penguin Books.

Lyson, T. (1989). *Two sides to the sunbelt*. New York: Praeger.

McGranahan, D. (1987). The role of rural workers in the national economy. In D. Brown & K. Deavers (Eds.), *Rural economic development in the 1980s* (ERS Staff Report No. AGES870724; Chapter 2). Washington, DC: U.S. Department of Agriculture, Economic Research Service. (ERIC Document Reproduction Service No. ED 313 211)

National Rural Development Institute. (1990). *A national study regarding at-risk students*. Bellingham, WA: Author.

O'Hare, W. (1988). *The rise of poverty in rural America*. Washington, DC: Population Reference Bureau. (ERIC Document Reproduction Service No. ED 302 350)

Page, A., & Clelland, D. (1978). The Kanawha county textbook controversy: A study of the politics of life style concern. *Social Forces, 57*(1), 265–281.

Perkinson, H. (1991). *The imperfect panacea: American faith in education, 1865–1990*. New York: McGraw-Hill.

Podgursky, M. (1988). *Job displacement and the rural worker*. Washington, DC: Economic Policy Institute. (ERIC Document Reproduction Service No. ED 325 281)

Porter, K. (1989). *Poverty in rural America: A national overview.* Washington, DC: Center on Budget and Policy Priorities. (ERIC Document Reproduction Service No. ED 309 901)

Reid, J. (1990, April). *Education and rural development: A review of recent evidence.* Paper presented at the annual meeting of the American Educational Research Association, Boston.

Schultz, T. (1981). *Investing in people.* Berkeley: University of California Press.

Sher, J. P. (1986). *Heavy meddle.* Raleigh: North Carolina School Boards Association.

Stephens, R., & Perry, W. (1991). A proposed federal and state policy agenda for rural education in the decade of the 1990s. In A. J. DeYoung (Ed.), *Rural education: Issues and practice* (pp. 333–394). New York: Garland.

Tyack, D. (1974). *The one best system: A history of American urban education.* Cambridge, MA: Harvard University Press.

Part IV

FRAMEWORKS FOR CHANGE

The two chapters in this part build upon the preceding parts and attempt to draw together findings and conclusions to form frameworks for educational change. In Chapter 12, James McPartland integrates the work of other chapter authors with results from new analyses to bolster support for a fourfold typology posited as a general framework for understanding student motivation and student willingness to remain enrolled in school. In Chapter 13, Samuel Stringfield sees in all that has been learned an absence of attention to the seriousness of the problem of school failure. He challenges policy makers, researchers, and practitioners to think of schools as High Reliability Organizations whose failure cannot and should not be tolerated.

These two chapters offer complementary perspectives on the next steps that should be taken to create meaningful improvements in our educational system. McPartland's typology suggests ways the experiences of students can be improved directly, and the High Reliability Organizations described by Stringfield suggest the sort of intense care, attention, and commitment needed to implement and sustain those improvements.

CHAPTER 12

Dropout Prevention in Theory and Practice

JAMES M. MCPARTLAND

Is there a small set of common themes in the various explanations for why certain students drop out of school and in the panoply of current programs to reduce these risks? Such an organizing scheme would be useful for both theory and practice, going beyond the usual categories of demographic risk factors to better understand students' own reasons for staying in school, and giving school planners a more comprehensive checklist of program components needed to increase the holding power of schools. A small set of program components with high priority in a clear theory of dropout prevention would also be useful in evaluating data on current dropout prevention efforts in American schools.

This chapter will present a fourfold typology developed as a general theory of student motivation to stay in school and work hard at learning tasks. To show its usefulness in organizing a rich array of ideas and potential solutions, major themes developed in other chapters of this volume and practical dropout prevention approaches described earlier will be located within this typology. In addition, the dropout component of the National Education Longitudinal Study of 1988 (NELS:88 Dropout Study), which covers a nationally representative sample of 1,034 recent student dropouts,[1] will be analyzed to validate the typology's categorization of dropout prevention approaches and to describe how well actual practice meets the needs identified in theory.

A TYPOLOGY OF SOURCES OF STUDENT MOTIVATION TO STAY IN SCHOOL

School officials designing a dropout prevention program for their own locality cannot easily learn from the experiences of others who have attempted the same thing, because each of the numerous written accounts of such efforts stands alone as a case study combining different features into a unique program for the given situation. It is unlikely that a *program* developed elsewhere can be duplicated exactly in another site, because local talents and priorities for school reform, the particular needs and interests of the students to be served, and the conditions of the school to be changed will differ. Instead of some brand-name, prepackaged, complete program to be replicated, local school reformers require a coherent set of general *components* to increase the holding power of schools serving students at risk, which can be adapted to fit local circumstances. Each of the components could then be given different priorities to fit professional judgments about the most serious problems at the local site, and each dimension could be implemented in different forms to meet the nuances of the school's own demography and resources.

For the same reason, it has also been difficult for educational researchers to get a handle on dropout prevention activities in American schools. Much previous research has focused solely on profiles of the dropout student population rather than on analyses of the interrelationships of school efforts at dropout prevention and learner needs. While existing surveys have revealed that almost every school with a significant dropout problem claims to have a "dropout prevention program," how does one assess what is actually going on in each school and what specific features are most effective? To further understand *why* particular approaches work better than others requires a testable theory that links particular general components of school reform to reductions in dropout rates of particular at-risk populations through some key student processes such as alienation or motivation.

A small group of researchers at the Johns Hopkins University Center for Research on Effective Schools for Disadvantaged Students has developed a conceptual framework on dropout prevention approaches to better organize case study materials on the issue and to provide a better research basis for developing and testing theories of the causes and alleviation of school dropouts.[2] We assembled existing accounts of dropout prevention programs and existing interview data from dropouts themselves, from which we sought to derive common themes. We decided to develop our conceptual framework from the perspective of the student, and how general sources of motivation to stay in school and engage with schoolwork are influenced by particular experiences with the school environment. So we also considered general treatments on different types of student motivation in developing our framework.[3] We present the resulting four-fold typology in this chapter, with some recent reformulations to meet the goals of this volume.

Any typology is a theoretical categorization produced by the cross-tabulation of two or more defining variables. Actually, we developed our fourfold typology as a stand-alone list of four generic categories before we recognized that the same categories could be generated by the intersection of two more general underlying variables. Figure 12.1 presents our typology in the more traditional format, using two initial variables to create the four key components.

We begin with the underlying variables of Type of Organizational Environment (Formal and Informal) and Nature of Organizational Problems (Internal and External). In terms of the school as the organization of interest, the distinction of Organizational Environment translates into the school's academic goals (as the Formal dimension) and the social relations of the school (as the Informal dimension). This distinction of school environments is similar to recent general theories of alternative schools developed by Wehlage and his co-workers (1989) and of effective lea. ning environments by Bryk and his associates (1990), who use the terms "bureaucratic goals" and "learning community goals" as their basic dimensions. The other underlying variable pertains to whether Organizational Problems exist that are Internal, concerning within-school experiences, or External, involving connections with the outside world. The intersection of these variables produces the four key components (described below) used to analyze different sources of student motivation to stay in school and work hard at school learning goals.

FIGURE 12.1 Typology of sources of student motivation to stay in school and work hard on school learning goals

		Type of Organizational Environment	
		Formal (School Academic Goals)	Informal (School Social Relations)
Nature of Organizational Problems	Internal (within school experiences)	Opportunities for success in schoolwork	Human climate of caring and support
	External (connections with the outside world)	Relevance of school to students' community and future	Help with student's personal problems

Opportunities for Success in Schoolwork

Students need to feel successful in schoolwork to continue giving their best efforts to classroom assignments, but many at-risk students experience only frustration and failure in their quest for academic recognition and rewards. When the National Education Longitudinal Study (NELS:88) Dropout Study asked students' reasons for leaving school on a checklist of 21 items, besides reporting the general reason "I didn't like school," the next most frequent responses included "I was failing school" and "I couldn't keep up with my schoolwork" (Ingels, Scott, Lindmark, Frankel, & Myers, 1992). Several correlational studies of factors that predict dropping out (e.g., Rumberger, 1987) also have found measures of school failure such as low report card marks and retention in grade to be the most powerful precursors of leaving school before graduation. On the recent survey, over 40% of high school dropouts had been held back a grade in school in the past 2 years. The importance of school success was also emphasized in the same survey when the major reason dropouts would consider returning to school from a list of 17 items was found to be "you felt sure you could graduate."

Lack of success at schoolwork deprives at-risk students of the motivation to stay in school that should come from the immediate rewards of good grades, teacher praise, and family pride. Without these positive responses to their efforts at classroom tasks, at-risk students lose their self-confidence as learners and stop caring about doing well in school. Rather than continue to pursue good grades, which they may find are out of their reach, they cease to place value on school success as something that reflects on their own worth and self-esteem (Natriello, 1989).

Many students from poor or minority backgrounds are particularly at risk of being deprived of opportunities for school success because they have weaker resources at home and in their communities to support learning of academic subjects. Although their families often care deeply about their school success, parents whose own educational accomplishments are weak and neighborhoods that have serious distractions from schoolwork place their students at a continuing disadvantage in competing for academic rewards. At-risk students usually begin school less well-prepared for schoolwork and remain well below average for their entire school careers.

Many ideas have been presented in the preceding chapters to increase opportunities for academic success of students at risk by changing specific school practices. In Chapter 2 Legters and McDill review offering intensive programs in the early grades to overcome initial disadvantages and build a firm foundation of basic reading skills; providing substantial extra help through peer tutoring or extended course time in later grades to prevent failures and grade retentions; and changing the criteria for school success to make academic rewards accessible to all students who work hard through added recognition for individual growth and improvement, or replacement of boring paper-and-pencil tests with a variety of assessment modalities where all students can show what they have learned and will care to do so. In Chapter 8 Fine outlines new assessment approaches to make schools in a large city work better for students at risk, including portfolios, exhibitions, performances, and other ways for students to demonstrate competencies beyond the traditional, short paper-and-pencil tests. In Chapter 11 DeYoung reports on a rural high school that was able to reduce its high dropout rate by instituting a new climate of success for all students, backed up by a number of new rewards for good attendance and coursework and extra help for individual students from counselors, one-on-one teacher tutors, and administrators who place emphasis on helping rather than punishing students who had problems in school.

The practical difficulties in bringing about real classroom reform are highlighted in Chapter 10 by Hess, who describes how school-based reforms in Chicago have initially favored "add-on" programs such as afterschool, preschool, or summer school programs. Hess reports that efforts to reform the regular classroom experiences of students have been much less frequent, in part because they require a high degree of teacher willingness to change and significant professional development time and staff support to implement new directions.

In Chapter 7 Rumberger and Larson describe how the ALAS program for junior high Chicano students provides immediate feedback on student behavior, including close monitoring of period-by-period attendance and regular (daily, if necessary) teacher feedback to students *and parents* on classroom performance and attendance. Boykin's analysis in Chapter 6 of the educational reforms best suited for African-American children includes a strong emphasis on talent development through routine opportunities for success experiences, as opposed to the penchant for assessing and sorting individuals, which he sees as the traditional overriding perspective in our school systems. For Hispanic learners, Valdivieso and Nicolau call in Chapter 5 for a standard core curriculum that includes no program or classroom tracking, is based on involved active learning activities, provides extra time and help from tutors, and provides added class time for any student who has serious English language deficits or who needs help to succeed in other core subjects.

Human Climate of Caring and Support

Students need to feel that the adults in their school are on their side and ready to help them in their pursuit of school goals. But many poor or minority students rarely experience a close positive experience with school adults or, even worse, come to believe that teachers and other school officials are there primarily to *sort* them into categories defined by lower grades and tracks rather than to *support* their efforts and ambitions as learners. Rather than seeing their school as a supportive "community of learners," as suggested by Wehlage, Rutter, Smith, Lesko, and Fernandez (1989), many students at risk see an impersonal institution that serves as an often hostile holding pen for them during their growing years. The NELS:88 survey of students' reasons for dropping out of school found that "I couldn't get along with the teachers" ranked close to the top, right after reasons concerning failure at schoolwork (Ingels et al., 1992). Negative perceptions of teachers and the general school climate are often strongly reinforced by student peer groups who share the same backgrounds and experiences. The same national survey shows that nearly three-quarters of recent dropouts had close friends who also left school before graduation, and almost the same percentage had high school-aged brothers or sisters who had also dropped out.

The motivation derived from teachers and peers can be a powerful force in how individual students approach their learning tasks. Teacher approval can be a strong influence on student efforts from the earliest grades, and peer acceptance emerges as another dominant factor as students move into early adolescence and adolescence. Teacher expectations of a student's abilities and peer norms for a student's behavior often become internalized as the individual student defines his or her own self-expectations and priorities. A teacher who communicates low expectations of a student's ability to learn challenging material will usually discourage the student's own confidence as a learner and interest in earning the teacher's recognition for good schoolwork. A peer group that places low value on doing well in schoolwork can enforce this viewpoint on its members and inhibit any contrary behavior.

Students from poor and minority backgrounds are especially likely to feel socially alienated from their schools and to be negatively influenced by the antischool feelings of their peer groups. Such students are more likely to be in schools segregated by lower socioeconomic class and race — schools in which academic norms for completing school and going on to college are often weak — and the school climate frequently fails to emphasize academic excellence. Disadvantaged students are much more likely to be assigned to the lower tracks and ability groups within their schools, where teacher expectations often are low and other learning resources weak. Such students in urban locations are more likely to be attending large departmentalized middle and high schools, where establishing a close positive relationship with teachers is difficult, especially if an individual is not a top student. And poor or minority students are often the victims of misunderstandings about teachers' directions or intentions because of the cultural differences between them, and are sometimes the targets of remaining prejudicial attitudes of some educators toward racial-ethnic minorities and lower socioeconomic-background students.

The preceding chapters have also covered this topic in numerous ways. Montgomery and Rossi (Chapter 1) delineate the ways in which risk factors that affect students may interact with school experiences to limit recognized attainments, while Gordon and Yowell (Chapter 3) emphasize the dynamic relationship between individuals and schools that can often produce at-risk conditions. Legters and McDill (Chapter 2) list several ideas for breaking down the anonymity of the large departmentalized school and for building a supportive human climate, and Fine (Chapter 8), in describing the development of urban "charter schools," shows that building a "community of learners" of teachers and students is possible when educators take on the task of defining the school climate and assuming real responsibility for each student's welfare.

Rumberger and Larson (Chapter 7) also focus on efforts to increase at-risk students' sense of membership or bonding to their school, describing how the ALAS program provides adult advocates and increased extracurricular activities in a large Los Angeles junior high school enrolling a high percentage of Chicano students. These authors describe principles the ALAS staff found important in establishing positive adult–student relationships. Valdivieso and Nicolau (Chapter 5) present similar themes in their description of the gulf between school and home perceptions of the expectations of schools, parental roles and responsibilities regarding their children's formal schooling, and proper behavioral manifestations of key attitudes such as respect, childhood conversations with adults, and family initiatives and relationships with agencies and officials.

Relevance of School to Students' Community and Future

Students need to relate schoolwork to their own lives and future goals if they are to give serious attention to their classroom learning activities. But schoolwork makes little sense to many poor or minority students, because their classroom tasks seem boring and meaningless, with little connection to their own experiences and expectations for later life. When dropouts reported on the NELS:88 Dropout Study that "I didn't like school" was their major reason for leaving school, it is safe to assume they rarely found much interest in their school assignments or could identify personal reasons for getting involved with schoolwork. The NELS:88 Dropout Study also shows that when dropouts consider reasons for returning to school, they list "you felt sure you could get a good job after graduation" and "school was more interesting to you" at the very top, just behind their desire to be academically successful in achieving graduation.

Students who see little relevance of school to their own experiences and futures are deprived of the intrinsic motivation that comes from interesting activities and of the instrumental motivation that comes from activities that have a strong payoff potential. Passive learning assignments delivered in the traditional teacher-lecture-and-student-listen modes give little opportunity for the initiative and spontaneity that can often be self-motivating to a learner. Intrinsic motivation must also be weak when the frequent learning objective for the student is to acquire a disconnected set of facts or algorithms to be regurgitated on the next test, rather than to acquire an understanding of a complex topic or to creatively apply higher-order skills to a challenging problem. Moreover, what students learn in many courses or how well they do in classwork is seldom linked to their instrumental motivation of getting a good job or entering a favored career. Research has shown that employers pay little attention to records of school performance when hiring for most jobs not requiring a college degree, which weakens student motivation to excel in schoolwork (Bishop, 1989). School curricula in the major subject areas rarely integrate academic and vocational or career emphases, which have remained separate programs and courses in most schools. Thus students may have a vague notion that their course content may be "useful" in later life, but few really understand how course skills might apply to real-world problems or how course content may be prerequisite knowledge for particular career goals or later life roles.

Poor and minority students face particularly strong barriers to motivation from the lack of relevance of their school experiences to current interests or future goals. The inherent content of classroom activities is most likely to be passive low-level, drill-and-practice learning tasks in the bottom tracks and ability groups where those students are overrepresented. The curriculum at all levels continues to give scant attention to the cultural traditions and historic individual contributions of minority students' own ethnic heritages, creating further daily barriers to finding inherent interest and stimulation in their schoolwork. Because poor and minority students have weaker prospects for going on to college, they will not make the instrumental links between current efforts at schoolwork and college admission, which sustain the efforts of many other students even when the classwork is dull. Connections between good school behavior and employment opportunities are also weakest for lower-level jobs, which are the only ones many poor and minority students will qualify for following high school.

This issue of relevance of school for student motivation has been prominent in several preceding chapters, especially reforms to imbue school curriculum with cultural referents and current experiences that students can relate to from the perspective of their racial-ethnic heritage and community. In Chapter 6 Boykin develops a multifaceted framework for understanding the importance of a culturally sensitive and culturally appropriate educational context for the schooling of African-American children. Boykin explains how children come to school with different sets of cultural rules that may interfere with learning by conflicting with their teachers' points of reference, regulations for behavior, or criteria for positive recognition. He also reviews modern theories of learning in contexts that prescribe using and building upon the backgrounds and experiences brought to school by children as the optimal basis for cognitive growth and motivation to learn. Valdivieso and Nicolau provide several ideas in Chapter 5 for tying the school program of Hispanic students to employment and college goals, including flexible schedules and work-study programs so high school students can combine school and work; strong counseling, especially for Hispanic females, to link current schoolwork to realistic educational and occupational ambitions; and providing incentives and support during middle and high school for advancement to postsecondary education. In Chapter 4 Noley describes the long history of denial of American Indian cultural heritage in their children's formal schooling, and recent efforts by American Indian educators to increase the numbers of role models in the classroom and the respect for cultural integrity in the curriculum.

Other ideas for making school more relevant can be found in Chapter 2 by Legters and McDill, including curriculum reform to introduce active learning of higher-order competencies (without tracking) for all students, connecting current schoolwork with college and employment opportunities through better information about the links for all parties, and integration of academic and career emphases in a common curriculum or in various career academic programs. In Chapter 8 Fine describes activities to support the transition from high school to college as one of the key ideas in the efforts to reform urban high schools, and she includes major changes in curriculum and instruction as another major theme in efforts to engage students in active, multicultural, collaborative learning to effect classroom relevance and interest for student motivation. Finally, in Chapter 11 DeYoung analyzes the difficulties faced by many rural schools in motivating students to stay in school when the local economy does not offer many employment opportunities that require a high school diploma or the advanced skills taught in the secondary grades. He reports that a new high school program to bring high school students in to local workplaces and to arrange student visits to higher education institutions has helped some students connect schoolwork to life after high school and has contributed to a reduction in the dropout rate.

Help with Students' Personal Problems

Students need to be free of serious personal problems — such as hunger, substance abuse, teenage parenthood, or abusive homes — if they are to concentrate on their proper school roles and responsibilities. But many students at risk have developed self-inhibiting personal activities or come from families or neighborhoods that present major obstacles to their attention and energies for schoolwork. For example, 15% of recent female dropouts gave the reason "I was pregnant" to account for their leaving school on the NELS:88 survey (Ingels et al., 1992). About 15% of surveyed dropouts also reported that being suspended or expelled from school led directly to their decision to drop out, suggesting that a mismatch of school demands and personal coping skills is another significant source of the problem. The same national survey indicates that the need to care for or support family members and to hold a job got in the way of staying in school for about 15% of recent dropouts, and about 10% had recently been in a drug or alcohol rehabilitation program. Such motivational distractions can make school concerns seem inconsequential for many troubled youth and rob them of their chance to experience and enjoy normal student life, which causes further estrangement from school roles and routines. Too often, the outside problems or added responsibilities simply negate any chance these individuals may have to think of themselves as students and participate in conventional school activities. The same national survey found that one-quarter of recent dropouts reported, "I felt I didn't belong in school."

Poor and minority students are especially at risk of falling prey to the various serious personal problems inside and outside of the school that can lead to dropping out. The unemployment, crime, and family instability in many poor neighborhoods create a breeding ground for various problems of youth and contribute to a sense of hopelessness that drives many youth to behaviors that damage their chances of getting a good education.

Preceding chapters describe these conditions and provide many ideas on how services provided by or coordinated with schools can help ameliorate outside problems of family or neighborhood. In Chapter 1 Montgomery and Rossi note that personal problems and conditions interrelate with school offerings within the more encompassing context of social and socioeconomic opportunities and limitations. They consider not only the need to directly counteract multiple risks in order to close disparities with which students may enter school, but also the requirement of new educational programs to strengthen the motivational power of positive school climates and interesting school activities that can attract and hold student energies and commitments. In Chapter 2 Legters and McDill review approaches to integrate social service agencies with school programs to address special students' needs and to create positive partnerships among school, home, and community representatives.

The New York City dropout prevention program, discussed by Grannis in Chapter 9, focused on first solving student problems outside of school so students and schools could then function successfully as intended. This chapter, in particular, highlights the problems and limitations of investing heavily in social services delivered by community-based organizations as a primary focus to reduce course failures, retentions, absenteeism, and dropouts. Besides the problems of coordination between different agencies and targeting of services to the most needy, who frequently have limited English proficiency, Grannis concludes that a social service-oriented solution for student needs may deflect attention away from the more fundamental changes by teachers and school programs that are needed to create climates and experiences to support student efforts at school completion. He cites evaluations that see merit in more flexible high school schedules (such as late afternoon makeup classes or opportunities to work for pay and earn a GED), as well as more accessible social support systems (such as peer tutors, peer mediation of conflicts, and smaller houses or subschools with adult mentors for each student).

Fine (Chapter 8) discusses how access to community-based services was a key element in a city's multiphased efforts to make high schools work better for disadvantaged students, and Rumberger and Larson (Chapter 7) describe how providing a direct problem-solving training program for students can reduce school problems such as truancy and classroom misbehavior, and how attending to students' home or family problems is often also needed to solve their school problems. Valdivieso and Nicolau (Chapter 5) also see professional social services as an essential component of an effective learning program for Hispanic students, including family life planning to avoid early adult responsibilities that curtail realistic education or career advancement, and school-based sexuality education and health clinics to reduce the risks of a variety of self-inhibiting behaviors. DeYoung (Chapter 11), describing factors that have helped a rural high school reduce its dropout rate, includes the integration of physical and mental health agency services into the school program, and Noley (Chapter 4) describes recent direct efforts to deal with student problems, such as drug and alcohol abuse and teen pregnancy, in American Indian schools.

Four Essential Components

The four components identified here as sources of student motivation to remain in school should be present in any dropout prevention program because the absence of any one component can be sufficient to create serious dropout problems and the presence of each component should serve to strengthen the efficacy of the remaining components. For example, if a high school student is having serious problems with either of the components related to connections with the outside world, such as seeing no relevance of schoolwork to future goals or being overwhelmed by personal family difficulties, it is unlikely that good internal school experiences, such as passing grades and caring teachers, will in themselves be enough to hold that individual in school as a conscientious student. On the other hand, if each component is established at a reasonable positive level, the combination should interact to prevent dropouts and engage student energies for schoolwork, as opportunities to succeed on meaningful learning tasks are bolstered by a supportive social climate uninhibited by negative outside distractions.

MATCHING THEORY AND PRACTICE: RESULTS FROM A NATIONAL SURVEY

The opportunity to assess actual practice in dropout prevention programs, in light of the theory-driven fourfold typology presented above, is provided by the School Principal First Follow-up Component of the National Education Longitudinal Study of 1988 (NELS:88 Principal Follow-up), which covers a subsample of 535 public high schools with dropout prevention programs and can be merged with the sample from the NELS:88 Dropout Study referred to earlier in this chapter.[4] The NELS:88 Principal Follow-up will be used to validate the typology as an organizing scheme for dropout prevention approaches and in combination with the NELS:88 Dropout Study to evaluate how well current programs match the actual needs and interests of students at risk.

The NELS:88 sample includes 535 public schools in which principals reported the existence of dropout prevention programs. These principals were asked several additional questions about their programs, including the number of students who participate; the bases on which students are recommended for participation; whether formal classes are included and when, where, and how often these classes are held; their opinions on factors influencing students to drop out; and the following two sets of questions, which we used to validate the typology.

- *Question Set One*. Principals were asked to indicate the level of emphases given by their programs to the following components of our fourfold typology:

    1. Providing opportunities for academic success
    2. Providing positive social relationships in school
    3. Communicating the relevance of education to future endeavors
    4. Reducing the negative impact of family or community

- *Question Set Two*. Principals were also asked to indicate which of the following services their dropout prevention program offered:

    1. Special instructional programs
    2. Tutoring by teachers
    3. Peer tutoring
    4. Incentives for better attendance or classroom performance
    5. Close monitoring of student attendance or classroom performance
    6. Individual or group counseling
    7. Career counseling
    8. Job placement assistance
    9. Health care
    10. Child care or nurseries for children of students

We analyzed whether this list of 10 items formed a smaller set of empirically related items and whether the resulting set matched up with our fourfold typology. A factor analysis (Varimax rotation) was performed on the 10-item checklist to derive categories of services that were most often provided together in the same school. Four clusters of items resulted: academic services (primary loadings from Items 1 and 5), tutoring and counseling services (Items 2, 3, and 6), employment services (Items 7 and 8), and social services (Items 9, 10, and 4). We then conducted a follow-up series of factor analyses, adding one component at a time from the four components included in Question Set One to the 10-item checklist of services in Question Set Two to study how each component lined up with the services factors. As shown in Table 12.1, the components of our typology fit the services factors as expected: "Providing opportunities for academic

TABLE 12.1 Loading of typology component on each service factor (read across for the same factor analysis)

	Academic Services	Tutoring and Counseling	Employment Services	Social Services
Opportunities for academic success	.726	.177	−.252	.056
Supportive human climate	−.144	.403		.219
Relevance of school	−.036	−.082	.785	.036
Help with outside problems	−.175	.405		.271

success" was most strongly associated with the academic services factor; "providing positive social relationships in school" (which we have called "supportive human climate") was most strongly associated with tutoring and counseling services; "communicating the relevance of education to future endeavors" (which we have called "relevance of school") was most strongly associated with employment services; and "reducing the negative impact of family or community" (which we have called "help with outside problems") was most strongly associated with either social services or tutoring and counseling services (depending on whether comparisons are made down the column or across the row of Table 12.1). These findings confirm that our fourfold typology provides four separate categories that cover a wide variety of existing and basic dropout prevention components, and that the categories define particular subsets of services that have similar substantive meaning and are likely to be used together in the same school dropout prevention programs.

MATCHING DROPOUT PREVENTION PROGRAMS
TO STUDENT NEEDS

NELS:88 data can also be used to study which dropout prevention components are used most frequently in different school situations and how well they address actual student needs. As expected, schools with higher dropout rates are much more likely to have instituted dropout prevention programs, and there is a clear rank ordering of major emphasis in these programs to each of our four components.

Ranked first for major emphasis in existing dropout preventions programs is "opportunities for academic success" with a probability of .84, followed by "relevance of school" with a probability of .76, "supportive human climate" with a probability of .67, and "help with outside problems" with a probability of .57. Recalling the examples of activities associated with each component, it appears that schools with serious dropout problems are most likely to offer some remedial courses to help with "opportunities for academic success" and to provide some career counseling or job-related coursework to help with "relevance," but to give less emphasis to improving the "human climate" or to providing "help with outside problems."

The national sample of dropout students was examined separately to investigate whether the particular dropout prevention programs available in their schools were given different emphases to match the particular reasons given for leaving school. Only about two out of three students of the NELS:88 Dropout Study sample had left a high school that offered any specific dropout prevention program at all, which, while better than the total national NELS:88 Principal Follow-up rate of about two out of five, indicates a serious shortfall in meeting the needs of at-risk high school students. Moreover, there were no patterns in the emphases given to different components of existing dropout prevention programs to match the particular reasons given by students who had dropped out. The school programs for students who had dropped out generally followed the same rank order of components regardless of the reasons given by the students, even though schools might be expected to know when they had serious specific problems such as student alienation or teenage pregnancies. In particular, the component "help with outside problems" invariably ranked lowest in emphasis, even in schools where students listed as reasons for dropping out personal problems such as disciplinary suspensions and expulsions from school or family responsibilities due to their teenage parenthood or problems at home.

Regardless of the presence of some prevention activities under one or more of the typology components, it seems evident that the activities are currently not up to the task of significantly increasing the holding power of schools for students at risk. Although most high school principals with dropout problems report prevention programs aimed at priority components, the dropout rates remain at alarming levels in a great many high schools. Clearly the current activities are not basic or intense enough to reform the primary causes of low student motivation to remain in high school that have been identified by educational theory. It seems that most current school programs are add-on or supplemental approaches that do not get at the basic structures and characteristics of schools that can turn off many students. For example, in addressing the component "opportunities for academic success," schools appear more likely to add remedial classes and services than to address the basic issues of tracking, grading, and promotion practices that contribute to student discouragement and failure in their academic pursuits. To be sure, investing in significant additional convenient resources can be very important in helping students who are well below average to meet core academic standards. But as long as grading practices give no recognition to individual improvements, and tracking with unequal resources and retention in grade are the primary school responses to student diversity, it is unlikely that opportunities for academic success will be expanded enough to make a major difference in dropout rates.

In addressing the "relevance of school" component, schools appear more likely to add vocational offerings and career counseling than to install basic curriculum changes that actively involve students in interesting learning activities connected with their own experiences and real-world issues or to experiment with more flexible arrangements that combine school and work experiences. Likewise, multicultural programs that go no further than recognition in textbooks of minority figures, with little change in minority adult role models on staff or desegregated schools and classrooms with cross-group support programs, are not likely to be effective.

"Supportive human climate" does not get the same attention in school dropout prevention programs as other components, even though students who drop out rank alienation from school staff as a prime reason for quitting school, second only to experiences of failure in coursework and grade promotions. The issue goes beyond the size and departmentalization of schools that limit chances for close relationships between teachers and students. It involves the perception by many students that school adults function to sort them, not support them in academic terms, and is reflected in the orientation of many teachers toward their subject-matter expertise rather than their share in responsibility for each student's academic success. Such a climate is sustained by the criteria used to assess students and evaluate teachers and by the structures of grades and tracks that condition relationships between students and adults in schools. Innovations in current practice, such as adult advisor-mentors and teams of students and teachers who work together and are judged together over sustained periods of a school career, can help penetrate these barriers. But basic reforms must also be made in setting and enforcing the priority goals of schools; that is, supporting the individual development of all students rather than sorting and selecting students for particular instructional experiences.

"Help with outside problems" is the component found to receive the least general attention in current dropout prevention programs, although it is needed as a first priority by some students at risk. Again, it is not so simple a matter as finding resources for more add-on programs in physical or mental health services or other social service assistance. To avoid another dumping ground for problem students removed from classrooms, it will be necessary to include the student's own regular school team of educators in any activities using outside professional help. We do not now understand how best to coordinate the work of different professionals focused on the problems and welfare of an individual student — because basic reform in bringing help from outside sources into the school context is not very far along.

Thus, in each key regard, incremental add-on changes have not proved to be powerful enough to solve continuing school dropout problems and are unlikely to make further inroads in keeping more students in school through high school graduation. More basic reforms are needed that address the underlying theory-based sources of student motivation in each key component.

IMPLICATIONS FOR NEW PROGRAM DIRECTIONS IN DROPOUT PREVENTION

Several of the chapters in this volume have argued persuasively that *implementation processes* need to be effective to bring new programs for dropout prevention into reality, including adequate resources for program design and staff development, and procedures to involve local educators throughout the design and implementation phases to gain strong local ownerships of reforms aimed at conditions of the local site. This chapter is about the *content* of dropout prevention approaches that is necessary for the programs to work well and includes recommendations on program content from other chapters, while assuming that strong implementation processes are used to elicit proper local variations and to support adequate staff development along the way.

This chapter's comparison of the theory and practice of dropout prevention in American schools suggests two dimensions of new directions required to make major improvements in reducing dropouts in the future: First, programs should be developed around key components of effective approaches, and second, the actual changes under each key component must involve basic reforms in the roles and responsibilities of students and staff and in the character of learning activities.

Components of Change

School district leaders and local school improvement teams working on dropout prevention goals should be encouraged to develop their programs around a small set of *key components* of school improvement, such as the fourfold typology offered in this chapter or any other theory-based outline of a comprehensive approach to attract the energy and commitment of students at risk.

A major advantage of building local school reforms around key components grounded in theories of the school factors leading to student dropout is that it forces local staff to better understand the school sources of dropout problems and to think about possible solutions in more creative ways. By considering the theory of how deficiencies in each key school component can destroy student motivation to stay in school, local educators can confront the ways schools themselves should change to reduce dropouts. Working through the theory-based reasons under each component that link particular school reforms to student motivation, local staff can decide which components should take priority at their own site and develop their own explanations for trying new approaches to increase the holding power of their school. Most important, with an understanding of the underlying component they seek to improve, local staff can find or invent the particular programmatic reforms that can address the generic component at their own site. For example, under the key component supportive human climate, there are numerous ways for a local staff to personalize positive student–adult relationships in the school for individual students, each way being suited to a somewhat different local organization of staffing, scheduling, or grouping and a particular redefinition and monitoring of staff roles and responsibilities.

The alternative is often to ask local staff to buy into some brand-name prepackaged program that has several facets intended to reduce dropouts, under the sponsorship of a well-known educational researcher or reformer or with a catchy title or acronym of appeal, such as "success," "accelerated," "community-based," "student-centered," or "SMART." Some packages actually are primarily concerned with the processes of implementing change and involving staff, providing few outlines or guidance on the content of change, which cannot of itself force staff attention on underlying factors that need reform. Some other packages may be based on well-grounded theories of particular school effects on students, but their adoption encourages local staff to implement particular formulas and practices rather than to understand the reasons the particular reforms might work and what modifications would not damage their essential features.

Many of the most promising current dropout prevention programs are based on short lists of key approaches, much like what is being recommended here, including the programs described in Chapters 7 and 8 of this volume. The best of these are more than lists, of course, including theory-based reasons why proposed categories of change will lead to better student engagement with school goals and school life. These provide local educators with the stimuli to set priorities among a broad range of changes and to develop a deep understanding of what each change should involve to implement local versions and monitor and modify them over time for true effectiveness.

Basic Reforms of Roles and Structures

The results of analyses of the match between dropout prevention theory and practice indicate that much more basic school reform under each component of the typology is needed if major inroads are to be made toward reducing dropout problems. Currently, most school administrators report they frequently give major emphases to many if not all of the components, but students continue to drop out from some schools at alarming rates, so the administrators' approaches are obviously not bold or intense enough to solve the problems.

Basic reforms are needed to change the content of learning activities and the criteria for evaluating and responding to student efforts; to redesign the curriculum toward problem-solving applications and regular references to each student's own community heritage; to change the atmosphere from the current emphases on control and sorting of students to support and caring of individual learners through major modifications in the roles and responsibilities of teachers and students; and to offer services to assist with students' personal, home, or community problems. Some of the approaches described in the chapters of this volume and some other small, experimental alternative schools (e.g., Wehlage et al., 1989) do attempt to motivate at-risk students in new ways to stay in school. If the continuing national dropout problem is to be solved, however, more bold ideas must be widely implemented to close the gap between good theory and actual practice of dropout prevention for students at risk.

NOTES

1. The NELS:88 Dropout Study is part of a comprehensive NELS:88 project conducted by the U.S. Department of Education to study a large nationally repre-

sentative sample of eighth-grade students who were administered tests and questionnaires in 1988 and will be followed up at two intervals through 1996, to collect information on a variety of attitudes, behaviors, and experiences in and outside of school. NELS:88 covered over 25,000 students in 1988 and is designed to include information from individual students' parents, teachers, and school administrators at various stages of base-year and follow-up studies. The NELS:88 Dropout Study was part of the first follow-up study of a subsample of 20,706 students conducted in 1990 that identifies 1,182 students who had dropped out of school between grade 8 and the end of grade 10, of whom 1,043 participated with survey questionnaire information.

2. This group included Jomills Braddock, Edward McDill, James McPartland, Gary Natriello, and Aaron Pallas. Earlier discussions of this work have been published in Natriello, Pallas, McDill, McPartland, and Royster, 1988; Natriello, McDill, and Pallas, 1990; McPartland and Slavin, 1990; and Braddock and McPartland, 1993.

3. Our sources included (1) student accounts of reasons why they drop out (Ekstrom, Goertz, Pollock, & Rock, 1986; Pallas, 1986; Peng & Takai, 1983; Rumberger, 1983; Wagenaar, 1987); (2) compendiums of dropout prevention programs (Branch, Miller, & Bumbaugh, 1986; Hahn & Danzberger, 1987; Natriello, McDill, & Pallas, 1990; NCCE, 1988; OERI, 1987; Orr, 1987; Rumberger, 1987; Slavin, Karweit, & Madden, 1989; USGAO, 1986; (3)academic theories of student motivation (Ames & Ames, 1984, 1985, 1989; Blumenfeld, Soloway, Marx, Krajcik, Guzdial, & Palincsar, 1991; Brophy, 1987; Lepper, 1988; Willis, 1991).

4. The NELS:88 Principal Follow-up covers 1,062 schools with grade 10 for which a survey questionnaire directed to the school principal in 1990 provided information on school characteristics, policies, practices, and programs as well as reports on student demography and teacher characteristics. Of this sample, 535 reported their school has a dropout prevention program and provided information about its characteristics. It is possible to merge data from the NELS:88 Principal Follow-up on characteristics of dropout prevention programs with data from the NELS:88 Dropout Study on student reasons for dropping out, by using a common code that identifies the school last attended by each dropout.

REFERENCES

Ames, R. E., & Ames, C. (1984, 1985, 1989). *Research on motivation in education* (Vols. 1–3). Orlando, FL: Academic Press.

Bishop, J. H. (1989). Why the apathy in American high schools? *Educational Researcher, 18,* 6–8.

Blumenfeld, P. C., Soloway, E., Marx, R. W., Krajcik, J. S., Guzdial, M., & Palincsar, A. (1991). Motivating project-based learning: Sustaining the doing, supporting the learning. *Educational Psychologist, 26*(3 & 4), 369–398.

Braddock, J. H., II, & McPartland, J. M. (1993). Education of early adolescents. *Review of Research in Education, 19,* 135–170.

Branch, A. Y., Miller, J., & Bumbaugh, J. (1986). *Summer Training and Education Program (STEP): Report on the 1985 summer experience.* Philadelphia: Public/Private Ventures.

Brophy, J. (1987). *Motivation in the classroom*. East Lansing: Michigan State University, Institute for Research on Teaching.

Bryk, A. S., Lee, V. E., & Smith, J. L. (1990). High school organization and its effects on teachers and students: An interpretive summary of the research. In W. H. Clune & J. B. Witte (Eds.), *Choice and control in American education* (Vol. 1; pp. 135–226). New York: Falmer Press.

Ekstrom, R. B., Goertz, M. E., Pollock, J. M., & Rock, D. A. (1986). Who drops out of high school and why? Findings from a national study. *Teachers College Record, 87*, 356–373.

Hahn, A., & Danzberger, J. (1987). *Dropouts in America: Enough is known for action*. Washington, DC: Institute for Educational Leadership.

Ingels, S. J., Scott, L. A., Lindmark, J. T., Frankel, M. R., & Myers, S. L. (1992). *National Education Longitudinal Study of 1988 first follow-up: Dropout component data file user's manual*. Washington, DC: U.S. Department of Education.

Lepper, M. R. (1988). Motivational considerations in the study of instruction. *Cognition and Instruction, 5*(4), 289–309.

McPartland, J. M., & Slavin, R. E. (1990). *Policy perspectives: Increasing achievement of at-risk students at each grade level*. Washington, DC: U.S. Government Printing Office.

National Committee for Citizens in Education. (1988). *Dropout prevention: A book of sources*. Columbia, MD: Author.

Natriello, G. (1989). The impact of evaluation processes on students. In R. E. Slavin (Ed.), *School and classroom organization* (pp. 227–246). Hillsdale, NJ: Lawrence Erlbaum.

Natriello, G., McDill, E. L., & Pallas, A. M. (1990). *Schooling disadvantaged children: Racing against catastrophe*. New York: Teachers College Press.

Natriello, G., Pallas, A. M., McDill, E. L., McPartland, J. M., & Royster, D. (1988). *An examination of the assumptions and evidence for alternative dropout prevention programs in high school* (Report No. 365). Baltimore, MD: Johns Hopkins University, Center for Social Organization of Schools.

OERI Urban Superintendents Network. (1987). *Dealing with dropouts: The urban superintendents' call to action*. Washington, DC: U.S. Department of Education.

Orr, M. T. (1987). *Keeping students in school*. San Francisco: Jossey-Bass.

Pallas, A. M. (1986). School dropouts in the United States. In J. D. Stern & M. F. Williams (Eds.), *The condition of education, 1986* (pp. 158–170). Washington, DC: U.S. Government Printing Office.

Peng, S., & Takai, R. (1983). *High school dropouts: Descriptive information from high school and beyond*. Washington, DC: National Center for Education Statistics.

Rumberger, R. W. (1983). Dropping out of high school: The influence of race, sex, and family background. *American Educational Research Journal, 20*, 199–220.

Rumberger, R. W. (1987). High school dropouts: A review of issues and evidence. *Review of Educational Research, 57*(2), 101–121.

Slavin, R. E., Karweit, N. L., & Madden, N. A. (Eds.). (1989). *Effective programs for students at-risk*. Needham Heights, MA: Allyn & Bacon.

U.S. General Accounting Office. (1986). *School dropouts: The extent and nature of the problem*. Washington, DC: Author.

Wagenaar, T. C. (1987). What do we know about dropping out of high school? In R. G. Corwin (Ed.), *Research in the sociology of education and socialization, 7* (pp. 161–190). Greenwich, CT: JAI.

Wehlage, G. G., Rutter, R. A., Smith, G. A., Lesko, N., & Fernandez, R. R. (1989). *Reducing the risk: Schools as communities of support.* Philadelphia: Falmer Press.

Willis, S. (1991). The complex art of motivating students. *Update, 33*(6), 1, 4–5.

CHAPTER 13

Identifying and Addressing Organizational Barriers to Reform

SAMUEL C. STRINGFIELD

Clearly, we know more than ever before about how to address the schooling needs of children at risk. Slavin, Madden, Karweit, Dolan, and Wasik's (1992) Success for All program, James Comer's (1988) School Development Program, Henry Levin's Accelerated Schools (1988), and such highly focused projects as Reading Recovery (Pinnell, 1988) show promise for improving the academic and more general well-being of students at risk. In this volume, Chapters 2 and 7 describe these and other efforts that show evidence of success. In addition to this programmatic knowledge, we know much more about what students at risk are capable of learning (much more than we're teaching, as exemplified in Chapter 6 in this volume) and about how we should structure learning experiences to tap individual potential. We know more about teaching them reading and math (Brophy, 1986) and "higher-order" or "advanced" skills (Means, Chelemer, & Knapp, 1991); as pointed out in Chapters 4, 5, 9, and 10 in this volume, we know more about the school structures needed to sustain higher student achievement (Good & Brophy, 1986; Stringfield & Teddlie, 1991; Teddlie & Stringfield, 1993).

If we understand this much, why do we have more and more young people who are at risk of school failure and dropping out? It's a fair question, and it can not be answered simply. What can be done is to describe a route toward addressing the question and to map our progress toward a satisfactory answer.

A few years ago I had the great fortune of receiving a 3-year Kellogg Fellowship. Among other activities, the foundation brought its fellows together twice a year to interact with experts from around the world as they presented the problems of their fields and the steps they were taking to address them. Presenters included management gurus, politicians, philosophers, social advocates, and leaders in medicine, public health, agriculture, and education. While the content areas and contexts of the presentations varied widely, a common theme was that problems are solved when talented people understand problems, identify plausible solutions, garner adequate resources, identify a plausible path between current realities and goals, create necessary alliances, act, and evaluate/react. In short, they all advocated contextually sensitive organizational development.

If the problems of students at risk are to be successfully addressed, schools must be improved. For schools to improve, educators, parents, and other concerned citizens must engage in contextually sensitive organizational development. This seems so obvious that it raises the additional question, "Why has that not already happened, or not happened often enough?"

WHAT ARE THE PROBLEMS?

Imagine visiting an organization that has the following general characteristics: Widespread low employee morale is evident, and ongoing labor–management conflicts are contributing to carelessness. Staff reductions are perceived as having directly contributed to a rise in accidents and an eroded emergency human backup capability. Workers have inadequate training and staff development to meet the changing demands of their jobs. Management and staff have little information regarding the potential short- and long-term hazards of not doing their jobs well. Management has failed to investigate the causes of previous poor performance, and staff are not carrying out several of the crucial tasks of the facility. Backup and support systems are either nonoperational or of such poor quality as to be irrelevant. Moreover, the central administration of the larger system views the facility as having low importance. Equipment and materials sent to the building are often inadequate or substandard.

I have visited schools that fit this description in rural and ghetto America. Several such schools were negative outliers in the Louisiana School Effectiveness Study (LSES) (Teddlie & Stringfield, 1993). However, the above description is of Union Carbide's now infamous chemical plant at Bhopal, India (Shrivastava, 1986).

The above example should make two points clear. First, as many of our problems are "human" as technological; and second, solutions to many are as near as our collective will and wisdom. Just as Bhopal was avoidable, many of the problems involved in educating students at risk are avoidable and/or addressable.

The societal-level problems have been identified in such recent works as Kozol's *Savage Inequalities* (1991), Kotlowitz's *There Are No Children Here* (1991), and Natriello, McDill, and Pallas's *Schooling Disadvantaged Children: Racing Against Catastrophe* (1990). These problems include the facts that many students must face inadequate food, shelter, and safety; an insufficient number of highly skilled teachers is willing to work in high-poverty, inner-city and rural areas; school resources are inadequate and occasionally misused; and motivation to improve the education of students at risk is apparently less than universal. I will say little more about these, focusing instead on the organizational problems within our schools. This is not to imply that these problems are not important or are unaddressable, only that I believe they may best be attacked by giving preeminent focus to improved school experiences for all. In fact, successful schools will, of necessity, address many of these problems in formulating their goals and strategies, and others of these problems are best addressed by schools that are effectively functioning for all students.

Within schooling, there are at least five reasons why organizational reforms that would benefit students at risk have not taken place. First, having been criticized from without so often, educators are often loathe to openly discuss problems from within. Not clearly understanding and stating our problems makes it unlikely that we will choose the best available solutions. Second, once problems have been identified, clear solutions are not always readily available. Third, for "programs that work" to work in a specific context, they need to be compatible with the current strengths of the schools in which they will be placed. Fourth, in the rare instances where proven programs exist in sufficiently detailed forms, practitioners, administrators, and boards often underestimate the human and fiscal costs of effective implementation. Staff development and training time are the most commonly miscalculated components of implementation plans. Finally, in our time there seems to be a profound individual and societal ambivalence about action in the public good. Voters are particularly skeptical of cost-bearing programs designed to help poor people. Programs that address the five problems or barriers already mentioned will not be free. Achieving taxpayer support of at-risk program improvement becomes a final challenge.

STEPS FOR OVERCOMING BARRIERS

The five barriers noted above are not easily hurdled. Following is a discussion of necessary but not always sufficient steps to overcoming those barriers.

Specify the Problems

As noted above, I believe that one of the greatest barriers to improving the academic lot of children at risk is a reticence on the part of educators to describe the problems educators face at various levels. Regardless of justification, this lack of specificity leads to an endless searching for someone "out there" to blame. Parents blame schools; teachers blame parents and administrators; administrators blame teachers, unions, colleges, and voters; affluent taxpayers blame all of the above and move to suburbs that have reputations for "good schools." Generic blaming of others will only continue the current gridlock and perpetuate current problems.

Teachers, principals, and schools provide three examples of the fallacy of generic statements of "the problem."

Teachers. Some of the world's most remarkable people are teachers. Some of these people provide extraordinarily high quality instruction under almost unbelievably trying circumstances. And yet, some who are paid to be teachers sit behind their desks, hand out ditto sheets, make assignments, and criticize young people for not being "attentive." Brophy (1988) notes that the teacher-effects literature best differentiates the top 75% of teachers from the remaining 25%. Education is a long-term proposition. From kindergarten through middle school, most students have at least a dozen teachers. We need to not generalize about the "goodness" of teachers. Some are wonderful, and others, as in an example provided by Michelle Fine (1992), criticize "those damn enthusiastic teachers." Some teachers are virtual saints; others need a great deal of support and training, or gentle but firm encouragement to find careers for which they are better-suited and less harmful.

Schools and principals. Schools can be a large part of "the solution." Levine and Lezotte (1990) describe many characteristics that are often shared among "highly effective" schools and principals. Lightfoot (1983) provides rich descriptions of several remarkable schools and principals. Many of us have visited schools that made us wonder, "What's the problem? Education's in great shape."

However, the very presence of unusually "effective" schools implies the existence of unusually "ineffective" schools. Stringfield and Teddlie (1988) describe a path for creating ineffective schools. That downward spiral, repeated hundreds of times a year, includes appointing an administrator with little prior successful experience and even less training in working with students at risk. That principal should visit classrooms only in order to comply with state or local evaluation requirements. He or she should take no interest in curricula or instruction, or in hiring (which can be managed from the district) or firing (which can be difficult). If such a person is placed in charge of a school serving an affluent community, beyond a point the community will push for the replacement of the principal. In a school serving families who already feel powerless and alienated from public institutions, the principal may stay for decades. Given that such a person does not conduct meaningful personnel evaluations, teachers who sit and pass out assignments will "like" teaching at those schools and stay. More energized staff will find the situation increasingly frustrating and tend to transfer out. Over time, these schools, typically serving poor communities, come to be led by at best indifferent administrators, and they will be staffed with more than their share of at best marginal teachers. The cumulative effect is not merely school ineffectiveness, but a virtual immunization against school improvement processes.

In short, some schools are wonderful. Others may require substantial changes before any new program or restructuring process can succeed. Most generalizations about "schools" fail to consider complex local realities. If schools are going to improve, they and their supporting districts need to begin with an honest, if not necessarily published, assessment of the strengths and weaknesses that exist in individual classrooms and individual schools, not generic schools or even generic schools serving Latino (or African-American or American Indian) students.

Seek Proven Solutions

There is one national problem about which generalizations are possible. Funding for research and development of "programs" has been inadequate. Many programs that have been developed have not been independently validated. Currently a cacophony is created from developers' claims that their programs "have been shown by research to work." What are needed are independently funded evaluations of promising programs and funded efforts to develop promising new programs. No less a fiscal authority than the accounting firm of Arthur Andersen & Company has concluded that these studies should be undertaken as soon as possible and could most efficiently be funded at the federal level (Measelle & Egol, 1990).

In the absence of such independent evaluations, a few programs could be tentatively recommended. Who should create the list becomes no small problem. Both of the programs described in Chapters 7 and 8 in this volume should be complimented for their data-gathering and analytic efforts. Other programs that are gathering data on their efforts include

Reading Recovery, the Comer School Development Program, and Success for All. A few others could arguably qualify as effective (see *Effective Programs for Students at Risk*, Slavin, Karweit, & Madden, 1989). But for a nation of a quarter of a billion people, our list of independently verified effective programs is far too short and must be expanded. Schools need options worthy of attempting.

Seek Compatible Solutions

It does little good to undertake a potentially valuable program if, for example, its basic tenants are at odds with those of the school or district. The Comer program has many attractive features, but if the local principal is unwilling to share decision making with the faculty, the program will not work. Similarly, a faculty committed to "whole language" instruction may not become enthusiastic about Success for All. A district committed to bringing Chapter 1 services into regular classrooms should not consider Reading Recovery. It is not enough to find a good program; a school-to-program match is also critical. The demands and limitations of the chosen program must be understood. Even a program independently validated and compatible with local predilections has limitations that must be addressed. Programs that may be worthwhile—for example, the Coalition of Essential Schools (CES)—deliberately do not specify curricula at any level of detail. Local faculty must develop units that are compatible with the CES philosophy. This requires time, effort, and development skills not currently found on all faculties. Success for All requires a full-time implementer. Reading Recovery requires extensive staff development for specified teachers, and that training often is not locally available. Failure to build skills and to provide the time necessary to meet these sorts of demands will result in failed implementations. When dealing with students at risk, "success for most" is not a satisfactory compromise.

Understand the Implementation Requirements

The areas probably most often miscalculated in implementing programs are staff development and planning times. CES assumes shared planning times, yet many schools have attempted to embrace CES principles without scheduling and budgeting the time required. Success for All requires the purchase of an extensive set of materials. The necessary levels of ongoing staff development to successfully implement such programs as the Paideia Proposal are almost invariably underestimated.

Showers, Joyce, and Bennett (1987) note that in order for staff development to actually change teaching, it must include presentation of theory, modeling, time to practice, and immediate, supportive feedback. These are characteristics that make a great deal of sense, yet they are rare in schools. Real change requires all of these elements, and the time and money required to implement such changes must be built into change efforts from the onset.

To this end, it is important to educate both the education bureaucracy and elected officials as to the need for support of full implementation. When fiscal crises come, as they inevitably do, the first thing most boards and superintendents cut is staff development. For programs to become implemented and institutionalized, staff must receive long-term training support.

It is not clear that the public has the political will to underwrite the costs associated with improvement. John Kenneth Galbraith (1992) recently dubbed ours the "contented society." By that he meant that the middle and upper classes have found ways to make government serve their needs (e.g., loans for college students, deductions for mortgage payments, Social Security, Medicare). These middle- and upper-class citizens, who are the chief taxpayers and, more important, voters, are frequently indifferent to the needs of the poor, who often don't vote. This is a troubling development because there can be little doubt that reforms of schools serving high concentrations of children at risk will require tax support.

One bright side of this concern is that Congress has increased funding of Chapter 1 by more than 90% over the past 6 years. If the trend continues, and if the U.S. Department of Education loosens its regulations regarding the expenditure of Chapter 1 funds, perhaps Chapter 1 can be used to overcome other areas of voter nonsupport for children at risk.

TOWARD SCHOOLS AS HIGH RELIABILITY ORGANIZATIONS

I believe that a major part of the problem of educating students at risk is concerned not merely with how we think about students at risk or teachers or schools or programs, but our assumptions about school organization in America. If we want to argue that all students can learn, that schools can teach them, and that the barriers to reform noted above are addressable, we need to create structures in which that happens. Our culture has produced examples of remarkable children, teachers, schools, and programs that have succeeded in the face of extraordinary difficulties; but to date we have not produced examples of school systems in which *all* children learn. If we are to address the needs of all children at risk, whole systems must work with levels of reliability that surpass the U.S. experience to date.

Current theorizing in education, like that in industry, is largely devoted to explaining trial-and-error, failure-tolerant, low reliability organizations. This was appropriate for the industries and schools of the past. However, the current generation of demands placed on education, such as the high goals stated in America 2000 (U.S. Department of Education, 1991), are, at heart, that *all* students must succeed in school. This is a demand that is novel in the history of U.S. education.

In some areas of modern culture, institutions and technologies have emerged that have great productive as well as destructive powers. As stated by LaPorte and Consolini (1991), "increasingly, any failure of these technologies is perceived by both their operators and the public to have such potentially grave consequences as to warrant the absolute avoidance of failure" (p. 19). The issue is not whether the technology can usually function correctly; that is a given. Rather, the requirement is that the technology never malfunction. The issue is not validity, which is assumed, but extraordinarily high reliability. In order to educate those U.S. students who are now deemed "at risk," in order for those students to achieve the educational accomplishments that are already being experienced by many students, we will need a similar increase in the *reliability* of schooling for U.S. children. We will need to create school systems that exhibit an "absolute avoidance of [student] failure."

In several areas deemed critical to the public interest, such as the operation of nuclear power plants and aircraft control towers, new types of organizational structures have evolved to meet the requirements of virtual 100% reliability. These organizations are required to engage not in trial-and-error improvement, as is common both to much of industry and management. Rather, the organizations are expected to operate "trials without errors" (LaPorte & Consolini, 1991, p. 20). Researchers investigating the characteristics of these systems have referred to them as high reliability organizations (HROs) (Roberts, 1990).

If one accepts the goals of America 2000, then it is no longer acceptable for significant numbers of students to not learn "the basics," or for only *many* students to learn them well. It is no longer acceptable for large numbers of students to drop out of school or to remain and be provided with a substandard curriculum. The costs to individuals and to society, once low, have become too high. Schools are no longer afforded the luxury of blaming the students and their families for students' failures. Schools are now seen as accountable for the successes and failures of *virtually all* of their students. In order to respond to these new realities, schools and school districts will have to abandon industrial efficiency models and take on the operating characteristics of HROs. Failure to do so will cripple any efforts at educational reforms designed to aid students at risk.

CHARACTERISTICS OF HIGH RELIABILITY ORGANIZATIONS

The following discussion presents an overview of the primary characteristics of HROs (adapted from LaPorte & Consolini, 1991; Pfeiffer, 1989; Roberts, 1990). Each characteristic is followed by my impressions of the status of U.S. education on the dimension at present.

Clarity of Goals

HROs require clarity regarding goals. Staff in HROs have a strong sense of their primary mission. Unlike most other first-world nations, the United States historically has chosen to decentralize goal setting in education. However, the America 2000 goals are a clear reversal of this historical tendency. Such goals as all students entering first grade ready to learn, reducing the high school dropout rate by over 50 %, and raising the mathematics and science achievements of all U.S. students to very high levels, have all been achieved in some U.S. schools. America 2000 requires that these goals be achieved in virtually all schools, including those serving highly disadvantaged students.

Establishing and maintaining clear goals has been one of the most frequently cited characteristics of the school-effects research base (Edmonds, 1979; Good & Brophy, 1986; Levine & Lezotte, 1990). Stringfield and Teddlie (1988) and Teddlie and Stringfield (1993) find that a cacophony of "most important" goals often resulted in a lack of clear, unifying goals for the faculties and students in low-achieving schools.

Development and Maintenance of Optimum Operating Procedures

HROs extend formal, logical decision analysis, based on standard operating procedures, as far as extant knowledge allows. At the time of the publication of the first *Handbook of Research on Teaching* (Gage, 1963), there was not a sufficient body of educational research to guide the development of standard operating procedures for schooling in any rational way. In the absence of such knowledge, and in the absence of clear national or state goals, districts developed local procedures. Districts, local superintendents, and principals often abdicated these responsibilities to teachers, with virtually no monitoring of resulting classroom practices. By the publication of the third *Handbook* (Wittrock, 1986), the research situation had changed considerably. The rudiments of a science of education now exist. However, practice has been slow to follow.

An important link between school-effects research and HRO literature is provided by two studies of teachers' behavior in more and less effective schools. Both Mortimore, Sammons, Stoll, Lewis, and Ecob (1988) and Teddlie and Stringfield (1993) found that teachers in high-outlier schools behaved in manners more like those predicted by the teacher-effects literature (Brophy, 1986). Perhaps as important, these studies found greater *consistency* among teachers in more effective schools. Teachers were more likely to be moving students through their lessons at a good pace, and fewer teachers allowed high rates of time off task in effective schools. Teddlie and Stringfield (1993) found that this higher rate of consistency on the part of teachers was clearly related to the behaviors of the principals, and not related to the income levels of the communities being served. Some principals are already insisting on, and getting, relatively high reliability in instructional delivery. Others are not.

Extensive Staff Recruitment and Training

HROs recruit and train extensively in order to compel adherence to standard operating procedures. Kozol (1991) repeatedly observed that children at risk need the highest quality teachers, yet often do not get them. There is, however, very little research on teacher, principal, and superintendent recruitment, and essentially none on the "effects" of recruitment. (For an initial effort that deserves multiple replications, see Wise et al., 1987.) Research on the "how to" of effective training has made much greater progress (Fullan, 1991; Lewis & Miles, 1990; Showers, Joyce, & Bennett, 1987). Ward and Tikunoff (1989) and Kirby, Stringfield, Teddlie, and Wimpelberg (1992) have conducted detailed studies of teacher induction programs, both of which found school-level effects. However, much more research on the long-term effects of various induction and staff development programs is needed.

Stringfield and Teddlie (1991) found that principals in positive-outlier schools were more likely to take an intense interest in staff recruitment. They found that, by contrast, principals in low-outlier schools passively accepted "what they [central administration] send us." This was particularly true in schools that served high numbers of students at risk.

Identification and Correction of Procedural Problems

HROs have initiatives that identify flaws in standard operating procedures and nominate and validate changes in those that prove inadequate.

I am unaware of large-scale research on school or district-level efforts at systematic, organizational efforts to identify flaws within schools and correct them. However, Mortimore and co-authors (1988) and Stringfield and Teddlie (1991) describe principal and staff actions in more effective schools that might serve to identify problems within schools and facilitate correction. Stringfield and Yoder (1992) present a case study of an exemplary school serving highly disadvantaged Hispanic children. That school consistently developed standard operating procedures and with equal frequency sought out methods for improving those procedures.

The 1988 Hawkins-Stafford Amendments to the U.S. compensatory education laws mandate a self-study and program improvement process for schools in which compensatory education students are not making adequate academic gains (LeTendre, 1991). Thousands of schools have been so identified nationwide (Heid, 1991), and in several states those schools have entered into an extended self-study with the eventual goal of school-directed improvement (see Stringfield, Billig, & Davis, 1991).

However, it is probably safe to say that the typical U.S. teacher does not view herself or himself as having open access to processes that could change significant school and district procedures. If schools and districts are to reliably educate virtually all students at risk, teachers and principals must have more voice in establishing and modifying school procedures.

Attention to Performance Evaluation

HROs are sensitive to the areas in which judgment-based, incremental strategies are required. They therefore pay considerable attention to performance, evaluation, and analysis to improve the processes of the organizations. U.S. education is currently undergoing increased emphasis on performance-based evaluation of teachers (Millman, 1981). Bridges (1986) has conducted a scholarly analysis of procedures for managing incompetent teachers, and his work demonstrates that effective action is possible, although rarely undertaken. He concedes that the majority of incompetent teachers are allowed to continue to intervene in the educational lives of children. Obviously, this derails all efforts at raising education's reliability.

Stringfield and Teddlie (1991) reported that principals in more effective schools took teacher recruitment, development, and evaluation more seriously than did principals in negative-outlier schools. Most of the principals in the positive-outlier schools had counseled out, forced the transfer of, or otherwise removed one or more teachers from their staffs. That was rarely true of principals in negative-outlier schools.

Mutual Monitoring by Administrators and Staff

In HROs, monitoring is mutual (administrators and line staff) without counterproductive loss of overall autonomy and confidence. In the United States currently there is minimal evaluation of teachers by administrators or fellow teachers, and virtually no evaluation of administrators by teachers. Rumberger and Larson (Chapter 7) and Fine (Chapter 8) present systems in which peers become much more aware of each other's teaching. This is a step toward institutional reliability.

Vigilance to System Lapses

HROs are alert to surprises or lapses. The experience of HROs is that small failures could cascade into major system failures and hence are monitored carefully. I am unaware of studies focused specifically on schools' responses to surprises or lapses. Mortimore and co-authors' (1988) "purposeful leadership," "maximum communication between teachers and students," and "record keeping," all found to be characteristics of more effective schools, would logically lead to quicker responses to surprises or lapses. Similarly, Stringfield and Teddlie's (1991) "attention to daily academic functioning," as a school-level predictor of school effects, might lead to quicker discovery of and response to lapses. The teaming in urban charter schools or in several Coalition of Essential Schools projects almost certainly leads to quicker identification of problems and responses to lapses.

In many schools serving students at risk, significant percentages of students arrive in second and even third grade unable to read. It is not plausible that previous teachers have not noticed these deficiencies. Yet adequate remediation had not been instituted. Such programs as Success for All (Slavin et al., 1992) and Reading Recovery (Pinnell, 1988) show that these situations are in no way inevitable; rather they are allowed to happen. For the error of not teaching a child to read to be allowed to cascade through several grades, a school must be operating at a low reliability level. We will not achieve the America 2000 goals with such performances. High reliability organizations point to a different structure and results.

Reliance on Staff Competence

HROs are hierarchically structured, but during times of peak loads, HROs emphasize a second layer of behavior that emphasizes collegial decision making regardless of rank. This second layer is characterized by cooperation and coordination. At times of peak activity, line staff are expected to exercise considerable discretion. U.S. schools are hierarchically structured. Expectations during "peak" times have not been systematically studied, but probably vary greatly. My impression is that during peak times at some schools, accommodations are made, everyone pitches in, and important functions continue to operate. By contrast, in some schools, temporarily heavy loads become excuses for nonperformance by key staff members. Things break down. To educate all students at risk, systems must be in place that rarely break down and invariably catch the breakdowns and correct them. HROs rely on the competence of all professionals in the facility and distribute responsibility accordingly.

Flexibility Toward Rules

HROs regularly respond to potentially disastrous situations as being far too important to trust to rules alone. Authority patterns shift from hierarchical to functional skill-based authority, as needs arise. Large U.S. school districts generally, and "special education" programs in particular, are rule-focused and rule-driven. In some schools and districts, exceptions to rules are almost never tolerated. This is often to the short- and long-term detriment of specific children. Schools and districts must be responsive to the needs of students who might fall through the cracks in a rule-driven system. Madden, Slavin, Karweit, Dolan, & Wasik (1992) offer examples of systems designed so that professionals "catch" students who might fall behind.

Interdependence of Staff

Especially during times of peak performance, HRO staff are able to assume a close interdependence. Relationships are complex, coupled, and sometimes urgent. A high level of coordination between compensatory and regular classrooms was found to be a characteristic of more effective compensatory education programs in the United States (Allington & Johnston, 1989; Griswold, Cotton, & Hansen, 1985). Mortimore and coauthors (1988) found that involvement of teachers in decision making and consistent teacher inservice programs were both related to school effectiveness. Stringfield and Teddlie (1991) also report that high levels of cross-classroom and cross-grade coordination were positive predictors of school effects. Professional isolation is the enemy of any program trying to truly serve students at risk.

Maintenance of Equipment

HRO equipment is maintained and kept in the highest working order. Responsibility for checking the readiness of key equipment is shared equally by all who come in contact with it. This is not true in most U.S. schools, where nonfunctioning equipment often sits unrepaired for months or years. A striking feature of equipment maintenance in many schools is the extent to which unnamed persons beyond the school are often viewed as being responsible for maintenance. This situation may in part be a result of many educational administrators viewing no equipment, beyond heaters and an office telephone, as "key" and deserving of their personal attention.

Central Administration Support

HROs are invariably valued by their supervising organizations. There is some evidence (e.g., Wimpelberg, Teddlie, & Stringfield, 1989) that school districts provide more attention and support to some schools than others, and that it is often the schools in the least advantaged neighborhoods that receive the least attention and local support. Stringfield and Teddlie (1988) observe that some school districts, rather than retraining or terminating manifestly unskilled teachers and principals, assign them to schools serving the least advantaged families. Such actions do not indicate high valuing of *all* students and schools by central offices.

The accountability requirements of the Hawkins-Stafford Chapter 1 Amendments of 1988 (Public Law 100–297) have led some districts to pay increased attention to schools serving higher percentages of students at risk. Winfield (1991) reports that in order to facilitate a shift to "schoolwide-project" use of federal compensatory education funds for schools serving students 75% or more of whom receive free lunches, one large school district discontinued its practice of requiring some schools to accept the involuntary transfer of probationary teachers. This would appear to be evidence of increased valuing by central administration of schools serving high percentages of students at risk.

Emphasis on Long-Term Reliability

In HROs, short-term efficiency takes a backseat to very high reliability. U.S. education has spent much of the past 30 years attempting to become more efficient, and much public dialogue concerns ridding education of "wasteful management." For the charter schools to succeed, Fine notes (Chapter 8, this volume) that teachers need to work together over time, and that the school district undermines these efforts when it "bounce[s] teachers out of the charter because the school has a momentary drop in enrollment." If the goal is restructuring, some short-term efficiencies must be temporarily set aside.

IMPLICATIONS FOR SCHOOLS OF HRO STATUS

In summary, the literature on HROs describes 13 characteristics of organizations that are necessary for them to operate trials without cascading errors. This is the requirement increasingly being made of schools. Several school-effects studies suggest linkages with the HRO literature. However, for a typical school serving large numbers of students at risk to become an HRO, it would need to make major changes. Some of those changes would require support from above the school.

The most important shift in considering HROs, however, is not in the specific characteristics of the organizations — rather, it is the intellectual shift that must precede the evolution of the characteristics. The most important characteristic of HROs is a perception, held by the public and the employees, that failures within the organization would be disastrous. Bhopal was disastrous. Three Mile Island was very nearly disastrous. Schools serving children at risk will increase the reliability of their work as the public and the professionals working within the schools come to view children's not learning to read as constituting individual travesties and public disasters. HROs evolve; they do not arrive complete. They evolve because the public demands them and pays for them.

Throughout the history of public education, the responsibility of schools has been to provide instructional processes to those deemed by the schools to be willing and able to benefit from schooling. It was presumed that others, including students who would now be described as "at risk," would drop out. Gradually over the past several decades and rapidly today, the mandate to educators has changed. The new mandate, clearly expressed in America 2000 and other policy documents, is that schools be responsible for producing high achievement levels among *all* students. Given that schools have previously demonstrated competence at educating many students, the new issue is one of much higher reliability.

To date, the field of school-effectiveness research has focused much of its energy on identifying variables that explain differences between schools in which students score higher or lower on achievement tests, attend school with greater or lesser regularity, and so on. The practical implications of this research were assumed to follow naturally. If researchers could determine what the best schools had, and if practitioners could provide it to all schools, all students' achievement levels would rise.

The HRO literature offers support for some of the findings of previous research. In particular, it supports the familiar characteristics of clear goals, attention to evaluations, and close coordination. However, the HRO literature suggests several other areas that may require attention for schools to serve all students well. Those areas clearly merit practical attention and academic study. The development and maintenance of standard procedures, where appropriate; the extensive use of staff development; the importance of open lines of communication; mutual monitoring; alertness to surprises or lapses; and the maintenance of equipment may be among the most important factors affecting the quality of educational services provided to students at risk.

The federal government could play an important role in improving school reliability. By loosening regulations and increasing a focus on staff development regarding the use of $6 billion a year in Chapter 1 funding, the federal government would increase the value of human capital serving students at risk in Chapter 1 schools. By modifying the "supplement not supplant" rule so as to require coordination among service providers, Chapter 1 could reduce professional isolation, particularly as it relates to service for individual children at risk. By entering into a greatly expanded program of national research on teacher, school, and program effects, the federal government could greatly assist local districts that seek proven options for improving services to children at risk. By funding the continued development and expansion of programs that have been proven to work, and by providing independent evaluations and cost analyses for implementation and institutionalization of the programs in various contexts, the federal government could provide invaluable assistance as schools seek not just "programs that work," but programs that are well-suited to the particular conditions faced by a specific community and school.

Two areas suggested by HRO researchers seem particularly worthy of future research on the education of at-risk students. These are clear evidence of valuing of schools by central offices, and the primacy of high reliability over short-term efficiency. There is no systematic literature on the role of central offices in creating school effects. Wimpelberg (1987) makes a first approach at defining "a central role for the central office," and Fullan (1991) notes several features of districts and higher levels of government that facilitate innovation. The HRO literature would suggest that unless the central office places considerable value on the performance of students within *each* school, long-term school effectiveness is unlikely.

HROs are created when, as stated by LaPorte and Consolini (1991), any failure of their technologies is generally recognized as having such potentially dire circumstances that failure must be avoided. If schools are being counted on to produce more and more nearly universal high rates of student achievement, then over time all schools will be asked to become HROs. This will be most difficult for schools serving large numbers of students at risk. Research on school and program effects now demonstrates overlap with the HRO literature. This suggests a systematic path toward progress.

An important policy-relevant conclusion concerns fiscal support for public schooling. HROs cost more than traditional industrial plants. They cost more because they operate under different demands. Efficiency assumes a certain level of fault tolerance. The greater the tolerance for occasional failures, the greater the possible efficiencies. HROs are designed to achieve trials without errors. If the political rhetoric of America 2000 and similar documents is to be taken seriously, then the supporters of that rhetoric need to understand that higher reliability is, in the middle term, more expensive. It will help if our political leaders remember that in the long run it would have cost less to have operated the Three Mile Island nuclear facility reliably than it is costing to clean it up. It will cost less to provide highly reliable schools for students at risk than to pay for continued expansion of welfare, police, and prison programs.

We now know enough to improve the reliability of schools for students at risk. Many of the systemic-, school-, and classroom-level changes can be described and undertaken. Whether as a conglomeration of over 15,000 school districts and as one nation we can muster the will to achieve universally high quality schooling for students remains an unanswered question.

REFERENCES

Allington, R., & Johnston, P. (1989). Coordination, collaboration, and consistency: The redesign of compensatory and special education interventions. In R. E. Slavin, N. L. Karweit, & N. A. Madden (Eds.), *Effective programs for students at risk* (pp. 320–354). Needham Heights, MA: Allyn & Bacon.

Bridges, E. (1986). *The incompetent teacher*. Philadelphia: Falmer Press.

Brophy J. (1986). Research linking teacher behavior to student achievement: Potential implications for instruction of Chapter 1 students. In B. Williams, P. Richmond, & B. Mason (Eds.), *Designs for compensatory education: Conference proceedings and papers*. Washington, DC: Research and Evaluation Associates.

Brophy J. (1988). Research on teacher effects: Uses and abuses. *Elementary School Journal, 89*(1), 3–22.

Comer, J. (1988). Educating poor minority children. *Scientific American, 259*(5), 42–48.

Edmonds, R. (1979). Effective schools for the urban poor. *Educational Leadership, 37,* 15–27.

Fine, M. (1992, April). *Barriers and incentives to implementing reforms.* Paper presented at the National Conference on Educational Reforms and At-Risk Students, San Francisco.

Fullan, M. (1991). *The new meaning of educational change.* New York: Teachers College Press.

Gage, N. (1963). *Handbook of research on teaching.* Chicago: Rand McNally.

Galbraith, J. (1992). *The culture of contentment.* Boston: Houghton Mifflin.

Good, T., & Brophy, J. (1986). School effects. In M. Wittrock (Ed.), *Handbook of research on teaching* (3rd ed.). New York: Macmillan.

Griswold, P., Cotton, K., & Hansen, J. (1985). *Effective compensatory education sourcebook* (Vol. I). Washington, DC: U.S. Department of Education.

Heid, C. (1991). The dilemma of Chapter 1 program improvement. *Educational Evaluation and Policy Analysis, 13*(4), 394–398.

Kirby, P., Stringfield, S., Teddlie, C., & Wimpelberg, R. (1992). Teacher induction in more and less effective schools. *School Effectiveness and School Improvement, 3*(3), 187–203.

Kotlowitz, A. (1991). *There are no children here.* New York: Doubleday.

Kozol, J. (1991). *Savage inequalities.* New York: Crown.

LaPorte, T., & Consolini, P. (1991). Working in practice but not in theory: Theoretical challenges of "high-reliability organizations." *Journal of Public Administration Research and Theory, 1*(1), 19–48.

LeTendre, M. (1991). The continuing evolution of a federal role in compensatory education. *Educational Evaluation and Policy Analysis, 13*(4), 328–334.

Levin, H. (1988). *Accelerated schools for at-risk students.* Rutgers, NJ: Center for Policy Research in Education.

Levine, D., & Lezotte, L. (1990). *Unusually effective schools.* Madison, WI: National Center for Effective Schools Research and Development.

Lewis, K., & Miles, M. (1990). *Improving the urban high school.* New York: Teachers College Press.

Lightfoot, S. (1983). *The good high school.* New York: Basic Books.

Madden, N., Slavin, R., Karweit, N., Dolan, L., & Wasik, B. (1992). Success for all. *Phi Delta Kappan, 72*(8), 593–599.

Means, B., Chelemer, C., & Knapp, M. (1991). *Teaching advanced skills to at-risk students.* San Francisco: Jossey-Bass.

Measelle, R., & Egol, M. (1990). *A new system of education: World-class and customer-focused.* New York: Arthur Andersen & Company.

Millman, J. (1981). *Handbook of teacher evaluation.* Beverly Hills: Sage.

Mortimore, P., Sammons, P., Stoll, L., Lewis, D., & Ecob, R. (1988). *School matters.* Somerset, UK: Open Books.

Natriello, G., McDill, E. L., & Pallas, A. M. (1990). *Schooling disadvantaged children: Racing against catastrophe.* New York: Teachers College Press.

Pfeiffer, J. (1989). The secret of life at the limits: Cogs become big wheels. *Smithsonian, 20*(4), 38–48.

Pinnell, G. (1988, April). *Sustained effects of a strategy-centered early intervention program in reading.* Paper presented at the annual convention of the American Educational Research Association, New Orleans.

Roberts, C. (1990). Some characteristics of high reliability organizations. *Organizational Science, 1*(2), 1–17.

Showers, B., Joyce, B., & Bennett, B. (1987). Synthesis of research on staff development: A framework for future study and a state-of-the-art analysis. *Educational Leadership, 45*(3), 87–97.

Shrivastava, P. (1986). *Bhopal.* New York: Basic Books.

Slavin, R. E., Karweit, N. L., & Madden, N. A. (Eds.). (1989). *Effective programs for students at risk.* Needham Heights, MA: Allyn & Bacon.

Slavin, R. E., Madden, N. A., Karweit, N. L., Dolan, L., & Wasik, B. (1992). *Success for all: A relentless approach to prevention and early intervention in elementary schools.* Arlington, VA: Educational Research Service.

Stringfield, S., Billig, S., & Davis, A. (1991). A research-based program improvement process for Chapter 1 schools: A model and early results. *Phi Delta Kappan, 72*(8), 600–606.

Stringfield, S., & Teddlie, C. (1988). A time to summarize: Six years and three phases of the Louisiana School Effectiveness Study. *Educational Leadership, 46*(2), 43–49.

Stringfield, S., & Teddlie, C. (1991). Observers as predictors of schools' multi-year outlier status. *Elementary School Journal, 91*(4), 357–376.

Stringfield, S., & Yoder, N. (1992). Toward a model of elementary grades Chapter 1 effectiveness. In H. C. Waxman, J. W. de Felix, J. E. Anderson, & H. P. Baptiste, Jr. (Eds.), *Students at risk in at-risk schools: Improving environments for learning* (pp. 203–221). Newbury Park, CA: Corwin Press.

Teddlie, C., & Stringfield, S. (1993). *Schools make a difference: Lessons learned from a ten-year study of school effects.* New York: Teachers College Press.

U.S. Department of Education. (1991). *America 2000: An educational strategy.* Washington, DC: U.S. Department of Education.

Ward, B., & Tikunoff, W. (1989). *New teacher retention project.* Los Alamitos, CA: Southwest Regional Educational Laboratory.

Wimpelberg, R. (1987). The dilemma of instructional leadership and a central role for central office. In W. Greenfield (Ed.), *Instructional Leadership* (pp. 100–117). Boston: Allyn & Bacon.

Wimpelberg, R., Teddlie, C., & Stringfield, S. (1989). Sensitivity to context: The past and future of effective schools research. *Educational Administration Quarterly, 25*(1), 82–107.

Winfield, L. (1991). Lessons from the field: Case studies of evolving schoolwide projects. *Educational Evaluation and Policy Analysis, 13*(4), 353–362.

Wise, A., Darling-Hammond, L., Berliner, D., Haller, E., Schlecty, P., Berry, B., Praskac, A., & Noblit, G. (1987). *Effective teacher selection: From recruitment to retention – case studies.* Santa Monica, CA: Rand.

Wittrock, M. (Ed.). (1986). *Handbook of research on teaching* (3rd ed.). New York: Macmillan.

About the Editor and the Contributors

Robert J. Rossi is a Principal Research Scientist and Director of the Youth and Community Research Group at the American Institutes for Research in Palo Alto, California. He currently directs studies evaluating dropout prevention programs and educational reforms for students at risk and is working with John W. Gardner on several efforts related to building community in workplace and school settings. He has authored or edited four books on education-related topics and written numerous journal articles and research monographs in the field. A former teacher of the educationally handicapped and teacher and director of migrant education programs, Dr. Rossi received his Ph.D. in Philosophy and Educational Research from Stanford University.

A. Wade Boykin is Professor of Psychology and Director of the Developmental Psychology Program at Howard University. He has studied and written extensively on African-American culture, socialization, and school performance and is currently conducting research on psychological stress, coping, and culture in an African-American population. He has written a plethora of journal articles and contributed chapters to numerous edited books, including *Advances in Black Psychology* and *Black Psychology*. Dr. Boykin received his Ph.D. from the University of Michigan and was awarded the Distinguished Scholar Award from the American Educational Research Association Committee on Minorities in 1988.

Alan J. DeYoung is Professor of Educational Policy Studies and Evaluation at the University of Kentucky and Faculty Associate in Sociology at the University's Appalachian Center. With support from the Appalachian Center, the U.S. Department of Education, and the Spencer Foundation, he has worked extensively to understand the historical, cultural, and socioeconomic dimensions of problems affecting rural schools. His publications include *Farewell, Little Kanawha: The Emergence, Decline and Demise of a Rural West Virginia High School*; *Struggling with Their Histories: Economic Decline and Educational Improvement in Four Rural South-*

297

eastern School Districts; and *Economics and American Education: A Historical and Critical Overview of the Impact of Economic Theories on Schooling in the United States.* He is the editor of *Rural Education: Issues and Practice* and has written numerous journal articles on rural education. Dr. DeYoung received his Ph.D. from Stanford University and has received five awards for outstanding achievement in research and scholarship from the University of Kentucky College of Education.

Michelle Fine is Professor of Psychology at the City University of New York Graduate Center. Concurrent with this position, she is Senior Consultant to the Philadelphia Schools Collaborative, which is engaged in restructuring comprehensive high schools. She has written many journal articles and chapters in edited books, and several books, the most recent of which is *Beyond Silenced Voices: Class, Race, and Gender in U.S. Schools* and the forthcoming *Chartering Urban School Reform: Reflections on Public High Schools in the Midst of Change*, published by Teachers College Press. She has also conducted research on educational equity and women with disabilities. Dr. Fine is the recipient of the Distinguished Publications Award from the Association of Women in Psychology and the Women Educators Research Award from the American Educational Research Award, among other honors. She received her Ph.D. in Social Psychology from Columbia University.

Edmund W. Gordon is a member of the permanent faculty at Yale University where he holds a primary appointment as the John M. Musser Professor of Psychology, Emeritus. His career spans life as a minister, clinical and counseling psychologist, research scientist, author, editor, and professor. Dr. Gordon's scholarship is documented in his authorship of more than 100 journal articles and book chapters, and in 10 books and monographs authored or edited by him. He served for 5 years as editor of the American Journal of Orthopsychiatry and for 3 years as editor of the annual review of Research in Education. Professor Gordon is best known for his research on diverse human characteristics and pedagogy, and the education of the low-status populations. His book, *Compensatory Education: Preschool Through College*, continues to be regarded as the classic work in its field. In 1978, Dr. Gordon was elected to membership in the National Academy of Education; he received his Ed.D. in Child Development and Guidance from Columbia University.

Joseph C. Grannis is Professor of Education, Department of Curriculum and Teaching, at Teachers College, Columbia University, and holds joint appointment as Associate Director of the University's Institute for Urban and Minority Education. He is currently directing the Institute's Stay in School Partnership Program, which is funded by New York State, and previously directed the Teachers College evaluation of the New York

City Dropout Prevention Initiative. His published writings and research projects encompass a range of educational issues, focusing most recently on dropout prevention and the stress of students in school. Dr. Grannis received his Ph.D. in Education from Washington University in St. Louis.

G. Alfred Hess, Jr. is Executive Director of the Chicago Panel on Public School Policy and Finance. An ethnographer by training, he has studied and written extensively on educational reforms and community development activities targeted at at-risk and disadvantaged youngsters. He is a former university professor and has been a guest lecturer in Educational Administration at the University of Illinois at Chicago, Loyola University, and Northwestern University. He has written widely about dropouts, particularly in Chicago, and his most recent writings concern school restructuring. He edited and contributed to *Empowering Teachers and Parents: School Restructuring Through the Eyes of Anthropologists* and is the author of *School Restructuring: Chicago Style*. In 1991 he received the Ben C. Hubbard Award for Educational Leadership in Illinois. Dr. Hess received his Ph.D. from Northwestern University.

Katherine A. Larson is a Senior Researcher at the University of California at Santa Barbara and is currently principal investigator of a 5-year study aimed at preventing school dropout in highest-risk Latino students. In 1988 she received a Distinguished Scholar Fellow Award from the U.S. Department of Education, OERI; previous honors included a Graduate Student of the Year Award at California State University, Los Angeles. Her publications include chapters on handicapped delinquent and adjudicated youngsters (in *International Encyclopedia of Education: Research and Studies Supplement*) and metacognition and learning disabilities (in *Current Perspectives in Learning Disabilities: Nature, Theory and Treatment*). Dr. Larson received her Ph.D. from the University of California at Santa Barbara.

Nettie Legters is a graduate student in the Department of Sociology and Research Assistant for the Center for Research on Effective Schooling of Disadvantaged Students at Johns Hopkins University. Ms. Legters received her B.A. from Whitman College.

Edward L. McDill is Professor of Sociology at Johns Hopkins University and is Co-Director of the Center for Social Organization of Schools. He has led several major evaluations of compensatory education programs and rigorously studied the academic impacts of school climates. His current work examines the effects and problems of an expanding population of disadvantaged students. Selected co-publications include *Schooling Disadvantaged Children: Racing Against Catastrophe*; *A Population at Risk: Potential Consequences of Tougher School Standards for Student Dropouts*; and *Performance Standards, Student Effort on Homework, and Aca-*

demic Achievement. Dr. McDill received his Ph.D. in Sociology from Vanderbilt University.

James M. McPartland is a Principal Research Scientist at Johns Hopkins University and, with Dr. McDill, is Co-Director of the Center for Social Organization of Schools. Dr. McPartland has written extensively on issues affecting school environments and school improvement, focusing much work on the problems of social justice, equality of opportunity, and desegregation of schools. His recent work includes the development of a typology of dropout prevention and field research in schools to develop effective instructional and organizational practices. Selected co-publications include *Policy Perspectives: Increasing Achievement of At-Risk Students at Each Grade Level* and *How Minorities Continue to Be Excluded from Equal Employment Opportunities: Research on Labor Market and Institutional Factors.* Dr. McPartland received his Ph.D. in Sociology from Johns Hopkins University.

Alesia F. Montgomery is a Research Associate at the American Institutes for Research and has been involved in studies of Chapter 1, dropout prevention programs, cultural diversity, and community building. Ms. Montgomery received her B.A. from the University of California at Irvine.

Siobhan Nicolau is President of the Hispanic Policy Development Project, which designs and administers national projects related to Hispanic American employment, training, and education. She developed and implemented large private-sector Hispanic American and Native American grant programs at the Ford Foundation. She now advises various foundations and corporations on Hispanic issues and the Hispanic market. Ms. Nicolau received her M.A. from New York University.

Grayson Noley is Associate Professor in the Division of Educational Leadership and Policy Studies at Arizona State University. Formerly he directed the Education Department of the Cherokee Nation of Oklahoma at Tahlequah. Dr. Noley has spent most of his professional career directing programs and studying initiatives aimed at providing meaningful educational opportunities to American Indian children and adolescents. He has been a frequent consultant to projects and committees working on issues in the areas of minority and multicultural education, and in 1989 he was honored with a Distinguished Scholar Award from the American Educational Association, Standing Committee on the Role of Status of Minorities in Educational Research and Development. Among his recent publications are chapters in *Indian Nations at Risk: Solutions for the 1990s* and *Race Relations in the 1980s and 1990s: Facts and Projects.* Dr. Noley received his Ph.D. from Pennsylvania State University.

Russell W. Rumberger is Director of the Educational Leadership Institute and Associate Professor of Education at the University of California at Santa Barbara. He has directed or been a principal associate on several major studies of dropout prevention, examining the economic consequences of dropping out of school for students as well as employers. Among his recent published work is "Chicago Dropouts: Research and Policy Issues" (a chapter in *Chicano School Failure and Success: Research and Policy Agendas for the 1990s*) and "Labor Market Outcomes as Indicators of Education Performance" (a chapter in *International Educational Indicators*). Dr. Rumberger received his Ph.D. in Administration and Policy Analysis/Economics of Education from Stanford University.

Samuel C. Stringfield is a Principal Research Scientist in the Center for Social Organization of Schools at Johns Hopkins University. He is currently conducting field studies of at-risk programs in selected areas throughout the country. He has specialized in the qualitative study of schools, particularly schools and school programs serving at-risk and disadvantaged students. He is co-author of a recent book, *Schools Make a Difference: Lessons Learned from a Ten-Year Study of School Effects*, and his other recent publications include a co-authored chapter in *Students at Risk in At-Risk Schools* and several journal articles on effective schools. Dr. Stringfield received his Ph.D. in Educational Psychology from Temple University.

Rafael Valdivieso is Vice President and Director of School and Community Services for the Academy for Educational Development. He currently either directs or is consultant to several projects that address the changing needs of in-school and out-of-school youngsters, with a particular focus on low-income, minority, and disadvantaged young people. Dr. Valdivieso serves on a number of advisory committees and recently participated as a member of the resource group on high school completion of the National Education Goals Panel. He is co-author, with Siobhan Nicolau, of *A More Perfect Union* and author of *Demographic Trends of the Mexican-American Population: Implications for Schools* and *U.S. Hispanics: Challenging Issues for the 1990s*, among other publications. Dr. Valdivieso received his Ph.D. in Sociology from New York University.

Constance Yowell is a doctoral student at Stanford University and was Research Assistant to Dr. Gordon at Yale University. Ms. Yowell received her B.A. from Yale University.

Index